THE SCREENPLAY
A Blend of Film Form and Content

THE SCREENPLAY
A Blend of Film Form and Content

Margaret Mehring

Focal Press

Boston   London

Focal Press is an imprint of Butterworth–Heinemann.

Library of Congress Cataloging-in-Publication Data

Mehring, Margaret.
    The screenplay : a blend of film form and content /
Margaret Mehring.
       p. cm.
    Bibliography: p.
    Includes index.
    ISBN 0-240-80007-9
    1. Motion picture plays—Technique.   2. Motion
picture authorship.   I. Title.
PN1996.M47   1989
808'.066791—dc19   88–13880
                                     CIP

British Library Cataloguing in Publication Data

Mehring, Margaret
    The screenplay: a blend of film form and content.
    1.Cinema
    films.Screenplays.Composition.Manuals
    I.Title
    808.2'3

    ISBN 0–240–80007–9

Butterworth–Heinemann
313 Washington Street
Newton, MA 02158–1626

10 9 8 7 6 5

7-14-97

❤ FOR BILL ❤

B~

Follow your dreams ~

Do this for you ...

not for me, not for anyone else.

I Love you,
Lin

CONTENTS

FOREWORD

As a young writer starting out, one of my first assignments was to work with the legendary director, King Vidor, on a proposed remake of his classic silent film *The Crowd*, this time, of course, as a "talkie."

While working with Mr. Vidor at his Paso Robles, California, ranch, conversation turned to the question of whether film, as an art form, was progressing or digressing. Mr. Vidor shocked me with his opinion that the sound era was still a long way from the level of excellence and artistry of the silent era. At first I tried to tell myself that he felt this way because his own best efforts had come before the advent of sound, but over the years— nearly fifteen now since that conversation—I have come to understand the brilliance of his perception.

Film as an art form is still in its infancy, by all of our standards, I'm sure, but there existed a period in the beginning, our silent period, when film-making had a purity to it, a simplicity of story-telling imagery that could be called its own halcyon, independent of what we writers and directors and producers have done to the medium since then. Go back and see *The Crowd* or *The Last Laugh* or *City Lights*. The use of "moving pictures" to tell a story, sans dialogue, was more poignant, more universal, less cluttered, more thematic, in short, more artistic than the majority of all the talkies we've made.

Sound, coming as it had from radio days, was a weird new bedpartner for the medium of moving pictures. There was a tendency to tell it all with words, to forget how much the picture might be saying. Writers were dialogue writers, assigned to work with directors, who were the "visual writers," if you will. It is only natural that these two "parents" of a project would clash severely over authorship. It is also no wonder why most modern films fail. A unity of sight and sound is not achieved and, all too often, the medium becomes a recording device rather than an art form.

Margaret Mehring is a visionary. In this remarkably entertaining and perceptive book, she addresses these central issues as squarely as anyone

I have encountered working in film: CAN FILM PROGRESS AS AN ART FORM WITHOUT FIRST TRAINING FILM WRITERS TO DEVELOP A SENSE FOR BOTH HALVES OF THEIR ART FORM, WHETHER THEY LATER DIRECT THEIR PROJECTS OR NOT? CAN THE TRUE ARTIST EVER SEPARATE WHAT IS TO BE SAID FROM THE WAY IT IS SAID?

In some lonely soul, the true heart of a film and its images must be hatched and nurtured first, for the film to have any chance of reaching its height during filming or later in the editing room. The screenwriter, not the director, is the best candidate to play this role since he or she is the one who generally comes to the project first.

Once we have raised a new generation of screenwriters who are expert blenders of sight and sound and who design their screenplays to use the "moving picture" art form to express their ideas, we can look forward to the brightest halcyon era film will ever know.

Douglas Day Stewart
Hollywood, California

PREFACE

At eleven o'clock on Wednesday morning of the seventh of May in 1980, the writing of *The Screenplay: A Blend of Film Form and Content* began. On this Wednesday morning a task force met in the "fireplace room" of the old Cinema "barracks" to begin the development of the new curriculum that would integrate and teach *Filmwriting and Design.*

The task force was composed of representative faculty members from the Production and Critical Studies emphases in the Division of Cinema-Television of the School of Performing Arts at the University of Southern California. This task force was formed and instructed to investigate and make recommendations leading to a course of study that would promote and encourage students to write screenplays utilizing the uniqueness of the motion picture medium.

Throughout the next two years we met, studied, and searched for the classes that would help the students identify with the aspirations and efforts of all humankind in all ages; classes that would sensitize students to the worlds within and around them; classes that would teach them the heart and craft of the storyteller; classes that would show them the varied and everchanging ways that artists have communicated their concerns; and classes that would teach and provide production experience with the very special elements unique to the art of moving images.

Two years after our first meeting, and after many hours spent researching, debating, compromising, and gaining curriculum approvals, the first group of students was admitted to study and receive a Bachelor of Fine Arts degree from the Filmic Writing Program.

The name of this new program—the Filmic Writing Program—was deliberately and thoughtfully chosen. We purposely chose not to call it a screenwriting program because we wanted to call attention to the fact that this new curriculum had a different emphasis—a different approach to teaching screenwriting. Instead of a more traditional and exclusive focus on the art of dramaturgy, our curriculum also focused on the art of film form. We wanted the name to symbolize this wedding of storytelling and filmic design.

The Program is now in its eighth year. We have graduated our first four groups of students. Some have already made major studio deals, many have secured representation, most are working in some aspect of the motion picture industry, and almost all are continuing to write screenplays.

By anyone's standards, the Filmic Writing Program is extremely successful and is producing some very imaginative and unique sceenwriters. However, this didn't happen instantaneously or miraculously. There were some turbulent times. Some of our ideas worked, others didn't; some people applauded our work, others scoffed; some members of the Program were fainthearted, others steadfast and courageous; but out of it all, through determination and devotion of students, faculty, and members of the professional motion picture community there emerged a very coherent, unique, and solid program.

Of particular importance to our growth and excellence are those members of the Writer's Guild of America, the Writer's Branch of the Academy of Motion Picture Arts and Sciences, and other distinguished members of the motion pictures industry who have served on our Council of Advisors, as faculty and as mentors for our upperclass students.

John Milius helped organize the Council of Advisors and served as its first chairperson. Douglas Day Stewart became the second chairperson and expanded its membership and functions. Members of the Council include Julian Blaustein, Allan Burns, Syd Field, Joe Gayton, Louis Garfinkle, Nelson Gidding, William Kelley, Max Lamb, Edmund North, Abraham Polonsky, David Rintels, Carol Sobieski, Jason Squire, and Jo Swerling. Syd Field, Nelson Gidding, Tom Joslin, William Kelley, Max Lamb, Edward Spiegel, Abraham Polonsky, Jason Squire, and Chuck Workman have served as faculty. A distinguished list of mentors includes Barry Beckerman, John D.F. Black, Robert Blees, Hal Bloom, Allan Burns, William Cannon, Morton Fine, Louis Garfinkle, William Kelley, Mark Norman, Edmund North, Norman Panama, Dan Petrie, Jr., Quinn Redeker, Eric Roth, Mann Rubin, Chuck Schyer, April Smith, Douglas Day Stewart, and Sid Stebel.

All have earned my most profound respect and gratitude for their support and involvement with the objectives of the Filmic Writing Program, their dedication to the screenwriting profession, and their commitment to helping young screenwriters become the very best they can be.

The Filmic Writing Program is also especially indebted to E. Russell McGregor, Melvin Sloan, and Karen Segal. E. Russell McGregor, as Co-Chairman of the Division of Cinema-Television, recognized the Division's need for a stronger emphasis on screenwriting. He initiated the development of the Program and facilitated its growth. Melvin Sloan, a dominant force in the creation of the USC Film School and a primary advocate of "filmic" storytelling, encouraged and participated in the formation of the Program's core curriculum. Karen Segal, the Director of the Thematic Option Program—a USC honors program—provided valuable advice and counsel for the selection of general education requirements and electives.

I am especially indebted to William Samuel Mehring. It was he who taught me the power of film form as a vehicle for communicating and shaping ideas of human importance.

The Screenplay: A Blend of Film Form and Content, now on its way to the publisher, becomes analogous to a still photograph. It becomes a fixed moment of thought. However, it is my earnest hope that it will be just one of many moments in the organic process of investigating and creating other thought on the blending of film form and film content.

Margaret Mehring
Director, Filmic Writing Program
School of Cinema-Television
University of Southern California
Los Angeles

ACKNOWLEDGMENTS

SPECIAL THANKS TO

Vincent Robert, Rosemary Taylor, and Jennifer Wilke who read the various drafts and unselfishly gave their time and counsel

Roberts Gannaway who brought his craftsmanship and insights to the creation of the drawings

Tony Gayton and Richard Ollis, former students, who gave me excellent examples for teaching some important concepts

Diane McLaughlin who helped me find time to write

Abraham Polonsky for being a beloved mentor

Douglas Day Stewart for his encouragement and support

and to all of the many Screenwriting Students who have taught me how to teach Screenwriting.

Also thanks to the screenwriters
William Kelly
Kurt Luedtke
Daniel Petrie, Jr.
Abraham Polonsky
Stewart Stern
Douglas Day Stewart
Earl W. Wallace

who wrote the excellent screenplays I have used to illustrate filmic writing.

INTRODUCTION

None of the "brick walls" in the motion picture industry can seem so high—so thick—or so long—as those encountered by the screenwriter who wants to have a screenplay produced as written!

The screenwriter has always been and continues to be the low person on the totem pole. The prevalent views in the industry presume that almost everyone can improve the final draft of a screenplay, that if one writer is good three more will be even better, and that writers do not and should not have control over what's produced from their material.

Historically the film director was the person with the original vision—the one who thought up a story, gathered a cast of performers and crew, and made a movie. Some actually wrote down their stories first, while others invented action as the cameras rolled. Louis and Auguste Lumiere, Georges Melies, Alice Guy, David Wark Griffith, Lois Weber, Mack Sennett, Charles Chaplin, and many others were truly "auteurs" of their produced work. Screen credits were virtually non-existent. Writers were first introduced to compose title cards for the silent films. These cards provided the necessary expository material, introduced the characters, and made occasional comments. Writers were associated with words, and until 1929, motion pictures had little need for "words" because no one spoke. The coming of sound created a demand for dialogue, and for photoPLAYS. The role of the writer changed. Now their "place" was to create conversation and staged plays to be photographed.

For centuries the function of a writer was to arrange words, just as painters were to arrange compositional elements, architects to arrange space, sculptors to arrange form, and composers to arrange musical notes. With the birth of motion pictures, this age-old role of a writer was passed on to the screenwriter. The fact that a new art form had emerged—an art form that was primarily a visual medium—did not alter the role expectations. The screenwriter was writing for pictures but was not supposed to be concerned with visual elements!

1

Producers bought this. Directors bought it. But most importantly, many screenwriters bought it—and then, having locked themselves into the role of second class citizenship, they gave away the key to the plantation's masters. There were those who laughed all the way to the bank. Nunnally Johnson contrasts the role of the playwright and the screenwriter by concluding that "You may give up your own property in the movies, but by God you're paid for it." (1) There were those who organized what became the Writers Guild of America to reclaim the key and those who have found that hyphenation *is* the key.* When asked what the screenwriter can do to gain better control of his or her work Edward Anhalt answered, "Well, I think by writing original material and refusing to part with it unless you have control, or some amount of control." (2) Yet, by and large, the screenwriter is, to use William Froug's words, "beaten, battered, and belittled." (3) This prevails in spite of the indisputable fact that no motion picture is ever made without a story—a scripted pre-plan, of some kind. Nothing happens until someone visualizes a story and then communicates that vision to others. Until then the cameras stay in their cases, the actors practice their art in actor's workshops, directors wait by their telephones, moviolas and steenbecks are silent, and heads of studios pace carpets in penthouse apartments. Why, then, when everything depends on a good story, do screenwriters remain in such a powerless position? A question for which there seems to be no valid answer! A problem for which there IS a solution.

Years of teaching filmwriting; even more years of writing, directing, and producing documentary, educational, and industrial films; and years of developing visual approaches to dramatic writing have created my definition of **a screenwriter.** A screenwriter is an artist who has something important to say. An artist who portrays the values of his or her culture, illuminates its issues, presents its problems, and dramatizes its struggles. The person who creates the dramatic structure and utilizes the filmic visual and aural design elements that will most effectively communicate his or her ideas. The person with the original vision.

Film form articulates the uniquenesses of the motion picture medium—the moving and audible image. It utilizes motion and sound, creates meaningful imagery, expands and contracts conventional time durations and relationships, and takes us to spaces that only exist in film. It makes it possible for us to ride on rollercoasters, chase after bandits, and dance on roof tops. It allows us the poetry of lonely crossroads, insight into tears of anger, the experience of a first day at school, and the ability to see the delicate shadings of a California Poppy in some brand new way. It takes us to outer space, into fairy tale land, puts the present before the past, and the past after the future. It's what makes film different from the novel, the stage play, short stories, and poetry.

---

* Writer-Director, Writer-Producer, Writer-Associate Producer.

Film form is how the screenwriter's ideas are realized on film. It's how things look and sound, but is not to be confused with the technicalities of film production. Film production is the process of executing the choices of film form that the screenwriter has written into the screenplay.

I define **filmic** as any device—visual and aural—that utilizes the potentialities basic and unique to the motion picture art form. These devices are multiple and varied. They're what I call filmic elements.

The **filmic elements** of a screenplay are derived from the nature of the motion picture art form. They are the result of the medium's ability to move, its ability to create both a time and a space that do not exist in reality, and its ability to present imagery and sound as abstractions of reality.

Filmic elements

Film content is what the screenwriter wants to say and the structure within which it is said. It's the story to be told, the characters to be met, the places to go, and the theme to be communicated. It's the stories that teach the children of the future the lessons of the past; the characters who help us understand ourselves by understanding who they are; the situations that show us brighter roads into the future and lead us to be more than we thought we could be. It's the ideas to be visualized in a structure that will involve us and make us a part of what is being said.

Film content

The characteristics of film content are derived from the ancient concepts of storytelling, modern conventions of dramaturgy, and current industry practices.

It is the blending of these two domains, form and content, that constitutes filmic writing.

Filmic writing, by my definition, is a process. A process of discovery and creation. A process that requires a knowledge of all filmic elements and an understanding of how these elements relate to each other and to dramatic structuring. A process that uses all filmic elements and deliberately blends film form and film content. It's what can make film content a universal masterpiece instead of just any story. It's combining the art of motion pictures with the art of storytelling.

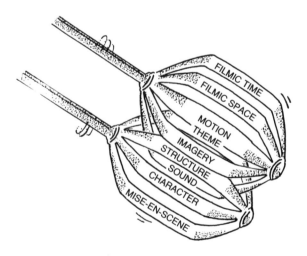

Filmic writing

There are some purists who will contend that filmic elements can only be related to the aesthetic attributes of filmmaking and that filmic elements in themselves rarely communicate story content. This is a much narrower definition and, although there are interesting arguments to support this position, I find it to be limiting and restrictive.

You may well ask, "Why me, why does the screenwriter need to know about film form?" V.I. Pudovkin answers that question on page 1 of his classic book, *Film Technique and Film Acting:* "In order to write a scenario suitable for filming, one must know the methods by which the spectator can be influenced from the screen." (4)

It was the claim of Slavko Vorkapich that "most of the films made so far are examples not of creative use of motion picture devices and techniques, but examples of their use as recording instruments and processes only." (5) These were his words in the 1950s and I suspect, with some notable exceptions, he would say the same thing today.

Unfortunately for the art of the film, in addition to combining all of the capabilities of all of the arts, motion pictures have become the means by which these arts can be reproduced. For many this represents the chief value of film and, all too often, film is looked upon as a recording medium rather than an interpretive medium. This denies the existence of film as a unique and sovereign art form.

It's the screenwriter who's in the best position to insure the production of *filmically* expressive screenplays rather than photographed stage plays. The screenwriter, as the creator of the journey, can establish its directions and destination. The screenwriter can create the screenplay that demands the utilization of the medium's full potential.

The motion picture is truly the most powerful of all media. It combines the best of all art forms and, in the combining, creates its own form. The power of this dynamic medium lies in the full utilization of its eclectic nature and the *deliberate* integration of its form and content. The initial creation of this integration is the responsibility of the screenwriter. This demands a complete and internalized understanding of what the medium can do and how the medium itself can contribute to the communication of the screenwriter's ideas.

Traditionally, film form and film content have been approached as separate entities—film form as belonging to production and film content as the domain of dramaturgy. It is the intent of this book to integrate the two and illustrate the expressive and interpretive power of film form. This is not the customary approach to teaching screenwriting. It is for precisely this reason that the words filmic writing have been chosen—to announce clearly the fact that a different approach is being used.

Film form IS the expression of film content. It's the vehicle that delivers film content. It is impossible for the screenwriter with a knowledge of the uniquenesses and power of the motion picture medium to separate form and content. This knowledge demands that you see and hear images as you create—not words. Words are simply the means of communicating your images. You hear the words your characters are saying and you see the things they are doing in a particular setting, surrounded by specific people, things, and sounds. It's the *total* image that contains the full meaning of your ideas, and as images appear in your mind they'll ultimately and effortlessly appear first in the screenplay and then on the screen.

When form and content are truly wed in the screenplay, they cannot be readily torn asunder. Content that depends on form for its full communication defies all attempts to separate the two. THIS IS THE SECRET OF A SCREENWRITER'S POWER! THIS IS THE WAY TO INSURE THAT THE SCREENPLAY IS PRODUCED AS WRITTEN—TO RETAIN THE ORIGINAL VISION. THIS IS THE SOLUTION. THIS IS THE WAY TO DISMANTLE THE BRICK WALLS—TO CLAIM THE POWER OF THE SCREENWRITER.

There is a power in the original vision that transcends all others. It is the source of our original inspiration, our moment of greatest clarity. Sergei Eisenstein wrote about the importance and the enduring quality of this first vision as he was working on *Ivan the Terrible:*

> The most important thing is to have the vision. The next is to grasp and hold it. In this there is no difference whether you are writing a film-script, pondering the plan of the production as a whole, or thinking out a solution for some particular detail.
>
> You must see and feel what you are thinking about. You must see and grasp it. You must hold and fix it in your memory and senses. And you must do it at once.
>
> When you are in a good working mood, images swarm through your busy imagination. Keeping up with them and catching them is very much like grappling with a run of herring.
>
> You suddenly see the outline of a whole scene and, rising simultaneously before this same inner eye, a close-up in full detail: a head nesting on a great white ruff.
>
> . . . Sometimes the hint fixed on paper will be developed and transferred to the screen. Sometimes it will be scrapped. Sometimes the contribution of an actor, or some unforeseen possibility (or more frequently, impossibility) of lighting, or any kind of production circumstance will alter or revise your first vision. But even here, by other means and methods, you will strive to convey in the finished work that invaluable seed that was present in your first vision of what you hoped to see on the screen. (6)

It is this first vision that the screenwriter needs to communicate to the film director so they can share the same inspiration and the same clarity.

This does *not* mean that the screenwriter usurps the responsibilities and prerogatives of the film director. On the contrary, it celebrates the importance of the film director as the interpreter of the original vision and the one best qualified to enhance and embellish that vision. As Stewart Stern puts it, "the thing we hope for as screenwriters is to have provided a blueprint, a platform you wear on your shoulders that a talented director can stand on and do a circus act. It's a pyramid—a reverse pyramid. But he [the director] has to share your vision with passion or you get a 'push me, pull you.' (7) However, in order to share the writer's "vision with passion," the screenwriter and the film director need to collaborate—as has been recognized and practiced by many of our finest screenwriters and film directors.*

Collaboration means working together in order to create a unified work of art. It means speaking the same language—the language of film form. It means the shared implementation of filmic elements—both aural and visual. It becomes the blending of different but interrelated talents. Thus—when the screenwriter utilizes filmic elements as the work is envisioned and structured, and when the film director understands, enhances and embellishes this same vision—a unified work of art will emerge.

The integration of film form and film content is by no means a new concept. It's been with us since the first images were photographed and projected. Film form was discovered and developed to be the handmaiden of film content. Filmmakers near and far, historically and recently, have refined, expanded, and continued this process. Many pages have been written about film history, film theory, and film criticism that document the extensive wedding of form and content. However, very few pages have been written to urge the germinating screenwriter to learn about film form as an expression of film content.

Screenwriters are special people. You have chosen one of the most pleasurable/painful, rewarding/defeating, powerful/humbling, and freeing/demanding of all professions. If asked why, I suspect you might say something like Cynthia Waite, a Filmic Writing student, said, "I think in terms of characters and stories that I need to share. Because if I don't share them, I'll explode." (8) This has been the compulsion of most artists throughout all time and it's what makes the artist so special—the need to explore, understand, and seek answers for human problems. The need to share.

Learning to write, for most, has always been a great deal more difficult than originally anticipated. Many young people wanting to become writers have grown up with a belief in the very old myth that people are "born writers," that this is a God-given gift and if you've been so endowed it

---

*Robert Riskin and Frank Capra, Kurt Luedtke and Sidney Pollack, Stuart Stern and Paul Newman, Nelson Gidding and Robert E. Wise, Dudley Nichols and John Ford, Irving Ravetch and Harriet Frank, Jr. and Martin Ritt, and I.A.L. Diamond and Billy Wilder.

will just happen. This, in my opinion, is the single most defeating factor confronting the beginning writer. It leads to the expectation that if you've got it, you'll do it, but if you can't do it, you haven't got it, and there's nothing you can do to get it. This is like expecting a person to become a surgeon without spending hours in an operating room, a swimmer to compete in the Olympics without months of daily practice, or a pianist to perform a Mozart concerto without years of preparation.

And, the very same people who would advise the aspiring concert pianist to start music lessons as early as possible and practice daily would tell the aspiring writer to go to school, learn all that can be learned, live and experience all human emotions and situations, and then, when older and with something to say, start writing. Of course, aspiring writers need to learn all they can learn, and, of course, they need to live and experience all human emotions and situations—but at the *same time* as they're studying writing and practicing it daily. And, my life experiences have taught me that no matter what you know, how old you are, or what you've experienced, you will always have something worthwhile to say.

Becoming a screenwriter is not an easy or instantaneous experience. It requires a broad general knowledge about all people past and present—their histories, art, literature, philosophies, and religions. It requires an understanding of how groups of people interact and influence each other, how individuals are shaped and personalities formed. It requires a knowledge of the history of motion pictures and television, filmic theories, criticism, and aesthetics. It requires insight about yourself—your thoughts and feelings. It requires that you learn how to observe the world with all its complexities and that you become aware of how you communicate with others and yourself. It takes knowledge of and practice with the structural conventions of classical and current storytelling and the accepted industry formats. It requires experience with general production techniques and the problems of those who will produce your screenplays. It requires an internalized knowledge of the uniqueness and design factors of audio and visual imagery. It demands the ability to use language correctly and expressively. Becoming a screenwriter is a lifetime adventure and utilizes every intellectual and emotional experience you'll ever encounter.

For the past twenty-eight years I've taught screenwriting and have worked with hundreds of students. Some took my class because it was required. Some were simply curious about screenwriting. Some came expecting the Muse to descend and declare them to be a screenwriter—and then left when the good goddess failed to appear. Some really wanted to become screenwriters. I've watched them all learn, struggle with growth, recognize their own strengths, create their scripts and their films, and then enter the film industry to become producers, directors, composers, cameramen and camerawomen, editors, grips, soundmen and soundwomen, production managers—and screenwriters. I've celebrated their successes, commiserated over their bad luck, watched them turn defeats into successes, applauded their tenacity, and understood their frustrations. And, I've heard the same question many many times, "What are my chances for becoming a successful screenwriter?"

My answer is always the same. If you're willing to commit yourself to a regular schedule of writing, if you gain an internalized understanding of the motion picture art form and the elements of storytelling, if you're willing to explore and know yourself, and if you're willing to reach out and experience all of life, then yes—the chances are very good that you'll become a successful screenwriter.

A screenplay is not a substance that can be called the sum of its parts. It doesn't have exact measurements of an exact number of elements that, when simply added together, will produce a screenplay.

A screenplay is organic. Like a person, it lives. It is conceived and nourished. It learns, grows, changes, matures. It is uniquely its own self. It has its own world view; its own personality; its own raison d'etre. It has certain characteristics in common with other screenplays but none are ever identical.

Most screenplays have plot, character, theme, and mise-en-scène. They have beginnings, middles, and ends. There's conflict, change, and resolution. There are acts, sequences, scenes, and shots. There's momentum, reversals, crises, climaxes, and tag lines. There's lighting, color, music, and composition. There's dialogue and externalized thoughts and feelings. There are locations and textures, rhythm, tempo, and pacing. There's complexity and simplicity. There's the creation of filmic time and filmic space. It's all of these, and more, that create the screenplay. It's all of these and the ways they interact and relate to each other that create the life and structure of a screenplay.

The structure of anything is generally defined as the aggregate of the elements of the entity in their relationship to each other. Using this definition, the **structure of a screenplay** can then be defined as the aggregate of the elements of film form and film content in their relationship to each other.

The structure of a screenplay is never an accident. It is deliberate. It is designed. Its elements are structured in a specific way for a specific reason within a specific time. Each one of the medium's elements—filmic time, filmic space, motion, imagery, and sound—has its specific characteristics. We will study these characteristics separately but always with the awareness that they operate simultaneously and gain their significance from their interdependence and interaction. And, always, as we study each of the medium's elements, we'll study them in the context of content and dramaturgy.

Most of the things that have been said—and will be said—about motion pictures are also applicable to television. There are, of course, significant differences between the two. These differences are largely the result of unique capabilities, limitations, and requirements of a technological and exhibitional nature. Also, when used to achieve its unique potential, television displays very powerful and exciting special characteristics. However, it is not the intent of this book to deal with either the special characteristics of television or the differences between the two media. We will deal with the many things they have in common, and their abundant similarities will be subsumed and dealt with under the verbal umbrella of film form.

Many pedagogical disciplines can be broken down into separate and exclusive segments. Learning the discipline can be accomplished by moving from one segment to the next; mastering each in its turn; and then, at the end, putting them all together for the full and complete knowledge. This is not true of most of the creative arts and is certainly not true for learning filmic writing. The study of filmic writing is a study of the relationships and interactions between all of its elements. The elements take their meanings from each other and only when combined do they serve their function. Although we will analyze the unique characteristics of each of the various components of film form and film content, it will always be in the context of their interdependence.

You will never, at least I hope you will never, approach conflict by scheduling a time to work on conflict, setting aside an afternoon for tempo, or tackling momentum during the weekend so you can develop reversals on Monday morning.

Hopefully, by having experienced, understood, and internalized each element of film form and film content and the various ways in which they interact and relate to each other, they will belong to you. They will all become a part of you and be operative at all times.

Think back to when you learned to drive an automobile or operate any complex piece of machinery. At first you had to examine, understand, and practice each step in the process. Then after you had driven or operated the machine for a given number of hours, the process became a part of you. You didn't have to think about what you were doing. The many steps blended into one and were activated by a single command.

The same phenomenon occurs as you learn to create screenplays. You consciously examine, understand, and practice each element. You grow to understand it, you practice it, and then, after a given number of pages, the many elements blend into one process.

Learning to become a screenwriter is, however, not as simple as learning to drive a car. There are no absolute rules or procedures that will result in a "good" screenplay. No formulas to memorize. No tests to pass. No "right" or "wrong" answers. Learning occurs by studying the elements of film form and film content and the ways in which the two can be combined. Learning occurs by trial and error, by trying different combinations of elements to see how they relate to each other. Learning occurs by asking for and receiving feedback about what works best and what doesn't work as well. Learning occurs by writing and rewriting—and rewriting.

Becoming a screenwriter is a pilgrimage that will lead you into many different areas, but areas that ultimately will merge and become one.

Our journey together will begin with the STATIC VISUAL IMAGE and we'll study it as an arrangement—a structure—within a framed static space. We'll examine how fixed visual elements communicate content and how the structure of content within the static frame is composed of the many spatial elements of line, shape, color, texture, lighting, rhythms, contradictions, balance, contrasts, and layering.

Then we'll move on to study the elements of the moving image. We'll look at moving images as an arrangement—a structure—within moving spaces and progressive time. We'll examine how moving visual and aural elements communiciate film content through theme, structure, character(s), and mise-en-scène, and how the structure of film content is composed of filmic time, filmic space, motion, imagery, and sound.

We'll start our exploration of the moving image with STRUCTURING FILMIC TIME to see how the modern screenplay follows the classical dramatic structure of Aristotle and how acts, sequences, scenes, and shots are structured through selected events in time.

Then we'll look at the ELEMENTS OF FILMIC TIME to see how selected "pieces" of time can be joined to create a unified entity; how time can be expanded, contracted, and rearranged; and how it can be speeded up, slowed down, reversed, and frozen.

Next we'll deal with the ELEMENTS OF FILMIC SPACE to see how selected "pieces" of places can be joined to create a space that can only exist on celluloid. We'll see how the reader/viewer is moved through space while remaining stationary, how the illusion of dimension is achieved, and we'll look at the many spaces available for containing information.

We'll look at the FILMIC ELEMENTS OF MOTION to see how motion does more than move people and things from one place to another, how expressive it can be, how actions are the voices of feelings and thoughts, and how the moving image creates tempo, rhythm, and pacing.

We'll look at IMAGERY to learn about the symbolic and poetic quality of images. We'll see how the mise-en-scène and the appearance of all visual elements influences what happens and what is communicated.

We'll explore the power of SOUND as an expressive element of the moving image. We'll look at the contributions to be made by situational and symbolic sounds, as well as those contributed by dialogue and music.

It is frequently said that the basis of a good story is a good character. We'll study CHARACTERIZATION to examine what constitutes a "good" character, how characters are created, and how they are revealed.

Discussions about THEME pervade the entire book, but we'll examine it more fully as the work of the artist and as the basis of storytelling throughout all time.

We'll look at the screenplay as a unique literary form and we'll examine the creative task of DESIGNING THE PAGE. We'll see how the form of the page can be used to help communicate content, how it can be used to paint the screenwriter's visions and involve the reader in imaging the unfolding drama.

Although the major focus of this book will be on the integration of film form and film content, I also hope to stimulate and develop your constant awareness of the worlds you live in, your relationships to these worlds, and your perceptions of these worlds. Your screenplays are the reforming and retelling of what you have experienced. You, as the receiver of experiences, are like a sponge taking everything into yourself to store away until you "squeeze" it out in a different form and for different purposes. It's important that you recognize this and then consciously work to build your large "storyhouse." Obviously, the larger the storyhouse the more stories you'll have to tell. So we'll explore THE CREATING PROCESS—and look at how you "soak up" your experiences, store them in your storyhouse and then squeeze them out.

Finally, we'll look at THE LAYERS OF WRITING—the various drafts of writing and rewriting that produce a screenplay.

Throughout this book, your active participation is required. This isn't a textbook that will "give" you answers. You won't be able to simply sit, read, and fill in the blanks. You will learn and internalize this knowledge by your involvement in specific experiments, activities, exercises, and fantasies.

I'll be asking you to put yourself in imaginary places and talk to imaginary characters, to engage yourself in specific explorations of your world, and to perform some simple tasks and exercises. Learning to become a screenwriter is an activity. You'll learn how by DOING it—not just reading or talking about how to do it. And the more fully you enter into the doing of these activities, exercises, and fantasies the more rapidly you'll learn.

The first thing I'm going to ask you to do is to obtain a Journal—a book with blank pages. This will be the book in which you'll write down the things you see, the sounds you hear, and the thoughts you want to keep. As time goes by you'll fill up many Journals. They'll be the "reference library" of your life and your training ground for daily writing. By making a habit of writing in your Journal every day you'll begin the "writer's habit." Writers write and writers write everyday. Choose a time in each day, a time to think and to write your thoughts, a time to write that becomes inviolate. Establish your writing routine. You may want to carry your Journal with you, keeping it handy to make notes the moment you collect your sights, sounds, and ideas. Or, maybe you'll want to jot down your thoughts on miscellaneous bits and pieces of paper to paste in your Journal, or to remind you of what you want to put in your Journal. Do whatever works the best for you.

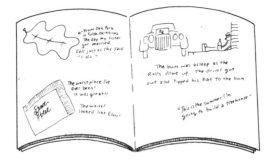

Generally speaking, film is studied by looking at examples of the finished and projected film. Filmic writing deals with images and content as created and described by the screenwriter, thus, the examples cited herein will be scenes and sequences from screenplays. In many cases the finished film duplicates the images as described on the pages of the screenplay. In others, the final and projected images may be substantially altered. This, however, had nothing to do with the selection of the excerpted scenes or sequences. The illustrations were chosen as excellent examples of how the screenwriter utilized film form to enhance the communication of film content.

The screenplays from which I have chosen extensive excerpts are Douglas Day Stewart's *An Officer and a Gentleman*, Abraham Polonsky's *Body and Soul*, Stewart Stern's *Rebel Without a Cause*, Daniel Petrie, Jr.'s *Beverly Hills Cop*, Kurt Luedtke's *Out of Africa* (adapted from "Out of Africa" and "Shadows on the Grass" by Isak Dinesen, "Isak Dinesen: The Life of a Storyteller" by Judith Thurman, and "Silence Will Speak" by Errol Trzebinski) and *Witness* written by Earl W. Wallace and William Kelley from a story by William Kelley and Pamela and Earl W. Wallace. We are all indebted to the screenwriters for having written such compelling stories with such creative uses of film form. Also, we are indebted to the producers and studios who have granted us permission to print the excerpts. They have given us the rare opportunity to fully study the actual words written by the screenwriters.

Aristotle begins the *Poetics* by writing:

> I propose to treat of Poetry in itself and of its various kinds, noting the essential quality of each; to inquire into the structure of the plot as requisite to a good poem; into the number and nature of the parts of which a poem is composed; and similarly into what else falls within the same inquiry. (9)

This has been the intent of most who have studied, written about, and taught the nature of storytelling, the essences of drama, the theories of playwriting, and the art of screenwriting.

However, it's with some caution that I approach the dissection of film form and film content and the selection of examples to illustrate their utilization. Listing and defining elements often leads to the creation of a formula for "how to" construct a screenplay. Concrete examples are often merely copied. Yet, both pedagogical methods are necessary for gaining an understanding and internalization of the concepts involved. So, hopefully, forewarned is forearmed and you'll avoid the pitfalls of formularizing and copying. Also, hopefully, this examination of the structural unity of film form and film content will only be used as a conceptual framework for your ideas, continuing questions and tentative answers, and the examples will simply become stimuli for your discovery of your own ways to blend the two.

REFERENCES

1. William Froug, *The Screenwriter Looks at the Screenwriter*, The Macmillan Company, New York, 1972, p. 237.
2. Op. Cit., Froug, p. 263.
3. Ibid, p. xi.
4. V. I. Pudovkin, *Film Technique and Film Acting,* Lear Publishers, Inc., New York, 1949, p. 1.
5. Lecture by Slavko Vorkapich, "Two Aspects of the Motion Picture: Recording and Creative and a Method of Teaching the Creative Use of the Medium." p. 1.
6. Sergei Eisenstein, *Film Form*, Harcourt, Brace & Co., New York, 1949, pp. 261, 263.
7. Stewart Stern, "Dialogue on Film," *American Film*, Oct. 1983, p. 21.
8. Filmic Writing Program, "Transcript", University of Southern California, May 5, 1986, p. 8.
9. *Aristotle's Poetics*, trans. by S. H. Butcher Hill and Wang, New York, 1961. p. 49.

THE STATIC IMAGE

Most classes and textbooks about screenwriting don't deal with the frame and the selection and arrangement of visual elements within it—mise-en-cadre—as a major concern for the screenwriter. Structuring the static image is generally taught and written about as the special province of the film director, the director of photography, and the art director. Indeed, the selection and arrangement of visual elements are a major responsibility of the production people, but they must also be the responsibility of the screenwriter.

It's the function of the screenwriter to create the characters, the action, the setting, and the emotional and intellectual communication for each frame. This function demands a knowledge of and participation in all aspects of the construction of a film. Screenwriters, as a general rule, see images in motion. You don't consciously image the static frame, and I'm not suggesting that you should. I am suggesting that an awareness of the principles of visual construction and visual perception, which are operative in each static frame, will provide you with insights and methods for the most effective communication of your ideas. At the very least, this aware-ness will increase both the quality and quantity of your visual and audio experiences. Then, whether consciously or unconsciously, you will utilize the visual and audio elements unique to the art of film.

The single static frame is the basic building block of the screenplay. The eye sees twenty-four of them each second, one thousand four hundred and forty each minute, and one hundred seventy-two thousand eight hundred during the viewing of a two-hour film. Through the use of shutters and intermittent drives, static images are first photographed and then projected onto a screen. When these images are shot at twenty-four frames per second and then projected at twenty-four frames per second, the impression of normal movement is created. A succession of frames becomes a shot, shots become a scene, scenes become a sequence, sequences become an act, and acts become a screenplay. Each of these—the frame, shot, scene, sequence, and act—is governed by different principles of visual construction and perception. Each contains different potentialities for cognitive and affective communication—intellectual and emotional communication. And yet, like the Russian toy that fits identical dolls within successively larger dolls, each is a microcosm of the bigger picture. The structural flow of each rests on the same elements.

The frame is a container of content. It holds the information you want to communicate. The frame contains energy. This energy comes from the elements you put within the frame, the way they're arranged to interact with each other, the way they interact with the frame itself, and the way the mind perceives these elements and their interactions.

The principles that govern visual construction—the nature of visual elements and their arrangement—have been most fully investigated and developed by visual communicators who predate motion pictures—painters, sculptors and architects, and, more recently, graphic designers.* The study of the principles of visual perception—the ways our eyes see and how our minds interpret, store, and retrieve information—is a relatively new science and has become a special interest of psychologists, educators, and graphic artists. Much has been written to analyze and explain their theories, research, and conclusions.** It is not my intent to involve you in a comprehensive review of these principles. It is my intent to introduce you to some of their basic concepts that are most pertinent to the work of the screenwriter and to sensitize you to the expressive world of imagery.

*I would especially refer you to Gyorgy Kepes, *Language of Vision*, Paul Theobald, Chicago, 1948; Laszio Moholy-Nagy, *Vision in Motion*, Paul Theobold & Company, Chicago, 1947; and Donis Adonis, *A Primer of Visual Literacy*, Massachusetts Institute of Technology Press, Cambridge, Ma., 1973.

** Of particular interest are the works of Rudolf Arnheim, *ART and Visual Perception*, 1954 and 1974 and *Visual Thinking*, 1969, both University of California Press, Berkeley and Los Angeles.

LINEAR AND LAYERED MOVEMENT

The images of a screenplay are both static and moving. A screenplay simultaneously is layered and moves forward.

The forward movement is linear. It is horizontal. It is created by the juxtaposing of frames, shots, sequences, and acts and the progressive introduction of new, motivated information, and change. The linear movement of motion pictures is often compared to the linear movement of literary material that juxtaposes words, sentences, paragraphs, and chapters. The structure of both calls for the building of information on information—one word, one frame at a time. Information accumulates, change and growth can occur, and the movement has a direction. It is the moment of juxtaposing—the end of one shot and the beginning of another—that creates much of the uniqueness of film. This, in its many aspects, will be dealt with in later chapters.

The layered movement has depth. It is vertical. It contains simultaneous and multiple amounts of information. It contains depth information about the setting, emotional information, and the opportunities for esthetic experiences. At the same time information is created by the frame itself—its size and boundaries; by the visual elements and their arrangements; by the relationship of the camera to the object(s) and/or person(s); and by the phenomena of visual perception exerted by and within the frame. There are many things going on at the same time—multiple information being presented and being presented in numerous ways—*simultaneous layers of content and form.*

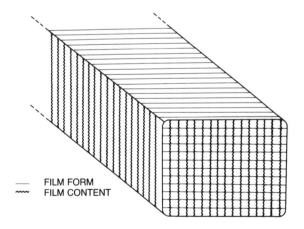

In order for you to understand and control this layered movement, it's necessary for you to understand mise-en-cadre and some of the principles of visual perception that govern the static frame.

The linear and layered movements in the screenplay correspond to linear and layered movements in music. In music the melody is developed in a linear fashion and the harmony and/or dissonance is layered. The melody carries the composition forward and the harmony and/or dissonance enriches. Without the layered and vertical movement the melody would seem naked and incomplete.

"FRAMED" SPACE

Art does not see through the eyes of real space. It sees through "the frame"—the boundaries—of a chosen medium. The most common "frame" of the screenplay and finished projected image is a view three units high and four units wide.

3:4 aspect ratio.

The wide screen frame stretches to an aspect ratio of 1:2.50 and in its most extreme extension can surround and tower above the viewer.

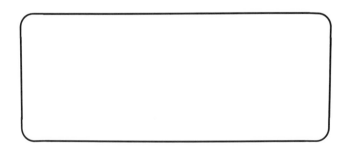

1:2.5 aspect ratio.

As the creator of what goes into the frame, you must learn to see your world and experiences through the motion picture frame. It's necessary for you to know the differences between real space and "framed" space. To help you gain these awarenesses, I'm going to ask you to create and then work with a paper viewfinder.

Put this book down and find a pair of scissors and several heavy pieces of paper. With these two items you'll be able to make two viewfinders, one a standard aspect ratio and the other a wide screen aspect ratio.

Do you have your scissors and paper? Don't make the mistake of just going on reading. It's the active participation and involvement in the learning exercises that'll help you internalize and own the abilities to become a screenwriter. So, if you haven't gotten these materials, do it now before you continue.

Do the standard frame size first.

Fold the paper—first in half and then in half again—so you have one quarter of the paper in front of you.

Then, from the point of the fold, measure and mark one inch along the edge.

From that designation, measure and mark three quarters of an inch away from the edge. These measurements tell you where to cut.

Cut and unfold.

Now you have a standard 3:4 frame.

Next do the wide screen frame. Do the same things except that for the wide screen frame you'll measure one and one-half inches along the edge and one-half inch away from the edge.

Now you have your viewfinders and you'll become the camera. First, hold the standard viewfinder up to one eye so you lose your peripheral vision.

Next choose some object within your view and, looking through your viewfinder, move close to it, around it, and away from it. Get down to ground level to look up at it—assume a "frog's eye" point of view. Stand on a chair to look down at it—from a "bird's eye" point of view. Look at it from your eye level—the normal point of view—and think about the differences between these three angles. Discover what this "framed" object looks like from as many different angles and distances as you possibly can. See what happens as you tilt up from the bottom of the object to its top and then from the top to its bottom. See how it changes as you walk around it, move toward it, and then move away.

Now, do these same things with the wide screen viewfinder and you'll see how much more the wide screen frame encompasses. This shows you how carefully you'll need to structure and control the visual elements to capture and direct the viewer's eye. When writing for the wide screen, this is a significant factor to deal with. You'll also see how differently the camera distance and angle affect the size and impact of wide screen images.

This is an exercise that needs to become a daily habit. Carry your view-finders with you and work with them several times a day. The time will come when your mind will automatically put a frame around the images you're working with but, at first, you'll need a viewfinder. The viewfinder will help you develop a conscious awareness of the differences between real space and screenplay space and the different ways in which the camera creates its own space. It will show you how the frame selects only certain things from real space, how the camera's distance from the object changes its apparent size and visual impact, and how the angle influences its af-

fective communication. It will show you the importance of what is *excluded* from the shot. What you choose to leave out of the shot is just as significant as what you choose to include in the shot. Also notice what your eyes do. They don't see the whole object in every detail all at once. They move from one aspect of the object to another and from one object to another.

The size and aspect ratio of the frame are important considerations and are generally a given. However, they can be changed to create a frame within the frame. This is achieved by masking or by splitting the actual frame.

Masking can be done optically or within the camera, by lighting, or by the way the shot is framed.

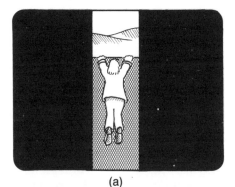

(a) Optical masking, (b) masking by lighting, (c) masking by framing.

(a)

(b)   (c)

It's also possible to optically mask—"iris" a small portion of the frame and then open it up to reveal a larger portion or the entire frame. Although seldom used, "irising" allows you to focus the attention of the viewer on a particular aspect of an event and can carry an emotional communication.

A split frame is almost always achieved by optical devices and allows you to present multiple information simultaneously.

A split frame.

The decision to mask or split the frame is most frequently a production decision, but if this technique would strengthen the communication of your idea it can be alluded to in the screenplay.

The size and shape of the frame can be changed, but it still remains a frame.

In addition to size and shape the frame has edges, corners and planes. The four edges and corners have a strong influence on the things inside the frame. Edges and corners are endowed with a magnetism that promotes or diminishes a sense of stability.

Put an object right in the center of the frame of your viewfinder. See how solidly it sits there. Now move the viewfinder so the object is off center and close to the left side of your frame. Chances are the object will appear to be drawn toward the left frame and will lose the stability formerly exhibited. Next, place the object in the upper left corner. See how the object appears to be drawn into that corner. Now place two people or objects within your frame. Look away and then look back. Which side of the frame did your eyes go to first? Chances are they focused first on the right side and then moved to the left, and chances are the first thing you focused on became the most important.

The final determination of object and subject placement within the frame is the responsibility of the production people. But, knowing about perceptual phenomena can lead you to describe your shots and scenes in such a way as to suggest their utilization. If the event you're presenting is one epitomized by stability and restfulness, the visual equilibrium should represent stability and restfulness. If it's excitement and tension, the image as well as the content should reflect excitement and tension.

There are three planes within the two dimensional frame—the horizontal, the vertical, and the depth plane. The horizontal plane runs from side to side. The vertical plane includes the area from top to bottom. The depth plane moves from the foreground to the middle ground and background.

Take your viewfinder outside among houses, trees, and automobiles or into a room that has a large area filled with furniture. Look through the frame and identify the grounds. Notice that the objects closest to you are in the foregound. The objects farthest away and toward the top of the viewfinder are in the background. The area in between is the middle ground. Actually these three grounds are an illusion since the frame actually has only two dimensions. The illusion is created by a comparision of the relative positions of objects. You can check this out by directing your viewfinder up toward a cloudless sky or a blank ceiling. Because you don't have a point of reference you don't see a foreground or background. These are aspects of our daily lives that we take for granted. As an artist, you want to look at them as tools for communication.

Now, move your finder to emphasize vertical things. Look up to the top of the tallest piece of furniture in your room or to the top branches of a tree. Note how different your image looks. There tends to be more energy and excitement in the vertical plane. It's new and unexplored territory—a different way of looking at your world.

Next emphasize the horizontal lines. Make the lines of your room or landscape the dominant things in the frame. This is your normal view. It's more restful, quieter.

Look now at what's closest to you—the things in the foreground. These are the things that show the most detail, that have the potential for "touching" you. The objects and people in the background have the least detail. They define the outer limit of your attention and, by their presence, are assumed to have some sort of impact upon the middle and foreground. It's the depth plane that's of primary importance to your work as a screenwriter. This plane provides you with multiple areas in which to place information—the events, characters, and objects you've selected to communicate your ideas. These elements, and the way you arrange them within the frame, cause the viewer's eyes to move and their minds to travel toward understanding what you want them to know. This is layered—inward—movement.

LINES

Dots create lines and lines create form—the boundaries, the details, and textures—but most importantly they create movement. Lines create movement by directing our eyes to follow where they're going and what they're doing. They take us along curves, into rooms, and up to the tops of buildings.

Lines take the viewer's eyes where you want them to go and lead them to see what you want them to see. They can expand or contract things, move up or down, right or left, and recede or advance. They can be curved or straight. Lines create shapes.

SHAPES

Shapes create the environment. They fill the space. Shapes require the active participation of the viewer to identify what they are and discover how they relate to other shapes within the same space. The identification of shapes is a cognitive activity. The mind sees the relationships between the parts, creates a whole and draws upon past experiences to give the shape a name and function.

There are three basic shapes—the square, the circle, and the triangle. Each of these shapes has acquired its own associative meanings. The square is associated with predictability, conservative ideologies, honesty, and masculinity. The circle is associated with warmth, caring, eternity, and femininity. The triangle is associated with excitement, tension, progressive ideologies, and action.

If it's predictability and honesty you're dealing with, the images should represent predictability and honesty.

(a)

If the event you are presenting is one epitomized by warmth and caring, the visual elements should reflect warmth and caring.

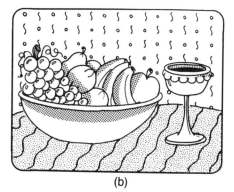

(b)

If it's excitement and action you're portraying, the images should communicate excitement and action.

Basic shapes: (a) square, (b) circle, and (c) triangle.

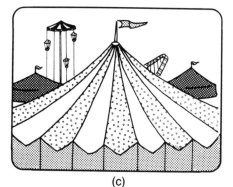

(c)

COLORS

Colors create lines and shapes. Experiencing color is a passive activity in the sense that you're not required to construct or identify it. It does, however, elicit an active emotional response. In fact, it's one of the most, if not *the* most, expressive of all of the visual elements. Colors emit energy and each color contains different associative meanings. The energy of the color and its associative meaning are linked to the event being presented. Red is commonly associated with excitement, passion, and anger. It's frequently thought to be warm, heavy, expansive, and very active. Blue is generally associated with sadness, compassion, veracity, and loyalty and often described as being cold, empty, light, contracting, and only moderately active. Playfulness, cowardice, and charm are commonly attributed to yellow; passivity, hope, and immortality to green; purity, enlightenment, and righteousness to white; and evilness, mystery, and death to black.

The symbolic nature of color is primarily culturally determined and the use of culturally accepted color symbols is common practice. However, it must be thoroughly understood that there is no such thing as a fixed and universal catalog of color symbols. You can develop your own color symbols as long as the symbolic relationship is clearly established. The classic illustration of this is the startling reversal of the use of black and white in Eisenstein's film *Alexander Nevsky*. The white robes worn by the enemy became associated with cruelty, oppression, and death while the black robes of the Russian soldiers symbolized heroism and patriotism.

There is much more that can be said about color—its relationship to other colors and to the backgrounds upon which it is placed, the effects of past color experiences, and the movement that can be induced by the juxtaposition of certain colors. For those of you particularly interested in exploring color in greater depth and detail, references are listed.*

My major concern is that you become aware of the emotional impact of color and that if, for example, the event you're presenting is one of anger, the colors used should reflect anger or if the event is one of mystery, the colors should represent mystery.

LIGHT

Light, like color, elicits an emotional response. In the extremes it can create an atmosphere that's ominous and depressed or happy and bright. We need light simply to see what's going on, but, as with all of the elements, it's the expressive nature of lighting that concerns you.

*Egbert Jacobson, *Basic Color*, Paul Theobald, Chicago, 1948; Faber Birren, *Color Psychology and Color Therapy*, rev. ed. University Books, Inc., New Hyde Park, NY, 1961; Faber Birren, *Color in Your World*, The Macmillan Company, New York, 1962; and Rudolf Arnheim, *Art and Visual Perception*, University of California Press, Berkeley, 1965.

Basically you're dealing with controlling two different things—the amount of light and the position of the source of light.

A high level of light that permeates the entire frame will create an up-beat mood. Conversely, a low level of light that illuminates only selected portions of the frame will create a down-beat mood. You can get a feel for this by working with your viewfinder and the ordinary lights in one of your rooms. Turn all the lights on and you get one feeling. Turn them off one by one and you'll get very different feelings. What you decide not to illuminate is just as important as what you illuminate. Also, notice how your eye is always attracted to the object receiving the most light.

A trip to your local art museum will also show you variations in the expressive quality of lighting. There you'll find examples of lighting that maximize the contrast between dark and light areas—chiaroscuro light-ing—and examples that minimize contrast and appear very flat. Flat light-ing has little, if any, emotional impact. It simply functions to provide illumination. Chiaroscuro lighting—often referred to as Rembrandt light-ing—can draw dramatic attention to the thematic elements within the frame and emphasize or create a mood.

(a)   (b)

(a) Flat lighting; (b) Rembrandt lighting.

Lighting can be used in many ways to achieve your dramatic objective. Selected performances can be spotlighted. Characters and objects can be lit to appear as silhouettes. Shadows can perform actions. Here again, using your viewfinder, you can experiment with ordinary lights to see the dif-ferent effects that can be achieved.

A light source that emanates from above eye level puts the viewer at ease. This is our normal experience with the sun and artifical lighting. Light that comes from below eye level is an unusual occurrence and creates a sense of uneasiness. You can easily see this by illuminating a person's face with a lamp held above your head and then lowered to beneath the person's face. See how different the person looks. The one is a normal view and the other may become grotesque.

It's the very creative and important job of the director of photography to illuminate the space, create the sense of depth, simulate the light source, emphasize or de-emphasize particular visual elements, and, most importantly, intensify the emotional tones of the screenplay. It's the job of the screenwriter to create those emotional tones and expressively communicate them so the director of photography can implement them.

As with all of the elements, lighting exists to contribute to the affective communication of the screenplay, and as you recognize and utilize the emotional power of illumination the images you create will become more expressive. If the event being presented is happy and lighthearted, the lighting must reflect that mood. If the event is one of fear and suspense, the lighting has to be one of fear and suspense.

TEXTURE

Texture is an element closely related to lighting because it is light that reveals the unique visual surface characteristics of any object or person. It is the presence of light and the position of the light source that reveals the absence of light. The absence of light creates shadows—and shadows reveal texture. Texture is patterns and rhythms of dark and light.

Textures contain affective meaning. They can represent feelings of softness, hardness, roughness, smoothness, coldness, warmth, quietude, and tension. There's a direct memory link between visual textures and the physical sense of touch. It's the memories of how things felt that evoke the emotional responses. We see patent leather shoes and feel smoothness; the furriness of a teddy bear is softness; the nubbiness of wool is warmth, and a thin edge of a knife is sharpness.

The sense of touch is the sense of texture and our sense of touch—like the sense of smell—is surrounded with many taboos. "Don't touch it. You'll break it!" "Don't use your fingers." "Keep your hands to yourself." "Hands off." "Watch but don't touch." "Touch and you'll get your hands slapped." These are commands we're all very familiar with. One of the greatest needs we all experienced at a very early age was the need to explore and learn about the world we lived in. We constantly reached out to investigate— to touch—but soon learned that touching often led to punishment. We learned "to keep our hands to ourselves." I'm suggesting that you now re-learn and reclaim this means of investigation and source of knowledge and pleasure.

In the context of being a screenwriter, it's important to know and utilize texture as a channel of affective communication and the wider the range of your textural experiences the greater will be your access to a full range of alternatives. For this reason alone, and there are certainly others, it's important that you continually update and increase your tactile experiences and inventory. Make it a practice to touch things. Deliberately run your hands over the surface of objects, linger to experience their physical characteristics, and then consciously recall your past experiences with similar objects and textures. Develop this as a conscious daily habit and texture will become an unconscious part of the images you select to communicate your ideas.

SPACE

Your ideas, by themselves, are abstractions. They become concrete and transferable only when translated into symbols and concrete images that exist in a space/time environment. In dealing with the static image, we're dealing primarily with space—with the arrangement of visual elements in a given area. Time, in the static image, is "frozen"—a captured moment. For the static image, there is fixed truth. For the moving image, there is emerging truth. The moving image is defined by the arrangements and continual re-arrangements of both time and space. The static image is defined by arrangements of space only—the space within the frame. A space that can be filled, in varying degrees, with many different types of information—information transmitted by characters; character actions and reactions; objects; locations and set design; costumes, hair styles and makeup; and music, sound effects, and dialogue.

The concepts of space are of great importance to the screenwriter because they speak about the many "spaces" upon which information can be placed. The ability to develop and convincingly portray events and characters depends upon the amount of cognitive and affective information conveyed within a given period of time. This is the screenwriter's constant concern. Each frame provides many "spaces"—layers—for information and each layer is related to all other layers, thus exponentially increasing the channels for communication.

Within the frame there is positive space and negative space. The entire frame is negative space until something is placed within it—a dot, a line, a shape. Negative space is empty space. Occupied areas are positive space. Too much positive space is crowded and too much negative space is vacant.

You can discover and feel the difference between the two by using your viewfinder. Fill your frame with a crowd of people or objects and then with just one or two persons or objects. Think about the emotional response stimulated by first one and then the other. Chances are you felt boxed in and confined with the heavily loaded positive space and isolated and lonely with the negative space. Normally you don't create either in this extreme but you can—if either of these responses is the one you want to elicit. In other words, if the event you're presenting is one of confinement, the image should elicit a response of confinement and if it's a lonely, cold event, the images should reflect that.

Normally the frame is composed of an interplay of positive and negative spaces, sometimes stressing one or the other and sometimes keeping them equal. The positive space may be very complex and contain a great deal of information or be very simple and contain little information. The density of the frame is primarily determined by the quantity and kind of people or objects you select to place in the frame, but can also be determined by the choice of the lens to be used.

LENSES

There are wide-angle lenses, long focal length (narrow-angle) lenses, and a normal angle lens. Your paper viewfinder won't show the difference between these types of lenses because the difference is created within the optics of each lens. The wide-angle lenses accept a wide angle of view and the long focal length lenses have a narrower angle of view that creates the illusion of magnification. In the middle, between the wide-angle and the long focal length lens, there's the normal angle lens that approximates the way the human eye sees things.

The long focal length lens acts like a pair of binoculars to bring faraway objects up close and reduce negative space by crowding things closely together. It diminishes the sense of individuality as behavior and structures appear homogeneous. The wide-angle lens spreads things out and enlarges the negative space. It increases the sense of depth and separation and allows the viewer to see a wide field of view. It allows for action to occur in the foreground, middle ground, and background. The decision about which lens to use is generally a production decision but may well be suggested by the idea and mood the screenwriter wants to communicate.

CAMERA POSITION

In addition to being aware of the amount and the arrangement of information, you need to think about how the information will be photographed and viewed. The position of the camera—its angle and distance from the subject or object—carries significant information in itself.

You've already become acquainted with the differences between the bird's eye, the frog's eye, and the normal view. You've seen the sense of power, the tension, and excitement created by low angles, and the feelings of submission and isolation created by high angles. Look through your viewfinder again and tilt slightly to the left or right. See how this angle distorts the image and causes you to become disoriented.

The size of the object or subject has an impact on how you perceive it. Placing the camera close to an object or subject is like standing there yourself. Think of how you respond when you stand within a few feet of another person. You see only the face and that in great detail. You may experience a strong sense of vulnerability because of the possibility of touching each other or you may enjoy the intimacy of being that close. Our normal vision of another person includes at least their shoulders and more frequently

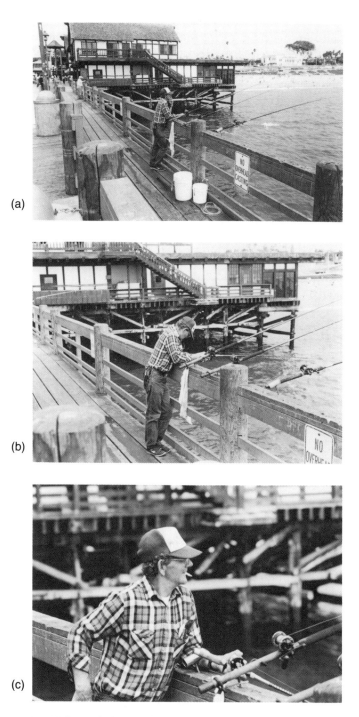

(a) Wide angle lense, (b) normal angle lense, and (c) long
focal length lense.

their waist as well. This is a distance we're used to and most comfortable with. The farther away we move the less detail we see and the less vulnerable and more detached we feel. Distance diminishes the power, the strength, and the importance of the subject or object. Use your viewfinder again to move close and then far away from a person. Stop at different points and experience your feelings at the different distances and angles.

MONTAGE

Normally we observe each "framed" space in a linear fashion—one space at a time—but, through the use of multiple exposures, it's possible to create a non-linear, simultaneous view of a number of different spaces. This capability allows the screenwriter to select and then to combine a variety of different spaces into one meaningful whole. It allows us to penetrate and look at the many sides of a person, object, or idea within a single frame. Multiple exposures are most frequently a part of motion picture montage. Motion montage will be discussed in a later chapter but now, within the context of the static image, multiple exposures need to be considered as another one of the visual elements that can be selected and arranged to communicate the thoughts and feelings of the screenwriter.

   Close your eyes and imagine a frame that contains a person engaged in some activity—playing a piano, weeding a garden, or eating an ice cream cone. Now imagine in the same frame the same person doing the same thing but at different ages, with the earliest age being the most dominant image. Your selection and arrangement of these multiple images communicates something about the activity that a single image alone would not do.

IMAGE SELECTION

The entire process of screenwriting is the process of selection and arrangement, and this process manifests itself within each frame of each shot. But screenwriting is not a process for its own sake. It is a process that fulfills the function of all art forms—the expression of ideas. In a lecture on "The Dynamic Image," Susanne K. Langer addressed this issue and defined the function and structure of a work of art.

> What is the work of art for—the dance, the virtual dynamic image? To express its creator's ideas of immediate, felt, emotive life. To set forth directly what feeling is like. A work of art is a composition of tensions and resolutions, balance and unbalance, rhythmic coherence, a precarious yet continuous unity. Life is a natural process of such tensions, balances, rhythms; it is these that we feel, in quietness or emotion, as the pulse of our own living. In the work of art they are expressed, symbolically shown, each aspect of feeling developed as one develops an idea, fitted together for clearest presentation. A dance is not a symptom of a dancer's feeling, but an expression of its composer's knowledge of many feelings. . . . Every work of art is such an image, whether it be a dance, a statue, a picture, a piece of music, or a work of poetry. It is an outward showing of inward nature, an objective presentation of subjective reality; and the reason that it can symbolize things of the inner life is that it has the same kinds of relations and elements. (1)

These ideas, as expressed by Susanne Langer, are commonly used in teaching screenwriting, especially as they relate to content. The objectification of subjective life is the essence of the content of a screenplay and the essence of each of the screenplay's images. It is the screenwriter's job to select the characters and events that create tension and resolution, balance and unbalance, and rhythm. It is the screenwriter's job to select the images that will evoke those same responses. The two jobs cannot be separated.

The choice of images is indeed a selection process. It can never be haphazard, willy-nilly. There must be a deliberate selection and arrangement of both story and visual elements to achieve a specific and common purpose. The strength and will of characters and events are pitted against each other but this strength and will must have line, shape, color, texture, direction, and position. It is when the two are synchronized—each expressing the same subjective life—that the communication is most clear and most powerful. This is the wedding of form and content. This is filmic writing!

TENSIONS AND RESOLUTIONS

Tensions and the need for resolutions are created by visual elements and plot events that confront and contradict each other—visual elements and plot events that are equal in strength but opposite in direction. This is the constant challenge confronting the screenwriter, and an endless number of alternative solutions are available. There are lines that intersect, colors that clash, shapes that dominate, movements that collide, textures that mismatch, positions that distort, directions that impact. There are battles to fight, races to run, goals that conflict, and incongruities that rub against each other. Collisions and contradictions create tensions and the need for resolution.

Imagine an image of a shabbily dressed, unshaven, very dirty man seated in an elegant restaurant. In all probability your mind will immediately go to work to resolve the apparent contradiction. You won't see the man as separate from the location. You'll see the two as having some necessary relationship and your mind will be forced to find a relationship to explain the seeming incongruity —perhaps he's an eccentric but wealthy celebrity, a relative of the owner, or a gunman holding the restaurant hostage. Your mind will be compelled to search for answers to explain the contradiction.

Think for a moment and remember images that compelled you to ask questions until you found a satisfactory answer. A beautiful doll lying in a mud puddle. Drops of blood on your kitchen floor. A drummer marching to his own music down a lonely road. Go in search of such images. Fill your Journal with these images.

Images that consist of elements equal in strength *and* equal in direction do not demand involvement. They're lifeless. There's no tension, no drama, and no need for resolution. Resolution occurs as the direct result of collisions and contradictions that demand involvement. Resolution occurs when we find or create a pattern, an order, that will tie things together so they make sense. Then, and only then, can we move on to participate in something else. This is a psychological phenomenon often referred to as the need for closure. It's a very active process and the process that involves us in any of the art forms—and life itself.

BALANCE AND UNBALANCE

Balance is extremely important to the human condition. It's what makes our worlds stable, comprehensible, and unambiguous. A balanced frame embodies visual unity and carries a clear message.

A balanced frame.

An unbalanced frame is incomplete and uncertain. It makes it hard, if not impossible, to grasp a meaning. An unbalanced frame may create the tension of frustration, but not the tension of involvement.

An unbalanced frame.

Balance is achieved when the visual forces compensate each other. It may be symmetrical or asymmetrical.

Arrangements that are totally symmetrically balanced contain very little tension and are the most stable. They communicate a sense of dependability, authority, and harmony.

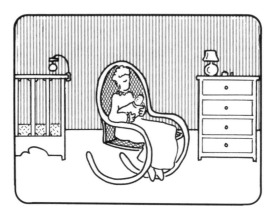

A symmetrically balanced frame.

Asymmetrical arrangements contain tension and communicate a sense of excitement, irregularity, and instability. Asymmetry is primarily created by the interplay of counterbalancing forces—size, shape, location, and color. It's the interdependence of these elements that holds each in its place. Each element demands the presence of a counterbalancing element.

This interplay involves the viewers, holds their attention, and leads them along a path of discovery toward understanding and resolution.

An asymmetrically balanced frame.

Understanding and imaging visual balance and tension serves two major purposes. First, it focuses your attention on the importance of including counterbalancing visual forces in the screenplay. Second, if you understand and internalize these concepts of visual balance and tension as they relate to the static frame, you may well find it easier to grasp and implement the creation of balance and tension in terms of character, plot, theme, and mise-en-scène.

The actual "framing" of a shot—establishing balance through the placement of the camera in relation to the arranged action and objects—is, of course, a production decision shared by the film director and the director of photography. The screenwriter has provided the ingredients and the production team "arranges" them to achieve the screenwriter's cognitive and affective objectives.

RHYTHMS

Visual rhythm is created by repeating and alternating similarities. It is action and repose, tension and release, and attachment and detachment. It is what keeps you involved with the image as your eye is guided from place to place within the frame. Although we normally think of rhythm as movement manifested in art forms such as dance or music, it can also be found in the single motion picture frame. There can be alternating and repeating shapes, colors, textures, positions, lengths, angles, curves, light, and directions. The image can be very still or vibrant.

Your eyes see the similarities and move from one to all others. The rhythm comes from the stimulus of the image and the response of the viewer.

(a)   (b)

(a) Still rhythms and (b) vibrant rhythms.

CONTRASTS

Contrast is another visual element of importance to you. Whereas rhythm depends upon similarities, and tension and the need for resolution rely upon contradictions that imply or create conflict, contrast explicitly shows differences. Conflict may result from these differences but need not. Differences can exist without conflict. Contrast is a means of sharpening your meaning. White next to black appears more white than if next to grey; silence juxtaposed with sound emphasizes each; gentleness beside roughness makes each more gentle and more rough.

Meaning exists in the context of polarities. Something is small only in contrast to that which is big. Spontaneity is recognized when it deviates from the predictable. Simplicity becomes apparent when coupled with complexity. All things are made of two sides. Love is the other side of hate, justice the other side of injustice, calm the other side of chaos. All things are on a continuum someplace on a scale between cold and hot, wealth and poverty, or war and peace.

The selection of contrasting images is important as a means of sharpening your meaning and, also, as a means of heightening the affective communication. A car careening out of control in a pastoral setting is more terrifying than in an urban setting. A lone figure seated in the center of a vacant room is more alienated than when seated among people. Kindness is more poignant when freely given in an atmosphere of anger.

THE WAY YOUR EYES SEE

As you've already discovered, your eyes don't "see" everything all at once. They can only look at one given area or object at a time. They move from individual configurations to a configuration of a whole. Your eyes enter the frame, move from place to place, and then exit the frame. This movement is determined by the selection and arrangement of the visual elements—the composition of the frame.

Your eyes will be drawn to the movement within the frame. Although the static frame is fixed, it still contains motion. It is implied motion—arrested motion—and indicates a direction. The direction can be vertical or horizontal, implosive or explosive, rapid or slow, and it can keep the viewer's eyes within the frame or force them to exit.

You eyes will be drawn to the characters or objects of the greatest size and weight. The colors that are the richest, strongest, and brightest will demand your attention. Objects and characters in full illumination and center foreground will be the most compelling.

A trip to your local art museum can greatly enhance your understanding of all of the concepts discussed in this chapter. Select a painting that intrigues you and become aware of how your eyes move and what they're drawn to. Explore the painting in great detail. Stay with it a long time.

Examine its lines, shapes, colors, textures, lighting, rhythms, contradictions, balance, contrasts, and how all of its layers combine to say something to you. Think about what it says to you and become aware of your affective response. Think about how the artist has used form to communicate his or her ideas. Acknowledge whether or not you feel connected with the artist and what he or she has wanted to say.

Always it is the work of the artist—poet, painter, dancer, or screenwriter—to present the stimuli that will elicit a response consistent with content. Always it is the work of artists to use the elements of their medium to achieve control over the viewer's responses. These are the tasks you are learning.

REFERENCE

1. Susanne Langer, *Problems of Art*, Charles Scribner's Sons, New York, 1957, p. 8.

2

STRUCTURING FILMIC TIME

Time is something we're all very familiar with. We know its meaning in many ways. We use time, mark time, waste time, pass time. There's double time and triple time, Christmastime, play time, and at this point in time. There's time past, the present time, and future time. There's a time to eat, a time to hand in assignments, a time to pick raspberries, and the need to get somewhere on time.

Time is a concept that deals with the order in which events occur and the measurement of how much time elapses between the beginnings and endings of given events. A structure becomes a specific shape of time. *A screenplay is a specific shape of time.*

There's a logical order to the passage of time because there's a logical order to events. You enter a room before you leave it, you have to have been asleep in order to awaken, you can only answer a letter after you have received it, and your last bite of dinner can only occur after a first bite.

Time is measured in a number of different ways. There's the natural way, which is based on natural processes: the return of days and nights, the seasons, gestation periods, births, and growth rings in trees.

There are artifical ways to measure time which establish a constant frequency element and a means of counting the elements: pocket watches, hourglasses, cuckoo clocks, and campaniles.

Then there's the filmic way. Filmic time is fragments of incidents selected to create an artificial order and progression of events occurring within an artificial period of time. Filmic time can condense events that would take two days or two decades of natural time into two minutes or two hours of actual viewing time. It can expand an event that would naturally take two minutes to occur into five or twenty-five minutes of viewing time. It can achieve a sense of experiencing different events simultaneously. It can mix time realities. Future events can precede present events and the past can follow the present. It can speed up, slow down, reverse, and freeze the natural motions of an event.

ELLIPSIS

It's a combination of the functioning of the human mind and the editorial process that makes the creation of filmic time possible.

The human mind constantly seeks cause and effect explanations and relationships between all things. Our minds find it very difficult to live in ambiguity. The need to hear the other shoe drop isn't limited to the telling of jokes. In all of life we're continually receiving stimuli that must be organized into meaningful structures. This phenomenon is the basis of the motion picture art form. By selectively adding one image to another, by combining these selected images into scenes, and scenes into sequences, we provide the stimuli for a progressive organization of meaning.

To look at a single shot is simply to know that particular event, object, or person. When a second shot is attached to the first, the mind seeks an understanding of a relationship between the two. Assuming that each individual shot already has its own and prior meaning, a relationship is assumed or discovered; a synthesis of the two is formed; and a new "shape" is created. A + B = C. This new gestalt may be a very obvious and simple one, as in the normal progression of an event, or it may require a mental leap from one thought to another. In screenwriting you work with both—the simple and complex. Both are conscious and deliberate choices.

This need for the integration and structuring of stimuli works for us, but it can also work against us. Given a minimum of information, the viewer will draw from his or her past experiences and fill in whatever additional information is needed to create a satisfactory meaning. Given a vacuum, the viewer will rush in to fill the void—"vacuum deduction." When this happens, the viewer becomes the screenwriter and you have become merely the supplier of stimuli. The solution for this lies in the careful selection and inclusion of all necessary information. Then, and only then, will the viewer walk along your chosen path rather than creating his or her own.

Our minds demand the integration and structuring of stimuli and they also make assumptions. Our minds assume that a process set into motion will continue until it's completed. We assume that our past knowledge of an event will apply to a similar event in the present and future.

These assumptions make ellipsis possible—they make it possible to el-lipse. Although not normal usage, but to emphasize the active nature of ellipsis, I will be using this word as a verb as well as a noun. Ellipsing is the elimination of any information that can be known and understood by inference. This is the process that allows you to shorten real time into filmic time. Ellipsis is not unique to screenwriting, but because of the high in-ferential value and multiple information layers of imagery it's a particularly effective filmic process.

Ellipsis is perhaps the most important thing for the screenwriter to know and deal with. Ellipsing *is* the process of structuring. The selection and ordering of the most important, most dramatic, most compelling moments of an event is the main task of the screenwriter. In its broadest sense, the discovery of the seed of a story is the first moment of ellipsing. It's the shedding of all that's insignificant and the grasping of the essence of the situation. It's the truth you want to write about. Then ellipsing—structuring—continues as all of the most important events are chosen to contribute to the telling of that truth.

Since a screenplay is a specific shape of time, screenplay structure must be studied in the context of filmic time. Concurrently, it can also be studied in the context of classical dramatic structure.

CLASSICAL DRAMATIC STRUCTURE

In the last quarter of the 20th century there is no absolute way to structure a screenplay, but the largest proportion of our contemporary screenplays utilize principles of storytelling that have been around for a very long time. As far back as 400 B.C., in his book *Poetics*, Aristotle analyzed both Comedy and Tragedy and defined Tragedy as

> . . . an imitation of an action that is complete, and whole, and of a certain magnitude; . . . A whole is that which has a beginning, a middle, and an end. A beginning is that which does not itself follow anything by causal necessity, but after which something naturally is or comes to be. An end, on the contrary, is that which itself naturally follows some other thing, either by necessity, or as a rule, but has nothing following it. A middle is that which follows something as some other thing follows it. A well-constructed plot, therefore, must neither begin nor end at haphazard, but conform to these principles. (1)

Whereas there are many excellent screenplays that do not "conform to these principles," it's important for you to understand and learn to implement them. Aristotle's *Poetics* is the basis for understanding all structures of storytelling. Then, if you wish, it can become a structure to *consciously* deviate from as you create your own "principles." Like painters learn basic methods of drawing and pianists learn scales and chords, writers learn classical—Aristotelian—dramatic structure.

It's certainly not strange that the principles expressed by Aristotle have been and continue to be the dominant structure of storytelling. All of life contains beginnings, middles, and ends: people are born, live, and die; the day starts, unfolds, and ends; a boy and girl meet, fall in love, and become mates; a journey begins, is traveled, and reaches its destination;

a child is conceived, develops, and is born. Beginnings, middles, and ends are the human experience—the way of life and the way we tell stories.

Kurt Luedtke's *Out of Africa* is the story of a woman's experiences in Africa during a loveless marriage of convenience and a turbulent love affair. The screenplay *begins* with scenes of Africa and establishes the fact that Karen Dinesen is about to marry Baron Bror Blixen, the twin of her former lover. She is exchanging her family's money for a title. The *middle* deals with her struggle to discover and maintain her identity and her experiences with Denys Finch-Hatton, the man she truly loves. The screenplay *ends* with her leaving Africa. She has lost everything. Her farm and coffee crop have burned. She is penniless and Denys has died in an airplane crash. She leaves, but she leaves with her own enhanced sense of self-esteem and the earned respect of all who have known her.

Beginnings

Most beginnings have the same ingredients—the principal characters are confronted with a *new experience* and a *problem to solve,* a problem that doesn't have an easy solution. In the beginning of *Out of Africa*, Karen is confronted with a new environment and a loveless marriage contract, and she must find a way to maintain her dignity and financial security in a situation where both are very tenuous.

The beginning starts the ball rolling. We meet the main characters, find out where the story's going to take place, learn about the situation, receive information about the characters' backstories, discover the characters' goals, and sense the source of the energy that will push the problem to its solution.

In approximately four pages, in his screenplay *Out of Africa*, Kurt Luedtke gives us all of this information.

INT/EXT/A BALCONIED BEDROOM AT MOMBASA
CLUB - DAY

CLOSE ON KAREN DINESEN in profile, glistening, slick with sweat. She drinks champagne, languidly strokes her face and neck, tastes her salt. Idle:

KAREN
When is it they marry us?

She is 28, aristocratic, rebellious, sardonic: a romantic protecting her heart by acting the realist. Her intellect is substantial, of little value to a woman of her time, her emotions those of a gifted child, unloved. Her masks fail to hide her vulnerability: about her always, a sense of yearning that is both appetite and hunger.

HER POV--FROM THE BALCONY

To establish Mombasa: a ribbon of surf, Fort Jesus looming
over the dhows in the harbor.

> BROR (O.S.)
> Tomorrow morning. Before
> the train. Do you plan to be
> there?

ANOTHER ANGLE

Her damp kimono gapes and clings. In a chair beside her,
cheerfully naked, BROR BLIXEN, 26, typically at ease, her
deerhound at his feet. Born to the Swedish purple, he is
without guile or guilt, an innocent hedonist unburdened by
complexities: there will always be something to ride after.

Their manner is peculiar: fond, familiar, yet detached.

> KAREN
> It's that or home to mother:
> I'll be there. Unless you find
> me . . dull.

> BROR
> In bed? Hardly. We surely
> frightened the dog. I've been
> wanting to do that with you
> for quite some time.

> KAREN
> Truly?

> BROR
> Since I was ten, as I
> remember. You were my
> Older Woman. By the time I
> knew how all the parts
> worked, you'd taken up with
> Hans.

> KAREN
> I don't believe I know him.

> BROR
> He *did* care about you, Tanne.

> KAREN
>
> Never

> BROR
>
> You were trying to own him.
> None of us wants that.

> KAREN
>
> Can't we send to the wharf to
> see about my crates? That's
> all my crystal. All my
> Limoges.

> BROR
>
> It's broken or it's not.
>   (beat)
> Is it strange, having been
> with twins?

> KAREN
>   (cool)
> It lacks variety, yes.

She steps into the room, looks for a cigarette. Above the
rumpled bed, mosquito netting tied to a ball. Bror and the dog
follow. He'll pour wine, sit on a stool.

> BROR
>   (a grin)
> Sorry.

> KAREN
>
> Tell me about the farm.

> BROR
>
> You must wait: it's a
> surprise.

> KAREN
>
> Tell me *something*, then.
> What are the women like?
> And don't say you don't
> know.

                    BROR
Just women. Less stuffy than
at home. They shoot well,
some of them.

                    KAREN
Better than I do?

                    BROR
Not birds. It will take a bit
for you to learn the game.

                    KAREN
I won't nag, but I don't want
you involved in anything
serious.

                    BROR
You're the one that's prone
to that.

                    KAREN
No more. If I fall in love with
anyone, I'll want it to be you.
          (beat)
I've talked you into this,
haven't I?

                    BROR
You *did* say I'd be a fool to
say no. Or was it idiot?

                    KAREN
There are other women with
money.

                    BROR
None I like as well.

He takes a sponge from a bowl on the bureau, wets his head.
Then, casual:

> BROR (cont'd)
> Hans says you want my title.

Her laughter, rich with candor, then, serious:

> KAREN
> You've never judged me, have
> you?

> BROR
> Often. You want much more
> than anyone can have—you
> may pay for that. But I like
> you for it. There's no point in
> living small.

> KAREN
> No.

He slips her gown to her waist, sponges her neck and
shoulders. She shudders at the water's trickle. And with
pleasure.

> KAREN (cont'd)
> I feel like an otter. Slippery.

> BROR
> (a grin)
> And behave like one.

He begins to sponge her breast. Her eyes close: she guides
his hand.

In less than five minutes we've met two of the principal characters and
we've learned many things about them and the situation. We now know
that the story will take place in Africa; Karen has proposed the marriage;
they have already had a sexual experience; Karen has had previous sexual
experiences and she has made love with Bror's twin brother. We have a
good sense of who these two people are: a man who is very casual and
sure of himself; and a woman who takes charge of her life, is concerned
about the things that belong to her, is sensuous, and who will not be forced
into a submissive position. We can already sense the strength within Karen
that will push the story forward. The seeds of the end are visible in the
beginning.

In real life this much information would rarely be revealed this fast, but
in drama it is the accepted convention, and is made possible by the selection

of only the most important dialogue and most revealing behavior—ellipsing.

The ball is rolling. We wonder what will happen in this relationship where status is important to one and money to the other, where one is ready to make a commitment and the other side-steps the issue, and where neither will accept domination by another.

Douglas Day Stewart's original screenplay *An Officer and a Gentleman* is the story of a young man who almost simultaneously realizes his professional and personal goals. In the beginning Zack is confronted with a new career goal which he has to achieve in a situation where everything is stacked against success. We immediately learn about Zack's background and his self-centered nature, we meet Staff Sergeant Emil Foley, the drill instructor; Sid, the man who's to become Zack's buddy; and Paula Pokrifki and Lynette Pomeroy, local girls in search of love and marriage. Foley's primary purpose is to weed out the candidates unsuited for a leadership role. He tells the candidates that he has a notch in his cane for every man he "got to D.O.R.—drop on request—from this program." He appears to delight in his mission and mercilessly rides the candidates, including Zack. Also, he tells the candidates about the local girls, ". . . Puget Sound Debs, poor girls who come across the Sound on the ferry every weekend for only one reason, to marry themselves a Naval aviator."

We're off and running. We've met the main characters, we know where the story is going to take place and the problems to be solved. Beginnings start the forward motion.

Middles

The middle picks it up and gathers speed as the main character struggles to achieve his or her goal. But, it's never easy for the main character—the protagonist—to achieve the desired goal. There are many obstacles and difficulties to overcome. The struggle is long and arduous. However, in the process of this struggle the protagonist will change and by the end will be different—different *because* of the things that will happen and *because* of the choices and decisions that will be made.

Zack must struggle to achieve his goal. He must survive and surmount all of the physical obstacles of the Officer Candidate School and learn to deal with his peers as a leader. The physical obstacles give him no trouble. Becoming a helping, caring person is his problem. We see this clearly in the images of his behavior at the obstacle course.

EXT. THE OBSTACLE COURSE - DAY

Foley is timing the class over the killer "O" Course. While most of his classmates are struggling to complete the course, Zack is breezing through it. As he finishes, he moves off by himself, aloof, confident. Foley watches him closely. He's the only one not rooting for his classmates.

In another scene between Zack and Casey, a female candidate, Stewart's images show us Zack's lack of concern for other people.

INT. SEEGER'S ROOM - DAY

Zack pushes the door open and stands there, grinning, as Gonzales rushes into her uniform. Seeger just sits there on her bunk, in her khaki pants and a bra, spit-shining her boonies [regulation shoes].

>   ZACK
>   Good morning, girls.

>   CASEY
>   Ever heard of knocking,
>   Mayo?

>   ZACK
>   Hey, did you hear? Sands and
>   Kantrowitz DORed last night.
>   (his killer grin)
>   Survival of the fittest.

>   CASEY
>   The whole world's a jungle,
>   huh, Mayo? Dog eat dog
>   down to the last one, right?

>   ZACK
>   You got it, Sweet Pea.
>   (eyeing her breasts)
>   Nice boonies, Seeger.

Casey smiles easily and Zack pushes off down the corridor.

But as the story unfolds and Zack risks deeper and deeper relationships with his buddy, Sid, and his girl friend, Paula, he begins to change, to grow.

Change/Growth

Change/growth is the essence of forward plot movement. A still picture, an unmodulated monotone, running in place, a continuous loop all represent status quo. They capture a moment in time without any observable attempt to move beyond that. On the other hand, we see successive and progressive moments of time as we watch the blossoms of an apple tree become small apples, become large, become ripe; infants crawl, then walk, then run; scribbles become letters, become words, become paragraphs, become stories; and Zack growing from self-centered, to giving, to sharing.

Change/growth is what keeps us finding excitement in a novel, in any human relationship, in fads and fashions and in screenplays. But it's not change just to change. It's not the flip of a coin, the turn of a switch, a non-sequitur.

Change has roots. Change happens in degrees and as the result of the interactions between people and events. For Zack, experiencing friendship and real love, finally releasing his stored-up anger, and receiving genuine help from Foley cause him, in the *end*, to change from being a taker to becoming a sharer. Stewart selected the important events that showed what Zack was in the beginning and the important events that could cause him to change. Obviously, we don't see all of the events that happened to Zack during his time at the Officer Candidate School. We only see the most important events—the rest are ellipsed. In screenplays we're involved with filmic time—not real time.

Forward plot movement comes from watching these changes occur, and the lack of an immediate resolution keeps the audience asking, "What will happen next and what will be the outcome?" In *An Officer and a Gentleman* this question is two-fold: Will Zack graduate and what will happen with Zack's and Paula's relationship?

There is external physical movement that involves the characters in activities that allow them to externalize their thoughts through actions rather than "talking" their thoughts. These activities have a forward momentum in themselves. For example, the Dilbert Dunker, one of the obstacles to be mastered in *An Officer and a Gentleman*, is a physical activity that advances the plot while at the same time it creates images of the characters in action.

INT. THE LARGE INDOOR POOL ON THE BASE - DAY

Our CAMERA is the first to ride the Dilbert Dunker, and we are suddenly shooting at high speed down a steep incline inside a cage-like contraption, painted red. Wham! We hit water at neck-wrenching speed and go under in a swirl of bubbles! Wait! What's happening? The goddamn cage is turning somersaults! Which way is up? Which way is up?? A strange-looking alien in a wetsuit and mask knifes toward us in the water. His hands work to extricate us. We rush toward

the promise of light and air at the surface. We can hear our
own tortured breathing. Will we make it?

CANDIDATE DELLA-SERRA REACHES THE SURFACE

gasping for air. The DILBERT DUNKER INSTRUCTOR stands
off to the side, giving him a thumbs down.

> INSTRUCTOR
> Back in line. That was totally
> unsat, Della-Serra!

Della-Serra clings to the side of the pool and vomits. He is
grateful to be alive.

There is internal movement—thought movement—actions, and dialogue
that show us and tell us how the characters are responding and moving
forward. Toward the end of the middle of the screenplay, Stewart clearly
shows Zack moving from being a self-centered loner to willingly sacrificing
a cherished goal to help a classmate.

EXT. THE OBSTACLE COURSE (VARIOUS SHOTS) - DAY

STARTING TIGHT on Seeger's face as Foley starts her.

> FOLEY
> Go!

He starts several of the others Ad-Lib. Then it's Zack's turn.

> FOLEY
> (continuing)
> Go!

Zack takes off across the course with a gleam in his eye. He
wants that record. Zack dances through the innertubes, hand
over hands the parallel bars, and churns his way through a
stretch of knee-deep sand, his classmates cheering him on,
wanting the record, too, wanting to leave their mark.
. . .

As Zack passes his slower classmates, they add their shouts
of encouragement to the cheering from the sidelines. "Do it,
Mayo!" "Put our name up there, Mayonaise!" "You can do it!"

Zack shimmies up a rope, yanks his body over the low
hurdles, crawls on his back under the low horizontal bars,
scampers up the angled beam, leaps the moat . . . and is
approaching the wall full tilt when he sees Seeger up ahead,
struggling as usual to get over it.

> ZACK
> Come on, Seeger! Let's go
> over it together!

He makes it in one leap but she falls back to the ground,
beaten. Zack pauses at the top of the wall and looks down at
her.

Foley watches from the distance.

Zack drops back down beside Seeger. She has tears of
frustration in her eyes. She's not going to make it and the
realization that she's come this far only to fail is crushing
her.

> CASEY
> Go on, Zack! Go for the
> record!

> ZACK
> Fuck the record. Now you
> listen to me and do exactly
> what I tell you.
>> (he draws a line with
>> his foot)
> Start back ten yards and take
> off from here. Not here . . .
> or there . . . but right here!
>> (the total officer)
> No excuses, Seeger! You are
> going to plant those legs
> here and then you're going to
> yank yourself over that wall
> because you have to! You
> want jets? Then do it,
> goddamnit!

Seeger nods, almost mesmerized by his decisive tone of voice,
his sudden emergence as a leader. She starts running, takes
off exactly on the mark, and struggles to the top of the wall.

She drops down on the other side and Zack joins her,
smiling, patting her on the back, as they run the rest of the
course together.

Goals

The middle is roughly half of your screenplay—around sixty pages. This
is a lot of film time and it demands that the protagonist have sufficient
energy to persist in the struggle to achieve his or her goals. The goals *have*
to be important and the protagonist *must* be compelled, no matter what
the obstacles, to pursue those goals. Each character has two goals. One is
a plot goal and one is a personal goal.

Plot goals are very specific. They're what people physically work toward
achieving. Things like becoming a famous pilot, being married to a wealthy
woman, capturing a notorious criminal, or earning a higher education
degree. Zack's plot goal is to become an officer in the Naval Air Corps.

Personal goals are what drive the characters to reach their plot goals—
personal goals like the need for security, recognition, revenge, self identity,
or dependence. They're the voices within the character that yearn for fulfillment, that must be satisfied. They're the needs that create the energy
to overcome obstacles. Zack's personal goal is his need to be loved, respected, and believed in. The character can clearly identify his or her plot
goal but is not able to articulate the personal goal—at least not until it is
achieved. It is the achievement of the personal goal, as a result of change/
growth, that enunciates the theme of the screenplay.

Zack was born out of wedlock and his father, Byron, deserted his mother
long before Zack was born. Zack's mother committed suicide when he was
only thirteen. It was then that Zack located his father in the Philippines
and went to live with him. Byron only reluctantly assumed responsibility
for young Zack and projected his own low sense of self-esteem upon the
boy. Zack never forgave his father for the way he treated his mother and
this anger created the energy for much of his behavior toward his father,
Foley, and Paula. There's an absolute necessity for this anger to surface
and be expressed. This necessity will be revealed in the ending.

Endings

Endings, sometimes referred to as the denouement, contain the resolution
to the problem first established in the beginning. The resolution is the
climax. The climax is the result of the final crisis and is followed by a tag
line or conclusion.

The **final crisis** is the event that makes the situation totally unbearable.
There have been crises—events happening throughout the screenplay that

have complicated the situation—but the final crisis is the most difficult, the most intolerable.

The *final crisis* in *An Officer and a Gentleman* starts building when Sid's girlfriend, Lynette, tells him she may be pregnant. This is the thing the candidates have been warned about and fear. Lynette confirms that she is pregnant and the tension escalates. Sid and Zack argue, Sid fails one of the mandatory tests and he DORs [drop on request]. When Sid tells Lynette that he dropped out she rejects his offer of marriage and announces that she really isn't pregnant. Sid commits suicide. This is *the final crisis*. Zack and Paula discover Sid hanging from a drain pipe in his motel room. Zack turns on Paula, accusing her of trying to trap him into marriage, leaves her, and heads for the base. This is the darkest moment.

The **climax** comes during the final crisis when the protagonist *must* make a decision that will reflect a substantial change within him or her and will create a substantial change in the situation. The protagonist can no longer straddle the issue, can no longer wait for additional information. An action must be taken. The climax is that moment when this decision is made and executed, the moment the change manifests itself. This is also the moment when the theme of the story becomes clear. The final change is what everything has been driving toward. This act embodies the screenwriter's theme.

In *An Officer and a Gentleman* the climax comes when Zack gets back to the barracks; he's determined to quit. He tries to talk to Foley. Foley refuses to hear Zack and orders him to participate with him in a martial arts demonstration. Zack's anger toward his father and all the bad things that have happened in his life are directed toward Foley. Amid cheers from his classmates Zack gets the best of Foley—until the very end.

> Zack offers him a hand. Foley looks up at him helplessly, shakes his head in defeat, and reaches out to accept his help. Then, with shocking suddenness, Foley coils his knees to his chest, yanks Zack toward him, and—at the same time—unleashes a kick straight to Zack's chin. Zack crumples to the canvas and lies there, barely conscious. Foley rises to his feet.

> FOLEY
> Oldest trick in the book. Now, is there anything you want to tell me, Mayo?

> Zack shakes his head, no.

Zack's anger was spent, his decision was made, and the situation was completely changed. This is the climax. An earlier climax had occurred when Zack made the decision to stop and help Casey get over the wall. It was at that point that we saw his ability to be a leader, but bigger questions were still to be answered—would he stick it out to the end to pass all of the tests and what would he do about Paula?

Resolution

The resolution is the climax—the change in the character and situation. If there is no change there is no resolution. Things would simply go on as they were in the beginning and the middle.

Conclusion

The rest of the film is the conclusion. Zack graduates, leaves the Naval Air Station, and appears in the paper mill where Paula works.

THE WOMEN ON THE NAPKIN LINE

send up a buzz of gossipy excitment as he strides past them. So clean. So handsome. So perfect. Every deb's fantasy.

HE WEARS THE DRESS WHITE UNIFORM WITH ENSIGN GOLD

and he wears it proudly as he strides through their ranks, toward the girl who is only now stopping to watch him approach.

PAULA CAN'T BELIEVE IT

Almost as she might have dreamed it long ago as a little girl, she watches him take her face in his hands and kiss her in such a romantic way that it's unlikely the women at National Paper, or any of us, will ever forget that kiss.

He has achieved both goals. He is an officer and he is loved, respected and believed in!

ACTS

Many scholars and teachers of screenwriting refer to the beginning, middle, and end as ACT I, ACT II, and ACT III. This terminology comes from the legitimate theater but in film and video, acts are utilized in different ways.

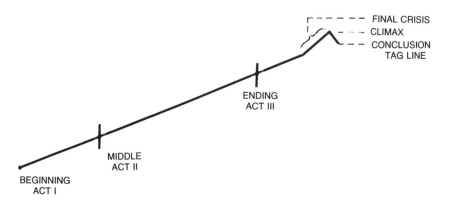

The classical story structure.

In some cases, particularly in television, the acts serve as breaking points and are constructed with each act ending either at the beginning or end of a very dramatic moment. This is done to lure the viewers back after the commercials to discover what will happen next or learn about the reaction to what has just happened. Here the division of a story into acts can be quite arbitrary. The acts are determined by programming requirements rather than story requirements.

There will always be a beginning, middle, and end no matter how the parts of the work are arranged and divided. This is the basic structure of storytelling. However, when acts are utilized in accordance with this basic structure they gain structural strength. This strength comes from the natural synchronization of the structure of storytelling with the structure of the presentation. The wedding of content and form!

In Stewart Stern's screenplay *Rebel Without a Cause*, Act I introduced us to the problems of three teenagers; Jim, the new kid on the block; Judy, a tender girl encased in a hard shell; and Plato, a near psychotic. It's Jim's story but all three are struggling with their need for love, companionship, and parental understanding. Act II presents their struggle to discover and prove themselves as they become involved with the police and make decisions about right and wrong. In Act III, Plato is killed, Jim and Judy learn the power within themselves and they reach a new understanding with their parents.

> Judy moves to Jim and touches his arm lightly. He looks down at her. Changes have happened to them both. Things have been shed and others come upon. He supports her as they move after the litter of Plato where the Negro Woman mourns. His arm is around her and his step is sure.

It is not a dirge as they walk behind the silent member, nor
the wedding march of children. It is that great first
promenade from the locked room of fears overcoming to the
open door of fears overcome where a father may be met and
pitied and released.*

When acts are used as developmental entities, with each act having its
particular function, each act will have its own particular direction. Act I
sets up the problem. Act II struggles to solve the problem. Act III resolves
the problem.

When the function of an act is fulfilled the story can and must move in
a different direction. It is a culminating event, a major reversal, that forces
the story to move in its new direction. These events are sometimes referred
to as plot points and usually occur at the end of Act I and Act II.

The first plot point in *Rebel Without a Cause* occurs when Jim decides to
confront the issue of his manhood by participating in the dangerous game
of chickie-run. His "sado-masochistic" opponent, Buzz, is accidentally killed
and the lives of Jim, Judy, and Plato are inexorably altered. The second
plot point occurs when Plato is tormented by Buzz's avengers, "soldiers
in search of an enemy" and loses his grasp on reality. This forces Jim and
his father into new behavior and a new relationship.

Whether we call these elements plot points, culminating events, major
reversals, Act I/Act II/Act III, or beginning/middle/end is irrelevant. The
important thing is that the elements, by whatever name, be understood
and designed to provide your screenplay with a basic structural unity.

Acts are the largest segments of the screenplay and each of them is built
out of smaller parts. Acts are made up of sequences, sequences are made
up of scenes, scenes are made up of shots, and shots are made up of
frames. Each of these successively smaller parts are stepping stones of
different magnitudes, but similar structures, that lead us along a path to
the resolution of the story problem.

SEQUENCE STRUCTURING

Sequences are defined as a series of scenes tied together by a single unifying
idea dealing with a major dramatic event. Each sequence represents a large
movement—a strong beat—in the protagonist's struggle to achieve his or
her goal.

In Stewart Stern's *Rebel Without a Cause* the first sequence introduces the
characters—the gang of rebellious trouble-makers, Jim and his family, Judy
and her family, and Plato and his caretaker. We see all of them in turmoil

---

* Note how Stern has summed up the entire screenplay and identified the beginning
("met"), middle ("pitied") and end ("released") in his scene description of this last
scene. Also note the poetic imagery of this scene description.

within themselves and among each other. The second sequence brings Jim and the gang together and sets a time and place for their joust of courage—a "chickie-run." The third sequence deals with Jim's decision to follow through on the "chickie-run," the event itself, and the death of Buzz, the gang's leader. In the fourth sequence Jim, Judy, and Plato share their fears and decide what to do and where to go. In the fifth sequence Jim, Judy, and Plato hide in a deserted mansion and pretend they're a "family" while the gang and police search for them. In the sixth sequence the gang and police discover the hiding place. Plato's tenuous mental health snaps and he shoots at members of the gang and at Jim. In the seventh sequence the police attempt to capture Plato. Jim and his father come together in acts of love and self-fulfillment and Jim goes to help Plato. The last sequence dramatizes the unnecessary death of Plato and the changes that occur within Jim and Judy and in their relationships with their parents.

Rebel Without a Cause contains eight sequences—eight dramatic events containing eight unifying ideas. This, generally speaking, is a typical number of sequences for a two-hour theatrical screenplay. There are those who will say there are thirteen, or seven, or even twenty-four, depending upon how they select and define the unifying event. If the unifying event is broadly defined, the number will be small and if narrowly defined, it will be larger. It's not important for you to determine the exact number of sequences. The important thing is to gain an understanding of sequence structuring, and the reasons for grouping certain events together within this structure.

Just as each screenplay has a beginning, middle, and end, so do sequences have beginnings, middles, and ends. And within each sequence there are elements that form its structure—a sequence goal, a strategy, struggle/conflict, a reversal, a realization, and a bridge.

Sequence Plot Goal and Strategy

In each sequence the protagonist sets out to achieve something—a sequence plot goal. This is a goal that the protagonist believes is "the pot of gold at the end of the rainbow." The goal is not necessarily articulated or even conscious, but it's there, and it's something the protagonist wants and wants very badly. On some conscious or unconscious level, the protagonist believes that by achieving this sequence plot goal the overall plot and personal goals will be achieved. The sequence goals are all related to and derived from the overall goal, but must always be different in each sequence. They are different and escalating. If they repeat themselves from sequence to sequence or if the goal is of little increased consequence, the dramatic tension levels off and the reader/viewer is no longer involved.

The strategy is the course of action the protagonist believes will achieve that sequence plot goal. It's what the protagonist does to try to get what he or she wants.

In sequence one of *Rebel Without a Cause*, Jim's sequence goal is to gain the attention of his parents. His strategy for achieving this is to get drunk and be picked up by the police. In sequence two his sequence goal is to be accepted by his peers. He tries to achieve this by attempting to emulate them. At no point does Jim state these sequence goals or strategies. They are unconscious but deliberate. They grew out of his personal goal—his personal need to discover himself and his values. In sequence three Jim wants guidance from his father and here he consciously asks for it: "What *can* you do when you have to be a man?" When his father avoids the question, Jim goes to discover his own answer. In sequence four Jim's sequence goal is to find answers about right and wrong. His strategy is to ask for help. He unsuccessfully asks his parents, fails in an attempt to see Ray, the Juvenile Officer, and then turns to Judy. In sequence five, all three, Jim, Judy, and Plato are seeking the closeness and comfort of belonging. They pretend to be a family. In sequence six Jim expresses his love for Judy and Plato. In sequence seven Jim again needs help from his father, again asks for it, and this time receives it. In sequence eight Jim wants to know himself. He does and his life will forever be different.

Jim's personal goal in *Rebel Without a Cause* is the search for self and self-esteem. The structure of *Rebel Without a Cause* is a series of events leading to Jim's discovery of self through acts of love and conscience. Each sequence goal on some level expresses this personal goal.

Struggle—*CONFLICT*

The major portion of a sequence is a struggle to make the strategy work. This struggle is not just one attempt, but *repeated attempts* that only stop when something unwanted and/or unexpected happens. In the first sequence of *Rebel Without a Cause* we watch Jim's struggle to get attention. He does many different things in his attempt to achieve this goal. He plays with a wind-up toy monkey; he imitates the wailing of police sirens; he offers his jacket to Plato; he ignores his parents; he hums "The Ride of the Valkyries" to himself; he shrugs when asked questions; he challenges his parents; he fights back his tears; he explodes; he rejects; and he acts tough.

The largest and most important ingredient in each sequence is struggle—conflict. This is the element that involves us and keeps us wondering what will happen next.

Conflict occurs when two opposing goals collide. If two persons (or groups of persons) want to travel on the same path but travel in different ways—have different goals—neither will achieve exactly what he or she wants. If they're on parallel or divergent paths, there's no problem. Each can easily achieve their goal because there's no opposition. But if they want to occupy the same time and space in order to achieve their goals, only one will succeed, or each must substantially alter their goal.

I think conflict is the most difficult thing the beginning screenwriter has to deal with. I believe this happens because our culture seeks to eliminate and deny conflict. Of course, we'd like to eliminate and deny global and national conflict. This is our ultimate and most worthwhile humanitarian goal and, happily, this isn't the kind of conflict elimination that would inhibit the ability to develop story conflict. Difficulty in creating story conflict comes from much more personal and individual sources. These sources are pervasive aspects of our culture that become internalized and are often invisible. They program us to avoid anything that "makes waves" and they surround conflict with nothing but unpleasant experiences. This, on a conscious and unconscious level, makes it difficult for the beginning student to embrace conflict. And, if the screenwriter cannot express conflict, it will be impossible for his or her characters to do so.

"Don't you talk back to your mother." "See no evil, hear no evil, speak no evil." "Stay in your room until you can be a nice person." "Don't argue." "Control your temper." "Watch your tongue." "Be a good girl." "Don't be upset." "Count your blessings." "Keep your mouth shut."

At almost every turn we're programmed to avoid the negative and look only to the positive. However, there *are* negative aspects in life and conflict *is* a reality. There's never enough wealth for all of us to have as much as we want; none of us ever is loved enough, listened to enough, or protected enough; we can't enter into every relationship we want when relationships require mutual desire; there's no possibility of always avoiding the forces of nature that destroy and change our lives; it's impossible to live as long as we want or be as healthy as we wish.

All of these things create conflict. When we want something we can't easily achieve and when we're committed to getting it no matter how difficult the task or how strongly opposed, there will be conflict.

Fortunately, in everyday life the occurrence of conflict is relatively limited and manageable, but in storytelling it's omnipresent, multi-layered, very concrete, unpredictable, and requires an enormous amount of energy on the part of the protagonist and antagonist. Conflict is not limited to chases, races, and combat. Conflict wears as many different clothes as there are different opposing goals; it ranges in intensity from disagreement to destruction; and it can surface intermittently or constantly. Conflict is always goal oriented. It is the necessary result of a struggle to achieve a competitive goal. An argument or discussion of different and conflicting ideas is not conflict in a storytelling sense. An argument exists for its own sake—not as a means to achieve a goal.

In the opening sequence of *Out of Africa* we immediately see at least five layers of conflict interacting simultaneously: the inevitable conflict of dominance between two people about to be married because of needs other than mutual love and respect; the sibling competition resulting from Karen's previous involvement with Bror's twin brother; Bror's manner of evading direct answers to many of Karen's questions; the sexual promiscuity of both; Karen's manner of abruptly changing the subject when an unpleasant topic is introduced.

The screenwriter deliberately creates the kinds of characters who'll come together with many built-in layers of conflict. They are then placed in situations where these multi-layered conflicts will collide, surface, and struggle. A single layer of conflict requires that the characters fight the same battle over and over. This becomes very repetitive and ceases to involve us. Multiple layers of confict create many different and escalating encounters and allow the kaleidoscopic interplay of all.

Karen and Bror's struggles with dominance interact with Bror's sibling jealousy; Karen's reluctance to deal with unpleasantness interacts with Bror's sexual activities; Bror's evasiveness impacts on Karen's need to have control.

In other words, story conflict is not simply a win/lose competition. It's not like a football game or a political election. There isn't the home team and the visitors or the Democrats and the Republicans. Characters don't win or lose on the basis of a single action or decision. As a matter of fact, in most stories, characters don't win or lose at all—*they change*. Conflict in storytelling is not there to create a contest. It's there to sharpen and to test the will of the characters. It's the vehicle that forces the characters to behave differently. It's the vehicle that creates change.

Conflict in screenplays is very specific, very concrete. It's a "belly-to-belly" interaction. It's characters dealing in the present on a face-to-face basis with obstacles keeping them from getting what they want.

Zack yells at his father at arms length and fights with Foley hand to hand. Karen personally sends both Bror and Denys out of her life. Jim touches his father as he pleads with him.

Conflict—struggle—contains back and forth motion. If two forces come together and one is immediately neutralized, there's no struggle. It's simply a happening. If the forces are equally matched so that neither can be neutralized, it becomes a stalemate, not a struggle. A struggle only occurs when one force is slightly more powerful than the other. When there's almost equal strength, the outcome is unknown. Each force tries to shape the events for its own benefit and tries to escape the difficulties and obstacles it confronts. It's like a tango with each dancer adjusting to the other's movements, creating a balance. It's this balancing act, the shifting of dominance, that creates tension and arouses the expectation that ultimately one force will change the other.

A good way to visualize the back and forth movement of story conflict is to watch two almost equally matched people arm wrestle. You'll see their arms moving back and forth and back and forth until one finally pushes the other's arm to the mat. If there's no movement, nothing is happening. It's a stalemate. If one person immediately wins, there's nothing to watch, nothing to become involved with. It's a happening.

Conflict requires strength—strength of will—not physical strength, although sometimes that will be required, too. There must be an absolute necessity for the characters to pursue their goals. They must have inexhaustable resources of strength that push them and allow them to bounce

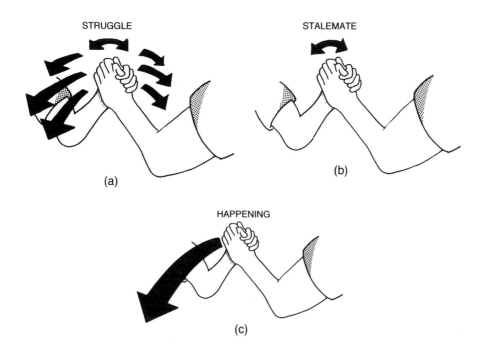

STRUGGLE

STALEMATE

(a)

(b)

HAPPENING

(c)

back when their efforts become fruitless. They must have boundless energy to seek other strategies, to look for alternative ways to control their destinies, and to deal with the unexpected and/or unwanted.

Reversals

In *Rebel Without a Cause*, after Jim's struggle and failure to gain attention from his parents, he does get attention, but from an unexpected, although motivated, source. Ray, a sympathetic juvenile officer, hears his pain. This is what is often referred to as a reversal. Jim talks about his feelings with Ray, is released, and apologizes to his parents. The unexpected ally in Ray created a change in direction.

Reversals—unexpected and often times unwanted events—appear in a number of different ways. There are the major reversals that completely alter the existing circumstances. These major reversals often come at the end of Act I and Act II and, as pointed out above, are sometimes called plot points. They're the events that force the protagonist to move in an entirely different direction. In *Rebel Without a Cause*, Buzz's death during the "chickie-run" places Jim in an entirely new set of circumstances. He must now face himself and define his value system. Another major reversal occurs when Plato "freaks out," turns his anger toward Jim, and starts shooting at the police. Again, Jim's world has changed. He's now compelled to risk his life as he attempts to save Plato.

Reversals, as a structural part of each sequence, are minor reversals compared to the reversals of plot points. Sequence reversals are the events that cause the protagonist to abandon the current sequence goal and strategy to move on to a new sequence goal and strategy. They make less radical changes in direction, but cause the story to "leap frog" from one sequence to the next.

Other reversals create events that simply advance the story and contribute to the character's change/growth. An excellent example of this occurs in *An Officer and a Gentleman*. Zack and his roommates Perryman and Sid are preparing for the weekend inspection. Perryman knows that Zack has a cache of perfectly shined boots and belt buckles hidden above the fiberboard in the ceiling.

> Perryman's problem is his belt buckle, which he is
> frantically trying to shine before Foley gets there. Zack
> stands casually by his locker, buffing his fingernails, his
> shoes and buckle shined to perfection, as always. CAMERA
> HOLDS on the fourth locker, the one that had belonged to
> Topper Daniels. The door to the locker is open and it's empty.
>
> [Daniels has DORed]
>
> > PERRYMAN
> > I'll never get it polished in
> > time. Give me a buckle, Zack.
> >
> > ZACK
> > I'd have to climb up there.
> > He might catch me.
> >
> > PERRYMAN
> > You'd make it. He's just
> > getting to the girls. Come on,
> > Zack. I gotta see my family,
> > man. I couldn't take it if he
> > keeps me here over the
> > weekend.
> >
> > ZACK
> > Sorry. I can't risk it.
>
> Sid gives him a dirty look but Zack ignores it. The SOUND OF
> harsh FOOTSTEPS approaching and the three candidates
> snap to rigid attention by their lockers.

Foley walks in and starts inspecting Perryman. Sweat runs down the black's face in rivers. Foley moves on to Sid, checks out his locker, then turns to Zack.

> FOLEY
> In every class there's a guy
> who thinks he's smarter
> than me. In this class, it's
> you, isn't it, Mayonnaise?

He brings his cane up so suddenly, like a majorette's baton and with one poke knocks the piece of fiberboard out of its place in the ceiling, allowing two pairs of shined boonies, a half dozen freshly-Brassoed belt buckles, and a little black book recording the monies owed him, to rain down.

> FOLEY
> No liberty this weekend for
> Mayo.

Zack is denied liberty and is required to participate in punitive exercises. During this time Foley leans on Zack, both physically and psychologically. At the point where Foley is pressing Zack's most vulnerable area, "a trio of mooners," Paula, Sid, and Lynette appear in the distance, making it easier for Zack to endure Foley's tactics. This gesture of caring and help has a profound effect on Zack and plays a major role in his change/growth.

> ZACK
> All week I kept thinking
> about you guys in that
> sailboat. Nobody ever did
> some thing like that for me
> before. Not my old lady. Not
> Byron. Nobody.

> PAULA
> Didn't you have friends in
> college?

> ZACK
> Not like this.

Some reversals, unexpected and/or unwanted events, are used for surprise or shock value. This is very frequently done in high adventure, horror, and science/fiction stories. Often these events become more a part of the mise-en-scène and are not a part of a structural development. There is a value in surprise and shocking events—a value that can be most effectively achieved when combined with sequence structuring.

Other types of unexpected and/or unwanted events can occur as a result of deliberate misinformation or concealment. Information is withheld or "red-herrings" are planted to keep the audience guessing and deliberately lead them in the wrong direction. These types of surprises are often used in detective and spy stories and may effectively develop suspense and momentary tension, but must be regarded as ornamentation and facade rather than as providing a strong foundation and sturdy framework. The work of the screenwriter more appropriately focuses on the reversals that contribute to the change/growth of the characters and the ultimate realization of his or her theme.

Realization

A realization follows the reversal. It's that moment when the protagonist realizes and accepts the fact that a particular sequence goal with a particular strategy just isn't going to work and is no longer worth the struggle. When Ray gives Jim the attention he so desperately needs, Jim can, at least momentarily, stop struggling to gain his parent's attention.

Actions are often the most powerful way of showing the moment of realization. In the "chickie run" sequence in *Rebel Without a Cause* Jim chooses to accept the challenge and to participate in this dangerous game. His goal is to prove he's "a man." Buzz is accidently killed.

TRAVELING SHOT JIM AT EDGE OF BLUFF

seen pushing through spectators revealed in the spotlight from below.

JIM
(a harsh whisper)
Where's Buzz! Where's Buzz!

TRAVELING SHOT PLATO

working his way through the crowd.

PLATO
(calling)
Jim! Jim!

CRUNCH

Crunch looks up as he hears Jim's repeated cry. Jim enters behind him, continuing blindly on his way. Crunch seizes him and thrusts him forward.

> CRUNCH
> (tight fury)
> Down there! Down there is
> Buzz!

Crunch tries to fling him over the edge. Jim wheels, sinks down behind Goon and retches.

It's at this moment that Jim realizes he hasn't achieved his goal. His involuntary behavior of retching communicates this realization.

Bridge

A bridge follows the realization. It is a transition into the next sequence. It ties the two together and sets the direction for the new sequence. In the first sequence of *Rebel Without a Cause*, after Ray tells Jim he is released and can go home, Jim goes up to his mother and "forces himself to kiss her." This is the bridge that links and moves the story into the second sequence.

At the end of the "chickie run" sequence, after Jim realizes the consequences of Buzz's death, he is momentarily immobilized and then takes his steps into the next sequence.

MED. SHOT JIM

seen between legs of hurrying kids. The siren and the pounding of their feet on the hard turf. Jim is sitting at the edge of the bluff. Plato rushes in, stops short as he sees him.

> PLATO
> Come on, Jim! We got to get
> out of here!

Jim doesn't move. Plato grabs his arm and yanks.

> PLATO
> Get up! Get up! Come on!

Jim stands. Plato pushes him.

PLATO

Go on! Move!

They start away, Plato still pushing from behind.

MED. SHOT JUDY

She is standing alone in the wind on the emptying plateau.
Jim and Plato move past in the distance. Jim sees her and
stops.

CLOSE SHOT JUDY

She is shuddering violently but there are no tears. She seems
not to see or hear or be aware of anything around her.

FULL SHOT JIM AND PLATO

watching Judy. Jim moves toward her, CAMERA PANNING
with him and leaving Plato behind.

Jim stands before Judy until she notices him. He shakes his
head for all the sorrow he feels, but no words come.
Tentatively he offers her his hand. After a moment, she takes
it. She knows only that help is being offered and that she
will accept it with trust. Jim leads her away toward the car.

DISSOLVE TO:

The members of the gang have shown their contempt for Jim, and his
wish to help Judy thrusts him back into action—and into the next sequence
with a new sequence goal, strategy, struggle, reversal, realization and
bridge for the next sequence.

This has the ring of a recipe, but it's certainly not a recipe. Recipes provide
exact measurements along with the list of ingredients. These are only
ingredients. Just as all summer picnics contain food, drinks, the sky, something to sit on, and flies or ants, each sequence contains its ingredients:
goal, strategy, struggle, reversal, realization, and bridge. Each summer
picnic is going to be different from all others because the ingredients will
come in different sizes, shapes, and amounts. Each sequence will be different because its ingredients will grow out of different ideas and be developed in varying degrees.

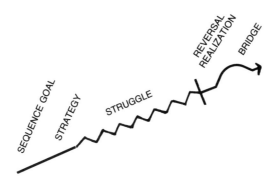

A model sequence.

SCENE STRUCTURING

As previously stated, the structuring of acts, sequences, scenes, and shots is the process of ellipsing—the process of creating filmic time. It's the act of selecting events and images that progressively and relentlessly drive toward the plot, personal, and sequence goals of the protagonist. Selecting the events for acts and sequences is a relatively generalized process. With sequences you're thinking in terms of broad strokes, but when you work with scenes the process is very specific. With scenes you're selecting precise images, the juxtaposition of images, and the amount of time to be devoted to each image. These are the images that tell exactly what the characters say and exactly what they do.

Scenes are the component parts of sequences. They're defined as a group of shots taking place within the same location and the same time frame. The forward movement in each scene represents a piece of the larger, forward movement of the sequence. Different scenes are structured in different ways and serve different objectives. There are scenes that are structured with the same elements that are found in sequences—beginning/middle/end and goal/strategy/struggle/reversal/realization/bridge—and there are scenes that are built out of implied information and do not contain a dramatic objective.

There are no rules that govern the length of a scene, its placement in the sequence, or its emotional weight. The purpose of a scene may be to serve as a transition, to provide complete or fragmentary plot or character information, to reveal emotional responses, precipitate change, or any combination of all of the above.

In the first sequence of *Witness*, a screenplay written by Earl W. Wallace and William Kelley, there's a scene that portrays the major plot event of the story and contains all of the elements of a sequence. *Witness* is the story of John Book, an undercover big city detective; Rachel Lapp, an Amish widow; and Samuel, Rachel's eight-year-old son. In the men's room of the Philadelphia train station Samuel witnesses a murder and John becomes the investigating officer. John discovers that his boss is involved in the murder, is critically injured by the murderer, and manages to escape into Amish country to return the mother and son to their home. Rachel nurses John back to health and they fall in love. John is ultimately discovered by the criminals but, with the help of the Amish, he survives and returns to the city—knowing that his and Rachel's worlds could never be joined.

In the beginning of the murder scene, Samuel goes into the men's room, during the middle of the scene he witnesses the murder, and in the end he evades detection. Samuel's goal—dramatic objective—in this scene is to avoid detection. His strategy is to remain hidden from sight. His struggle—the escalating action/reactions—is to make it impossible for the murderer to see him. The reversal occurs when the murderer's partner insists that they leave. Samuel has the realization that he can come out of hiding when he hears the men leave, and there is a bridge into the next sequence when Samuel fully views the murdered victim.

We come into the scene knowing that Samuel is inquisitive but naive and vulnerable.

ANGLE IN MEN'S ROOM

as Samuel enters.

It's a long row of sinks, urinals, and stalls . . . Samuel stops before one of the urinals—a long, trough-like affair with water drizzling down the rear porcelain panel.

It's set a little high for Samuel, and it is making GLUGGING-FLUSHING NOISES that are, at least, intimidating. Samuel stares for a moment, then turns, looks toward the stalls, stoops to see which are empty.

HIS POV - TOILETS

Beneath the row of doors we can see no feet visible. Samuel is alone in the restroom.

BACK TO SCENE

As Samuel proceeds along the row of doors, finally selects a stall near the end. He enters.

As he does so, a heavily bearded youth in a dirty sweatshirt enters.

With some urgency, he removes a small notebook from his pocket and places it behind a paper towel dispenser.

Suddenly he glances up.

Two other men have entered the men's room; one is a large BLACK MAN in a three-piece suit under an expensive overcoat. His PARTNER is a Caucasian in designer jeans, half boots and a short leather jacket.

They advance on the young man with unmistakable menace. The young man whirls in terror; his two assailants lunge for him . . . a savage, wordless struggle ensues in the close confines of the lavatory.

ANGLE IN SAMUEL'S STALL

as the struggling men bounce off the door of his stall . . . he can see their feet under the edge of the door.

BACK TO FIGHT

as the struggle builds to a climax . . . ends with the young man stiffening with a grunt, his face draining of color.

The two attackers step away, the blade in the black man's hand bloodstained. His partner stares at what they've accomplished with a stunned expression:

> PARTNER
> Jesus . . .

The young man's hand comes away from his belly covered with blood. He stares at it, staggers toward the sinks. Finally his bloodied hand reaches to smear at his face in the mirror. Then he collapses to the floor.

The black man motions for his partner to watch the door, then quickly reaches up and removes the notebook from behind the dispenser.

ANGLE IN SAMUEL'S STALL

as he edges open the stall door a crack. Over his shoulder we can see the black man, his BACK TO US, rifling the body. But beyond him, in the mirror on the far wall, we catch sight of the black man's face.

SAMUEL

as he stares out the narrow crack. A beat, then he closes the stall door.

ANGLE IN STALL

Samuel tries to make the latch work, but it's warped and won't fall closed.

BLACK MAN

as he checks the notebook before placing it in his pocket. His partner is covering the door, an automatic in his hand.

The black man makes for the exit, then on second thought, glances at the row of stalls.

HIS POV - STALLS

All quiet, but . . .

BACK TO SCENE

The black man whips out a .357 Magnum revolver, and, starting at the near end, starts pushing open the stall doors.

ANGLE IN SAM'S STALL

as the black man approaches, Samuel working desperately on the latch.

At the last minute he finally wedges it in.

BLACK MAN

He elbows Samuel's stall . . . the door won't open.

ANGLE IN SAM'S STALL

Fighting back panic, Samuel has retreated as far as he can.

BLACK MAN

as he gives the door a kick. It holds. He swears under his breath.

ANGLE IN SAM'S STALL

In desperation, Samuel does the only thing he can think of
. . . he slips under the partition into the neighboring stall
the black man just checked out. But he loses his hat in the
process. His hand snakes back INTO FRAME to snatch it just
as the black man gives the door a ferocious kick that
splinters the lock and nearly takes it off its hinges. He's
framed there, the big muzzle of the .357 looking down our
throats.

ANGLE

as his partner snaps from the doorway:

> PARTNER
> Will you come on, for Christ's
> sake!

A beat, then the black man holsters his weapon, turns to
follow the partner out.

BACK TO SAMUEL

as we hear the SOUND OF THE TWO MEN EXITING the
lavatory.

A long beat, then Samuel opens the stall door a crack.

HIS POV THROUGH DOOR

Samuel's own face reflected in the blood-smeared mirror . . .
then PANNING DOWN to the still figure of the young man
lying in the crimson pool of his own blood on the floor.

Dramatic Objectives

Every action in every scene has an objective. Some are dramatic objectives
and some are not. An objective becomes dramatic when it conflicts or
contradicts. An action of walking across a room to get to the other side
has its objective—to get to the other side—but it is not dramatic unless or
until something or someone tries to prevent it or to change it.

Just as sequence goals reflect overall plot and personal goals, a dramatic
objective reflects the sequence goal. In the first sequence of *Witness*, Samuel's sequence goal is to explore and to deal with what is for him a brand

new environment. His experience as a witness to the murder is a piece of that exploration and the dramatic objective of that "piece" is to survive it.

Actions/Reactions

Just as sequences have major dramatic movements, scenes have major, and very specific, dramatic movements—actions/reactions. Each actions/reactions represents a series of confrontive actions that have to culminate with one of the characters (objects or environment) reaching his or her objective. There are four actions/reactions in this scene from *Witness* and each is fraught with escalating tension. The murder takes place and Samuel immediately knows the danger he's in. He tries to lock the door. It doesn't work. The Black Man almost leaves but turns back. This is the first action/reaction. The second action/reaction consists of the Man searching the stalls and Samuel finally closing the latch. During the third action/reaction the Black Man discovers the locked door, Samuel retreats to the back wall, the Black Man kicks the door and it holds. Next, Samuel crawls into the next stall, he loses his hat and retrieves it just as the Black Man kicks in the door to find the stall empty. The Black Man and his Partner leave and Samuel comes out. This is the fourth and final action/reaction of the scene. Samuel achieved his dramatic objective. He remained undiscovered.

There are other actions/reactions of a lesser magnitude—minor obstacles that have to be dealt with in some way or other. In building a scene you deal with a multitude of obstacles. Nothing ever happens easily and very little ever happens by chance. At the beginning of the murder scene from *Witness* we see how Samuel is too small for this environment and immediately there are obstacles for him to deal with. The urinal is too high and even its noise is intimidating. This forces him into a stall. He doesn't just happen to go into a stall—he has to go there. The necessity to overcome or sidestep obstacles continually involves the reader/viewer and also serves to motivate a character's behavior. The choice of how to overcome or to sidestep an obstacle tells us about the character—his or her thoughts and background.

Actions/reactions are stepping stones to the dramatic objective. The stepping stones in this scene from *Witness* build a physical struggle—to get caught or not to get caught. Stepping stones in a scene from Abraham Polonsky's original screenplay, *Body and Soul*, builds a psychological struggle—to accede to the wishes of his mother or to deny them.

Body and Soul is a story about a boxer who has to make a comeback choice between wealth or self-esteem. The beginning of the screenplay establishes the fact that a deal has been made for Charley Davis to throw his last championship fight. The middle takes us back to Charley's teenage fight against poverty, his love for Peg Born, and his rise to fame, fortune, fast living, and loss of self-esteem. In the end he chooses to reclaim Peg and his self-esteem.

The scene that builds a psychological struggle between Charley and his mother is in the third sequence and takes place in the Davis kitchen.

Charley Davis has brought his girl friend, Peg Born, to meet Anna, his mother. Anna has opposed Charley's wish to be a fighter, in spite of the fact that they're very poor and this would be a way for Charley to earn a great deal of money. He has both the ability and opportunity to be a fighter. Charley deeply resents their poverty and Anna's control. In this scene, Anna, a proud woman, is assessing Peg's respectability and Charley is very embarrassed by this. Charley's all-consuming need and dramatic objective of this scene is to maintain a sense of pride and dignity. Into this already emotionally charged scene comes a social worker.

>   MISS TEDDER'S VOICE
>   May I come in? I heard your
>   voices in the kitchen.

Anna partly makes a way, and MISS TEDDER appears, not really in the room, but on the verge of it. She is a typical refined social worker doing good in the world. She carries both a briefcase and her social superiority.

>   MISS TEDDER
>   I'm from the Community
>   Charities, Mrs. Davis, in
>   reference to your letter.

The statement cuts through the warmth of the room. Anna's face grows fearful, Charley's white, staring. Shorty looks terribly embarrassed because he knows all about charities. Peg is at first puzzled, and then she reacts in terms of Anna's and Charley's humiliation.

>   ANNA
>   (caught before Charley)
>   Some other time . . .

>   MISS TEDDER
>   I'm terribly sorry to
>   interrupt your dinner. It's
>   hurry, hurry, hurry all the
>   time . . .
>   (she trips past Anna
>   to table, pushes dishes
>   aside, opens briefcase)
>   So many cases and so few
>   people . . . and so little
>   cooperation. I won't be long.
>   I have your letter here. Mrs.
>   Anna Davis. Is that right?

Anna looks around the room. But it is Charley whose gaze clashes with hers. Violence breeds hate in him. Anna accepts the inevitable now. She goes to the table.

>   ANNA
>   (in low voice)
>   Yes. I'm Anna Davis . . .

>   MISS TEDDER
>   Just a form so we can make
>   a proper check . . . Race:
>   white. Religion: Jewish.
>   Nationality: American . . .
>   (without looking up)
>   One of these boys your son?

>   CHARLEY
>   (exchanging look with
>   Shorty; defiantly)
>   I'm Charles Davis.

He keeps looking at his mother, who refuses his glance, then at Peg, who walks into the bedroom, still visible.

>   MISS TEDDER
>   You're unemployed?

>   CHARLEY
>   (impertinently)
>   Got a job for me?

The muscles of his face are frozen, his eyes like slits.

>   MISS TEDDER
>   Have you tried?

>   ANNA
>   He tried.

> MISS TEDDER
> All these questions must be
> answered. I'm sorry.
> (turning to Anna)
> Have you tried getting a job,
> Mrs. Davis?

> ANNA
> Would I be asking for a loan
> if I could find work?

> MISS TEDDER
> It's not personal. We're
> supposed to ask. Have you
> any resources . . . any
> jewelry?

Charley walks up to the table as Peg comes to the bedroom
door.

> CHARLEY
> (viciously)
> She has her wedding ring.

> MISS TEDDER
> (embarrassed)
> We don't ask our clients to
> sell their wedding rings.
> (to Charley)
> I wish you'd understand. I
> have to ask these questions.

> ANNA
> (desperately)
> Go in the other room,
> Charley.

Miss Tedder takes a glance at the old, dilapidated furniture in
the room.

> MISS TEDDER
> Is this furniture yours?

Charley suddenly grabs the form sheets from her hands. He
crumples them into a ball and throws them in her face.

>   CHARLEY
>   (yelling)
>   Get out of here! Get out!

He is beyond himself. His mother cries out . . .

>   ANNA
>   Charley!

Shorty takes Miss Tedder and leads her to the door, while Peg runs to Charley.

>   MISS TEDDER
>   You think I like asking these
>   questions? Someone has to
>   do it. We can't operate
>   without information. We
>   have to know if we're going
>   to help.

>   CHARLEY
>   (shouting)
>   Tell 'em we're dead and don't
>   need help! Ghosts don't eat!

Shorty closes the door behind Miss Tedder. Charley turns furiously on his mother.

>   ANNA
>   (low, desperately)
>   There was no money left.
>   Nothing, Charley, and I didn't
>   want you to . . .

>   CHARLEY
>   (wheeling to Shorty)
>   Get me that fight from
>   Quinn. I want money . . .
>   (hysterically)
>   Money! You understand?
>   *Money!*

ANNA
(with same hysteria
as Charley's)
I forbid! I forbid! Better take
a gun and shoot yourself.

CHARLEY
(yelling)
I need money to buy a
gun . . .

He runs from the kitchen, swinging the door open. It yawns as Anna, Shorty, and Peg stare after Charley. We HEAR his steps clatter up to the roof. Anna turns away and walks into the front room. Peg starts after Charley.

Here we've seen four actions/reactions—four places where Charley's dignity is questioned and he's compelled to respond. The first comes with his realization that Anna is asking for charity. The second is Miss Tedder's question about his employment. The third results from Miss Tedder's questions about their personal property and the fourth comes when Anna tells him they have no money left. The scene has moved from a gala occasion, where Charley is hoping to please his mother, to his defiance of her and the system he sees as a threat to his pride and dignity. The struggle here is not between Charley and Miss Tedder, albeit she exhibits very tactless and insensitive behavior. The struggle is between Charley and Anna. Anna will do anything to prevent Charley from going into the ring and Charley will do anything to avoid accepting charity.

Not all scenes are structured with dramatic development and the full enactment of a beginning, middle, and end. There are those that are structured with implied information. While every action has a beginning, a middle, and an end, it's not always necessary to portray the entire action. When information can be inferred from one or two parts of the action, the unnecessary parts can be eliminated.

In *Out of Africa*, Luedtke implies many miles and a great deal of action in three scenes—one on the lawn at Parklands, one in Denys's study, and one approaching the farm. At Parklands Karen and Bror are attending a lawn party in their honor. Karen is weary and the heat of the day causes her to faint.

BROR AND IDINA-MOMENTS LATER

> BROR
> So they're both of them
> naked and not a shrub in
> sight--

> A MAN
> Come give us a hand, will
> you Blix? Just sun, I think,
> but your wife's gone faint.

INT/DENYS'S STUDY-DAY-CLOSE ON FARAH

Turbaned, stiff on a camel saddle stool, inscrutable, waiting.
He is Somali, that race Hamitic: Pharaoh's son in blackface.
O.S., the MUTED NOISE of the PARTY. He stands.

ANOTHER ANGLE

Because Karen, lying on a couch, a cool cloth on her
forehead, is stirring, sits up, slow to wake.

> FARAH
> Msabu. I am Farah Aden. We
> can go now.

And abruptly departs. Karen looks about.

A great number of books, native art, a huge elephant tusk, a
half dozen hats, memorabilia of public school days, a littered
desk, some sheet music, a dehydrated orange, a gun cabinet
with a dozen rifles, and shotguns. As she moves to the door,
she pauses a moment to look at photographs of two women,
leaves the room.

EXT/APPROACHING THE FARM-NIGHT

Two ox-wagons loaded with her baggage move ponderously
in the night, native drivers silent, Farah on one wagon box,
Karen dozing on the other, Bror on horseback.

ANOTHER ANGLE

As they turn up the drive to the house, a substantial stone
bungalow, the grounds wild about it. From bomas off-screen,

the Kikuyu begin to gather, the children running, laughing, falling silent when they're near.

BROR
Hello the house!

And Karen wakes.

These three scenes take us from the party at Parklands to the farm and from day to night. It's implied that Karen was taken to Denys's study, that Farah was summoned to watch over her, that everything was loaded onto the ox-wagons, that farewells were exchanged, that the oxen were started down the road, and that the distance to the farm was traveled. Only the most significant and necessary information was selected. From this information our knowledge of what *must have happened* fills in the gaps.

These scenes from *Out of Africa* are there to span time and distance, but they also create a sense of place. They show the environment and relate and contrast the world of the white man with the world of the natives. Although they are devoid of dramatic objectives, internal escalation, and provide only fragmented information, these scenes are an important part of the progressive movement of the sequence.

The similarities between scenes and sequences again remind me of the Russian dolls—within a doll, within a doll, within a doll.

However, you must never lose sight of the fact that scenes are the heart-beat of the screenplay. It is within scenes that you capture the emotional essence of your plot, characters, and theme. Sequences are the aggregates of those essences.

SHOT STRUCTURING

Shots can be defined as the specific instructions that communicate how events are to say what they say and how they're to do what they do. Technically, shots are the strips of film that represent the interval between camera starts and camera stops. For the screenwriter, shots are the vessels for information that, when combined with other shots, will develop a cohesive communication about an event. Just as words develop the communication of a sentence and notes of music create the rhythms, shots create the scene.

You've undoubtedly noted that the murder scene from *Witness* breaks the action down into shots separated by SLUG LINES. Slug lines are the capitalized words at the beginning of the shot, such as ANGLE IN MEN'S ROOM and HIS POV—TOILETS, that communicate where the action occurs and who or what is included in the shot. The scene from *Body and Soul* doesn't do this. It's written as a **master scene.** In a master scene there's only one slug line and it is placed at the very beginning of the scene. But both of these scenes contain shots—because both specify the important and necessary dialogue and behavior. Each has provided the information that implies what is to be shot and how it is to be shot.

The final design of each shot during production is traditionally the collaborative work of the film director and the director of photography. Together they determine the final and exact placement of the camera, its angle and distance from the subject or object, the camera speed, lens, and movement. Screenwriters will, however, include specific and detailed instructions when a particular image is necessary for the development and enhancement of his or her dramatic purpose.

In the murder scene from *Witness*, Wallace and Kelly specify two important and precise camera positions, one at the beginning of the scene when Samuel looks beneath the stall doors and the other at the very end when Samuel looks first into the blood-smeared mirror and then at the murdered young man. Both of these are POV shots (point of view). The shot beneath the stall doors speaks about Samuel's curiosity and establishes the essence of the scene. The final POV shot reinforces and echos this essence. Samuel *is* a witness. The crime is seen from his point of view. The position of the camera communicates the idea. Wallace and Kelley also designate the camera movement in the final shot of the scene. They specify that the camera is to PAN DOWN from the mirror to the body on the floor. The movement of the camera becomes the movement of the boy's head, a further reinforcement of "the witness." They also specify that we are to see the black man over Samuel's shoulder and in the mirror.

The camera itself has a voice. A voice that speaks through its position and its movement. A voice that does much more than record what is happening in front of the camera lens.

Polonsky doesn't explicitly specify camera positions or movements but they are implied. When he describes Charley's facial expression, "The muscles of his face are frozen, his eyes like slits," Polonsky implies that there should be a close up. When Charley walks up to the table where the social worker is filling out her form, it is understood that the camera will move with him.

The shot is a series of static frames to be juxtaposed with another series of static frames. The shot is governed by the size, shape, and magnetism of the frame. The shot has layers, planes, and grounds. Lines within the shot direct our attention. Shapes, colors, light, and texture contain affective meaning. Space and lenses confine and compound and expand and simplify. The distance between the camera and subject/object creates involvement and isolation. Shots produce tensions and resolutions, balance and unbalance, rhythms and contrasts. Shots do more than contain content—they shape content.

REFERENCE

1. *Aristotle's Poetics,* translated by S. H. Butcher, introduction by Francis Fergusson. A Dramabook, New York: Hill and Wang, 1961, p. 65.

3

ELEMENTS OF FILMIC TIME

It's the job of the screenwriter to create the acts, sequences, scenes, and shots and it's primarily the job of the film editor to maximize the effectiveness of each. The screenwriter creates filmic time on paper. The production people break it apart and produce filmic time in bits and pieces on film. The editor puts it all back together and creates the illusion of reality.

Through the editing process real time is condensed and expanded to create filmic time. Real time can be condensed by continuity editing, reaction shots, cutaways, and intercutting. Real time can be expanded by cutaways and overlapping. By controlling camera speed, the time it takes to perform an action can be increased, decreased, reversed, or stopped all together. Through dialogue and behavior the passage of time can be communicated. Through montage multiple periods of time can be experienced simultaneously. Transitions form the bridges that connect different periods of time. Real time can be totally reorganized through flashbacks, flash forwards, dreams, and fantasies.

CONDENSING TIME

Continuity Editing

Ordinary continuity editing continues the ellipsing process—the selection and ordering of the most important, most dramatic, and most compelling aspects of an event. Continuity editing is what creates the illusion of reality—it maintains the sense of uninterrupted action and consistent screen directions and screen positions while creating filmic time. An action begins in one shot, the editor cuts to a different shot and then back to the original action which is now in a new and different position. There's no way the action could have happened that fast in reality, but in order to maintain the illusion that it's actually happening, our minds make that assumption. The intervening shot may be a different aspect of the action—something else happening as a part of the event. These intervening shots are called reaction shots and cutaways.

Reaction Shots and Cutaways

Reaction shots and continuity editing cutaways are customarily a part of the scene in which the primary action is being performed. A reaction shot shows how others are reacting to what's happening in the primary action. A cutaway shows something or someone else in the scene. Reaction shots and cutaways are not customarily specified as such in the screenplay. Reaction shots are traditionally a part of the film director's coverage of a scene. Cutaways may be suggested in the screenplay or may be developed during production from elements within the mise-en-scène or actor's business. "The cow shoots him a rather skeptical look over her shoulder," from the barn scene in *Witness* suggests a cutaway. "The Blue Angels scream over their heads . . ." in *An Officer and a Gentleman;* ". . . the old, dilapidated furniture . . ." in *Body and Soul;* and ". . . her deerhound at his feet" in *Out of Africa* all also suggest possible cutaways.

Intercutting

Intercutting—cutting back and forth between shots from two or more different scenes—is generally specified in the screenplay. This technique indicates that the actions are occurring simultaneously and/or reveals secondary but related actions. Intercutting is an integral part of the theme and structure of Daniel Petrie, Jr.'s original screenplay *Beverly Hills Cop.*

Beverly Hills Cop is a story of an unorthodox Detroit undercover cop, Axel Cobretti, who goes to Beverly Hills to capture a killer. Axel is a renegade, but honest, cop whose buddy is killed in his apartment. Axel's pursuit of his friend's killer takes him to Beverly Hills where he continually outmaneuvers the Sergeants Taggart and Siddon, members of the Beverly Hills Police Force; and ultimately discovers and captures the murderer, Paul Fleming. Sergeants Taggart and Siddons are assigned to a twenty-four hour tail of Axel. Axel's search for incriminating evidence on Fleming is intercut with Taggart's and Siddons' futile attempts to follow him.

EXPANDING TIME

Condensing time is a process of subtraction. Expanding time—creating an action that takes longer on film than it does in reality—is additive.

Additional Actions

Additional shots of other things within the scene can be used to stretch, rather than to condense. The primary action occurs in its normal amount of time, but is intercut with secondary actions or people interacting with the primary action. This technique is clearly employed by Stern in *Rebel Without a Cause*. Jim has decided to accept Buzz's "chickie-run" challenge. The two boys are to race stolen cars to the edge of a cliff and jump out of their cars just before reaching the edge. This event, viewed as a single action from the start of the race to the jump and crash, would take less than one minute. By breaking the action into different shots and cutting away from the primary action it lasts at least two to three minutes.

LONG SHOT PLATEAU

The cars are in close, seen from the rear. Judy is a small distant figure, arms stretched high. The exhaust blasts. Now she drops her arms. The cars leap ahead.

MED. SHOT JUDY

She whirls to see the cars snap by, then begins running up the center of the plateau between the lines of spectators.

FULL SHOT SPECTATORS

SHOOTING OVER their shoulders as the cars approach and scream past.

PIT SHOT CARS

As they approach, gaining speed, and thunder over the CAMERA.

INSIDE JIM'S CAR (PROCESS)

He is tense.

INSIDE BUZZ'S CAR (PROCESS)

His hands hard on the wheel. The comb is still between his teeth. He begins edging toward the door on his left.

MOVING CLOSE SHOT JUDY

biting hard on her finger, as she runs forward.

CLOSE SHOT PLATO

Both hands cover his mouth. The fingers are still crossed.

INSIDE JIM'S CAR (PROCESS)

As he edges to his left. He is driving with one hand. He opens the door, gets set for his jump.

INSIDE BUZZ'S CAR (PROCESS)

He reaches for the door handle and misses. As he raises his arm to reach again, the strap of his windbreaker sleeve slips over the handle. He looks down in panic, then back at the drop ahead. He tugs but cannot get the sleeve loose.

CLOSEUP PLATO

staring. He shuts his eyes tight and keeps them shut.

INSIDE JIM'S CAR (PROCESS)

His face is soaked. He looks once toward Buzz—then ahead. His eyes widen in fear. He shoves left and flings himself forward, and out.

OUTSIDE JIM'S CAR

As he sprawls forward—into CAMERA

INSIDE BUZZ'S CAR (PROCESS)

Buzz leans way forward now. He seems to rise in his seat. His mouth opens and the comb falls out.

FULL SHOT SPECTATORS

Staring in disbelief. Suddenly a youth ducks his face into the neck of his girl friend so he cannot see. At the same instant -

                    CROWD
                (in a single breath)
        Oh!

REAR VIEW EDGE OF THE BLUFF

as the two cars go over. There is NO human SOUND.

CLOSE SHOT JIM

as he stops rolling.

BUZZ'S CAR IN FLIGHT (PROCESS EFFECT)

The car soars through the night, the vehicle of a terrible journey.

MED. SHOT BUZZ (PROCESS)

Surprise has gone. He rides lightly on the thrill of his last moment—then suddenly, his face twists in a spasm of protest and loss.

THE KIDS

staring at his flight.

JIM

unaware of the disaster—glad he made it.

LOW ANGLE EDGE OF THE BLUFF

With headllights blazing, both cars dive down. Buzz's car strikes a projection and bursts into flame. As if fired from a catapult, it bounces forward and OVER our heads.

MED. SHOT JUDY

standing frozen as the spectators shove past and around her.

WIDE ANGLE EDGE OF THE BLUFF

as spectators swarm to it, stand looking down.

JIM

On hands and knees trying to rise. Legs rush by him, knock him onto his face.

REVERSE SHOT STEEP ANGLE FROM BLUFF

Both cars leap completely over the highway, bounce high, crash forward into the flat area beyond.

Overlapping Actions

Another method of expanding time is to overlap action. This is done by repeating parts of the same action from a different angle and/or distance. Expanding time by overlapping is not a common practice, but if the story calls for a very intense event or mood it can be an extremely expressive technique. Athough rarely used in contemporary films, this technique was effectively developed by Sergei Eisenstein in his early experimentations with film form. The drawbridge sequence in *Ten Days that Shook the World* is a classic metaphoric example of overlapping action.

Ten Days that Shook the World dramatizes the fall of the Russian Czar and the establishment of the Kerensky provisional goverment. In the draw-bridge sequence people are fleeing from the Czarist soldiers, trying to escape over a drawbridge that's being raised to prevent their escape. A horse and carriage are caught on one side of the rising bridge and the body of a dead girl on the other. Viewers experience the terror and relentlessness of the entrapment through the frenzy of the struggling horse and the image of the dead girl's hair slipping inch by inch into the opening of the ever-rising drawbridge. The event is broken into many different shots and the progression of the event is repeated and photographed from many different angles and distances. The suspense is extended and prolonged until finally the dead girl falls and the horse and carriage plummet to the bottom. The form and the content worked together to communicate both the affective and cognitive information.

CAMERA SPEED

Altering the speed at which film moves through the camera is another way of creating filmic time. This is done by increasing or decreasing the camera speed. Normal motion, as it is performed and observed, is photographed and projected at twenty-four still pictures per second.

In order to make this same motion appear to occur more rapidly, we can slow down the camera speed while maintaining the same projector speed. If, for example, we set the camera speed at twelve still pictures per second there are half as many frames for the same action. This causes the action to occur in half the normal amount of time and creates a filmic time that can never exist in reality.

By decreasing the number of pictures for a given action there are gaps in that action. Only one half of what actually happens is photographed,

(a)   (b)   (c)   (d)

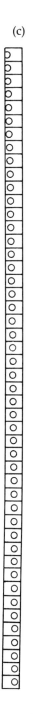

(a) Standard 24 frames-per-second camera speed; (b) 12 frames-per-second camera speed; (c) 48 frames-per-second camera speed; (d) 24 frames of freeze frame.

making things appear to jump from position to position. This kind of "jumpy" movement appears incongruous and is sometimes used to create a comic effect. Although infrequently used, you may develop scenes where this kind of abnormal movement and compression of information serves your dramatic purpose. Compression squeezes out all non-essential parts of a piece of information and can intensify an event.

The reverse occurs when the camera speed is accelerated. When more frames record the motion and the projector speed remains at twenty-four frames per second, the amount of time required to complete that motion is increased. If forty-eight still frames of an action are photographed instead of the normal twenty-four frames, we see the action occurring in twice as many positions and twice as much time.

In addition to expanding the amount of time required to perform the action, a feeling of unreality is introduced and the communication becomes highly subjective. This utilization of film form through the manipulation of camera speed can reflect the psychological state of the character, seemingly intensify his or her physical effort, vary the rhythm of the action and scene, depict the underlying mood of an event or action, and control the audience involvement. In these ways form and content blend to be and to say the same thing.

In *An Officer and a Gentleman* Stewart suggests the manipulation of camera speed to achieve all of these dramatic values. Zack and Sid are being challenged by one of the local residents and it becomes impossible for Zack to avoid a fight.

VARIOUS SHOTS OF THE FIGHT, IF YOU CAN CALL IT A
FIGHT

Zack turns around and hits Troy in the face with two very
fast punches, a left and a right.

Before his assailant can recover, Zack delivers a strange,
roundhouse kind of kick that seems to come out of him in
slow motion, then gathers incredible speed, until it's
slamming with the force of a mulekick into Troy's face. Troy
goes down gushing blood from flattened nostrils.

The freeze frame stops the passage of time completely. This is a single frame that's repeated over and over. The literary idea that "time seemed to stand still" can be portrayed by film form.

This method of controlling time may be used in a number of different ways. It can present a fixed moment for the careful examination of all of its elements. It can signify the end result of a struggle. It can communicate a subjective state of mind.

In addition to being able to increase, decrease, and stop time, the motion picture medium can reverse time. Although this technique is rarely used, film form can literally "turn back the pages [frames] of time" by running the film backwards so what was the last frame is first and the first frame becomes the last.

AUDIO AND VISUAL TIME-TELLING EVENTS

The passage of time can be shown through the handling of objects, through dialogue and through events that in themselves show a movement through time.

In the beginning of *Witness*, Book arrives at the Lapp farm expecting to drop off Rachel and Samuel and to leave immediately. He turns his car around and heads out of the barnyard. Samuel, Rachel, and Eli watch him start to leave.

    THEIR POV - BOOK'S CAR

    The car has failed to take a bend in the road and is now
    bouncing across an adjoining ploughed field. It's knocked
    over a tall birdhouse by the roadside. The car finally comes
    to rest against a bank of earth.

Later, toward the middle of the screenplay, and after Book has recovered enough to be up and doing things around the farm he ". . . gathered up the pieces of the birdhouse . . ." and ". . . works on repairing the broken birdhouse . . .". Then toward the end of the screenplay,

    INT/EXT. RACHEL'S POV - LATE AFTERNOON

    The distant figure of Book and Eli working on the birdhouse.
    Eli walks toward the house.

This action announces to Rachel that Book is about to leave. It marks the passage of time.

In *An Officer and a Gentleman* the length of hair shows the passage of time. In the beginning we see the candidates getting their hair shaved off.

    INT. THE BASE BARBER SHOP - DAY

    STARTING CLOSE ON shears as they cut a swath through a
    forest of hair. In a matter of seconds, DELLA-SERRA, a 22-
    year-old New Yorker, is converted from a longhaired
    individualist into a cypher, balder than a baby's butt.

When Zack and Sid first see Paula and Lynette the passage of time is linked to the length of their hair.

>   LYNETTE
>   (calling to them)
>   See you in a month when
>   you get liberty!

>   PAULA
>   (calls)
>   Don't worry. It grows out
>   about an inch by then.

Then, about five pages later Stewart tells us how much time has passed.

> . . . his [Zack's] hair is now about an inch long. He pats it
> back with his hands, primping.

>   DELLA-SERRA
>   Another week or two, you'll
>   have that ducktail back,
>   Mayo.

And finally, when the month has passed and on their first night of liberty, Zack and Sid again encounter Paula and Lynette.

>   ZACK
>   (rubbing his head)
>   You told us it would grow
>   out an inch.

All but the most important events of that month have been ellipsed and the various lengths of hair have marked the passage of time.

In *Body and Soul*, Polonsky informs us of the passage of time through dialogue.

ON COUCH

>   PEG
>   It's been a long year,
>   Charley . . .

CHARLEY
Yeah . . . twenty-one fights
. . . nineteen knockouts, two
decisions . . .

PEG
A lonely year . . .

This is at the beginning, just before Charley's championship fight. Then at the end, when he returns to Peg, she reminds us of how much time has elapsed.

PEG
(without hostility)
Last year you dropped in
because you were bored. The
year before you were lonely
. . . Once it was your
birthday, twice it was mine
. . . What's the occasion this
time?

MONTAGE

Montage, as another element of filmic time, is defined and utilized in a variety of ways. For some Europeans, and especially some early Russians, montage referred to the entire editing process and embodied their philosophical and often political beliefs. Montage, in the American sense of the term, primarily deals with the contraction and expansion of time; the expressive characterization of a time, place, event, or state of mind; and may be totally representational or expressive and symbolic. This is achieved by joining different times, places, and expressive characterizations into a compact unity of filmic time. These events may pertain to a single event or a particular idea and create an overall impression of the event or idea—such as a wedding or battle sequence. This type of montage is usually achieved by direct cuts from one shot to another. Another type of montage is created by multiple superimposures. This technique can be used to show thoughts, dreams, fantasies, as well as changes in time or place. Then there are the montages that establish interrelationships between images by the use of optical effects to create multiple and changing images: wipes, irises, split screens, and dissolves.

In *Beverly Hills Cop* an opening montage introduces and makes a statement about the City of Detroit at sunrise.

EXT. THE CITY OF DETROIT—HELICOPTER SHOT—DAWN

An icy March wind blasts across Lake St. Clair and roars
through the downtown streets. We HEAR a pounding, high
energy Soul/Rock song that captures the city heartbeat.

EXT. DETROIT STREETS—VARIOUS ANGLES—DAWN

As the song continues we see quick images of Detroit at
sunrise:

—A BLACK KID who's been up all night shivers as he bops
along, ghetto blaster on his shoulder.

—A United Auto Workers billboard reading: "We don't like
your Japanese car. Park it in Tokyo."

—Several HOOKERS in miniskirts wait outside a steel plant
for the shift to change.

—A group of what politicians call the "hardcore
unemployed" try to keep warm around a fire burning in a
55-gallon oil drum.

This selection of images and music is a combination of shots portraying
the awakening of a city and emphasizing elements of poverty within a
particular part of that city.

In *Body and Soul* a flashback montage shows and comments on the path
of brutality that brought Charley to the eve of his first championship fight.

MONTAGE

Overprinting Charley's face as he lies on the rubbing table in
the present, his voice in narration continuing:

> CHARLEY'S VOICE
> I got claws for everybody but
> you, Peg . . .

To kaleidoscope of scenes in which Charley is surrounded by
the bodies of his fallen opponents, as he and Shorty move by
train from the prelims up to the main events. We see
Charley's face emerge through the blood, the cuts, the
bruises, the beatings he takes changing him, the knockouts
he gives changing him, the life he leads changing him, a long

rush of fierceness, of time serving across the continent
until . . .

DISSOLVE TO:

CLOSE SHOT - STEAM LOCOMOTIVE (1934) - DAY to create a
sense of the levers pumping like knees and the whistle cry
above the pump of steam. As the whistle shrieks for a
crossing and the train slows for a coming station . . .

The montage ends with this visual simile and leads into the announcement of arrangements for "the big fight."

In *Witness* there's a montage that contracts time to show and characterize
Samuel encountering a new and somewhat frightening world.

SAMUEL'S ODYSSEY

A SERIES OF CUTS as Samuel examines some of the products
of the twentieth century.

He stares long and hard as a man punches the buttons on a
pay phone.

He's wide-eyed and a little frightened by an escalator.

He looks up at the gargantuan war memorial statue of an
angel holding a dead soldier, which hovers over the bustle of
the station.

Rachel takes his hand and gently leads him away, the boy all
the while looking back over his shoulder at the face of the
angel.

This montage shows events over a relatively short period of time. It's
more of a vehicle for characterization than an advancement of plot or
establishment of setting.

TRANSITIONS

Transitions are another means of creating filmic time. They are a screenwriter's bridges and an integral part of the screenplay's unity. Transitions
are the glue that solidifies the ellipsed elements of a story. They're the
connecting links, the passageways, that carry us on an uninterrupted jour-

ney from the beginning, through the middle, and to the end. The nature of this function demands that transitions call attention to themselves. They announce to the viewer that a change is occurring.

Transitions are accomplished in a variety of ways—through the use of optical effects, imagery, dialogue, motivated or expressive sound effects, and music. Whichever, all transitions show relationships and similarities, push the story forward, and, at the same time, may make a comment about some aspect of character, theme, structure or mise-en-scène.

Optical Effects*

The least imaginative but, nonetheless, very effective transitional devices are optical effects. Over the years, optical effects have been the transitional devices most frequently used and have acquired special and different meanings to denote the passage of time.

FADE IN and FADE OUT signify a long passage of time. The FADE IN starts with no image and ends with the image fully revealed. The FADE OUT starts with the image fully revealed and ends with the image completely gone.

The DISSOLVE signifies a shorter passage of time. In the DISSOLVE one image fades out as another is fading in. In other words, the images overlap each other.

The WIPE may signify a very short passage of time or simultaneity of time. In the WIPE one image appears to be pushed off the screen by another image replacing it.

When any of these devices are amplified by the addition of such things as a BLUR or one of many diffusion techniques, it often signifies the entry into the past, the far future, a dream or fantasy scene or sequence. A blur is achieved by a rapid movement away from the subject/object to cause everything to go out of focus. The same thing can be accomplished by keeping the camera stationary and changing the focus of the lens. Oil, diffusion filters, or nylon fabrics may be directly applied to the surface of the lens to cause the appearance of a "hazy" focus.

---

*The words signifying optical effects are always capitalized in the screenplay.

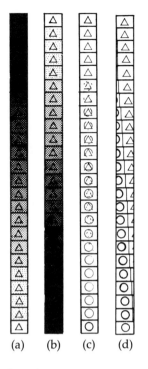

(a) (b) (c) (d)

(a) A fade-in; (b) a fade-out; (c) a dissolve; (d) a wipe.

Aural and Visual Transitional Devices

Aural and visual transitional devices are discovered and emerge from the form and content of the time to be left behind and the time to be entered. Something is taken from the past and present into the future so we know and understand the relationship between where we've been, where we are, and where we're going. Therefore, the operative concepts in filmic transitions are similarity and continuation—similarity and continuation of form, content, movement, action, object, texture, color, and sound.

Similarity of form.

Similarity of content.

Similarity of movement.

Similarity of action.

Similarity of object.

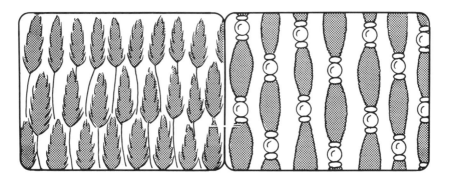

Similarity of texture.

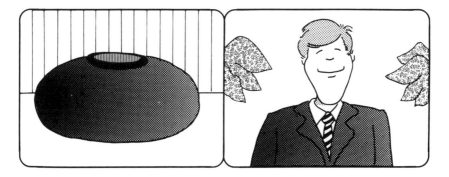

Similarity of color.

Similarity of sound.

In *Rebel Without a Cause* Stern uses the sound effect of a siren to carry us from Jim at the scene of a burglary to Jim at the Precinct Station. At the scene of the burglary "A siren is HEARD distantly, growing louder," and then, after the titles, the "SIREN rises piercingly close" to segue into "The siren SCREAMING wildly, then dying," as the police car pulls into the Precinct Station. Throughout the entire screenplay Stern reminds us of the conflict between the young people and the law and the omnipresent threat of impending danger through his repeated use of the siren sound effect. Granted, this is a motivated sound effect, a sound that was called for by the action itself, but Stern also uses it expressively.

Later, when Jim and Judy are running to hide from the Kids, Stern uses dialogue about water and the sound of water as a transition between locations and characters. Also, the last words of one scene express fear and anxiety and the first words of the next express the same emotion. The feelings of one scene carry over, contribute to, and prepare us for the feelings of the next.

> JUDY
> I feel as if I'm walking under
> water.

They start out.

> DISSOLVE TO:

INSIDE BATHROOM JIM'S HOUSE

The water is running in the sink and Jim's father is fixing a stomach settler. Gradually he grows aware of a heavy pounding which insinuates itself above the splash of water.

The father pauses, then turns off the tap. The pounding continues. Jim's mother appears at the bathroom door. She is seen in the mirror tying her robe.

> MOTHER
> Frank? I'm frightened.

The dialogue about water and the sound of water link the sequences, and then, later, when Jim, Judy and Plato pretend to be swimming in a pool without water, Judy says, "You can't talk underwater."

Through the similarities of images, sound, and content the screenwriter spins a continuous and ever-expanding web of relationships.

In *Body and Soul* Polonsky carries us from one time frame to another through the similarity of the sounds of rhythmic beats. Charley is being prepared for what is to be his last championship fight.

CLOSE SHOT - CHARLEY ON RUBBING TABLE

He wraps the bandage around his hand more and more slowly. He stops. Conflict, indecision, and memory touch his face. Suddenly he lies back on the table and covers his face with his hands. The bandage falls to the floor and unrolls.

> CHARLEY
> (murmuring)
> All gone now . . . all gone
> down the drain . . .
> everything down the
> drain . . .

The pounding of thousands of feet begins to shake the room. Charley slowly removes his hands from his face. The stomping booms louder, louder, rhythmical . . .

> BLUR DISSOLVE TO:

INT. TRIUMPH MEETING HALL - NIGHT - CLOSE SHOT - BASS DRUM marked: IROQUOIS DEMOCRATIC CLUB, and the painted head of an Indian. It beats time, drives into a drum roll, and the final clash of a cymbal, as the CAMERA MOVES to reveal SHELTON, standing in a spot on the dance floor. He has just signalled the end of the drum roll. Now he faces around and booms out.

The rhythmic beat of the stomping feet become the beat of the drum and an entrance into Charley's past. This transition is further strengthened by a BLUR DISSOLVE, calling attention to the fact that this is not an ordinary DISSOLVE.

Toward the end of the screenplay, when Charley goes down for a count, Polonsky uses the similarity of an action and the continuation of content to take the story back into the past again.

FROM CHARLEY UP TO REFEREE AND MARLOWE

Charley gazes into the blaze. The referee starts to count.

                    REFEREE
          One . . . two . . .

                                        OIL WIPE TO:

INT. GYM (A MODERN STILLMAN'S) - LATE AFTERNOON -
CLOSE SHOT - $1000 BILLS
being paid upon a rubbing table. This is a small dressing
room with lockers, etc.

                    ROBERTS' VOICE
              Fifty-seven, fifty-eight, fifty-
              nine, sixty thousand.

The CAMERA PULLS BACK to reveal Roberts and Charley facing each other across the rubbing table.

The counting in the ring becomes the counting of payoff money. The similarity of action and the cause/effect relationship of content move the story forward and cement the two scenes. And, here again, the use of an OIL WIPE communicates the fact that this is not to be regarded as a standard use of the wipe.

In *Witness*, where the use of direct cuts replaces the use of dissolves and wipes, Wallace and Kelly use a similarity of movement to bridge a time span.

EXT. 30TH STREET STATION - NIGHT

Deputy Chief SCHAEFFER sits in a car. Stan, a uniformed policeman, sits in the front. Schaeffer is in the back. Schaeffer leans forward to Stan.

> SCHAEFFER
> Will you ask that officer to
> come over.

Stan motions to a uniformed policeman to come to their car.
He rolls down the window.

> SCHAEFFER
> Will you get me Captain
> Book.

The uniformed officer nods and heads off.

BOOK

Book heads out of the station. He crosses through lots of
police vehicles and activity. He crosses over to Schaeffer's car
and gets in.

Here it is suggested that the cut be made on the movement of the uniformed officer who "heads off" and Book's movement as he "heads out."
In the screenplay of *Citizen Kane*, (1) the story of the newspaper tycoon's
fruitless struggle to love and be loved, a passage of time is shown through
the similarity of objects.

INT. THE GRAND HALL IN XANADU - 1925

CLOSEUP of an enormous jigsaw puzzle. A hand is putting in
the last piece. CAMERA MOVES BACK to reveal jigsaw puzzle
spread out on the floor—.

Susan is on the floor before her jigsaw puzzle. Kane is in an
easy chair. Behind them towers the massive Renaissance
fireplace. It is night and baroque candelabra illuminates the
scene.

> SUSAN
> (with a sigh)
> What time is it?

There is no answer.

> SUSAN (cont'd)
> Charlie! I said, what time is
> it?

> KANE
> (looks up—consults his
> watch)
> Half past eleven.

> SUSAN
> I mean in New York.

> KANE
> Half past eleven.

> SUSAN
> At night?

> KANE
> Yes. The bulldog's just gone
> to press.

> SUSAN
> (sarcastically)
> Hurray for the bulldog!
> (sighs)
> Half past eleven! The shows
> have just let out. People are
> going to night clubs and
> restaurants. Of course, we're
> different. We live in a
> palace—at the end of the
> world.

.   .   .

DISSOLVE OUT:

ANOTHER PICTURE PUZZLE - Susan's hands fitting in a
missing piece.

DISSOLVE:

ANOTHER PICTURE PUZZLE - Susan's hands fitting in a
missing piece.

DISSOLVE:

INT. XANADU - LIVING ROOM - DAY - 1928 ANOTHER
PICTURE PUZZLE

CAMERA PULLS BACK to show Kane and Susan in much the
same positions as before, except that they are older.

Susan's persistent questions about time introduce us to the transition.
The choice of the "enormous" jigsaw puzzles carries the intrinsic communication of a task that requires a long time to complete. The DISSOLVES
from one "enormous" jigsaw puzzle to another provide the fluidity of a
forward movement and we easily and comfortably accept the passage of
three years.

Musical Transitions

Musical transitions can repeat a familiar motif to recall a past event. They
can relate what has happened before to what is about to happen. Music
can create a musical mood similar to the mood being portrayed to communicate a continuation, or it can present a change in mood to prepare
the audience for change. In *Rebel Without a Cause*, Stern specifically calls
for "MORNING SONG by Grieg . . . " as a transition between the completion of the lecture at the Planetarium and the departure from the Planetarium.

REORGANIZING TIME

In addition to expanding, contracting, and transitioning time, the motion
picture medium can reorganize time. It can make the present come before
the past, the future precede the present, and the past follow the future. It
can make what's unreal seem real. The techniques for doing these omnipotent things are flashbacks, flash forwards, and dream and fantasy scenes
and sequences.

The manipulation of time and reality is one of the most challenging of
all filmic tools. It can be used very imaginatively or it can be used in a
pedestrian way. If used as an *integrated* element of memory, expectation,
anxiety, and desire, the manipulation itself can provide insight and clarity.
If used merely as exposition, to provide explanations, it calls attention to
itself as a device and disrupts the dramatic flow of the story. In other
words, the reorganization of time and reality must grow out of and serve
the story rather than be "tacked on." The difference lies in the intended
receiver of the information contained in the flashback, flash forward, dream,
or fantasy. When used as an expository device, the information is provided

for the audience, but when integrated into the story the information is intended *for the character.*

When manipulating time periods, it's important to immediately establish the rules of the game that will keep the audience aware of exactly what time frame they're experiencing. Transitions can help you do this. Transitions can reveal the reason for the time manipulation at the same time they're creating the connections that sustain forward movement and dramatic fluidity. There must be a compelling logic that demands the rearrangement of past, present and future. The mixing of time for the sake of mixing time is readily apparent and weakens structural unity. Each movement into a reorganization of normal time requires its individual motivation, and collectively they must all fit into a pattern that forms an overall structural unity.

The manipulation of time, and in particular the *manipulation of time realities,* is one of the things motion pictures do best. The printed and spoken word stimulates the mind to create its own visual images. The literary writer can only hope, but never be sure, that these images will approximate what he or she wanted to communicate. Projected images in motion juxtaposed with other images in motion communicate exactly what the screenwriter has in his or her mind. The transfer of imagery from the mind of the screenwriter to the mind of the viewer is both immediate and unambiguous. Because of this immediate and unambiguous communication, the viewer can rapidly and easily slip from one time reality to another.

In Stewart Stern's screenplay *Rachel, rachel* we are continuously moved from the present reality to past memories, to fantasies and daydreams, to thought processes, and to a simultaneity of past and present.

Rachel, rachel is the story of a small town old maid grade school teacher who finally admits and accepts her sexuality and desire for independence. Rachel confronts her past, her boredom with her present, her sexual desires, and her fears of parental and community disapproval and rejection. Stern portrays Rachel's turmoil and progression through his manipulation of non-linear, shifting time realities and inner dialogue. We're carried from one time frame to another through transitions that clearly emphasize the similarities in each. These methods are made very obvious in the beginning. Then, as the script moves forward and we've accepted the conventions of the screenplay, the transitions become more subtle.

These conventions are immediately established on the first three pages of the screenplay as Rachel is awakening and arguing with herself about whether or not she's having a heart attack.

>   RACHEL'S INNER VOICE
>   (continuing over above)
>   You've been having heart
>   attacks every morning for
>   seventeen years. Longer.

> Since before you even knew
> what they were. Every day
> it's the same - heart
> attacks—cancer. Get up!

During this, CAMERA has discovered Rachel's hands again, performing a shadow-play on a space of empty wall below the pictures. Shadow animals' heads snap at each other, drive each other off. For a moment, the wall is blank, then shadows enter again, and meet, smaller than they were.

PULL BACK to include the hands and arms of RACHEL AS A CHILD. CAMERA PANS DOWN to show that Rachel, the adult, has been replaced in bed by the Child Rachel. The VOICE OF THE MOTHER is heard, as if approaching from beyond the bedroom door.

> MOTHER'S VOICE
> (singing)
> Lazy Mary, will you get up!
> Will you get up, will you get
> up! Lazy Mary, will you get
> up! Or you'll be late for—
> *what?*

> CHILD RACHEL
> (calling out)
> *School!*

The child looks apprehensively at the closed door as the SOUND of the knob turning comes over.

RACHEL'S P.O.V. - BEDROOM DOOR

as it opens, revealing Rachel's MOTHER, wan and rumpled in her wrapper.

> MOTHER
> Good morning, Rachel dear --

MED SHOT - ADULT RACHEL

as she sits up, blinking sleeplessness out of her eyes, yawning and scratching her head.

RACHEL
Good morning, Mother --

While dressing, Rachel discovers a hole between the lace and the hem in her slip. "She puts a finger through it and wiggles it." Then, on her way to school, she fantasizes about what would happen if people saw that hole. This fantasy communicates her anxiety and fear of unfavorable parental and community opinions.

> . . . She tends to lumber a bit when she walks, leaning
> forward and hiding her breasts, as if pretending to search for
> some lost, irretrievable object.
>
> EXT: STREET - DAY TRAVELLING SHOT - RACHEL'S LEGS
> (HAND HELD)
>
> The legs walk briskly along. Three inches of slip show
> beneath the hem of the dress. The hole is very apparent. One
> hand reaches down to hike it all up, but the slip drops even
> lower. PAN UP to show Rachel frantic with embarrassment
> as she hurries along.
>
> TRAVELLING SHOT - RACHEL'S P.O.V. - CHILDREN (HAND
> HELD)
>
> CHILDREN en route to school are overtaken by the hurrying
> CAMERA. They all look up at the lens (Rachel's eyes), then
> down (at her slip), and react with giggles or head-slapping
> shock.
>
> TRAVELLING SHOT - RACHEL (HAND HELD)
>
> She jounces along, grim, humiliated, perspiring.

As the fantasy continues, Rachel is struck by an automobile, an ambulance arrives, and she is placed on a stretcher.

> CAMERA TILTS to show the Lady lift up the hem of Rachel's
> slip. It is full of holes, mended and unmended.

LADY
I'm amazed the school board
would hire someone who was
so careless about her
personal things.

Mother hears this and pales. CAMERA has been lifted into
the ambulance, head first, and now looks back out the doors
at the gawking witnesses in the street. We see Mother run
out of the crowd with a small cry, stricken. She totters in a
tight circle, like some delicate wounded antelope of advanced
age. Then she drops dead. The ambulance doors SLAM and a
SCHOOLBELL starts to ring as SIRENS moan away.

EXT: STREET - TRAVELLING CLOSE SHOT - RACHEL

walking as before. Nothing has happened. The SIREN FADES
away, but the BELL continues to ring.

> RACHEL'S INNER VOICE
> Stupid thought. Morbid. I
> mustn't give houseroom in
> my skull to that sort of
> thing. Whenever I find
> myself brooding like that, I'll
> simply have to turn it off and
> think about something else.

PAN with her to show the front of the school, and
CHILDREN hurrying toward the entrance.

We see Rachel's ever-emerging thoughts about sex during a fantasy that
occurs while she listens to a dinner invitation from the principal of her
school.

> WILLARD
> Oh! Well, Angela and I just
> wondered if you'd like to
> have a little supper with us
> at home tonight.

RACHEL'S P.O.V. - WILLARD'S HAND

resting on the seat-back. It is a spotted, furry hand. His
VOICE becomes low and indistinct, and the CHANTING of the
children diminishes too. It is as if Rachel's concentration
pre-empted them.

> WILLARD'S VOICE
> (indistinct)
> She'd really like it. So would
> I. We've been wanting to
> have you for a very long
> time --

CLOSE SHOT - RACHEL

She looks at Willard's hand, fascinated, then reaches in
through the window, unlocks the door, and leans into the
car.

> WILLARD'S VOICE
> (indistinct)
> —but Angela's been busy
> with out-of-town relations
> and somehow or other --

CLOSE SHOT - WILLARD'S HAND

as first Rachel's fingertips, then her lips, reach in and brush
across the furry knuckles.

> WILLARD'S VOICE
> (indistinct)
> --summer's here and we
> haven't invited our little
> Rachel in for a single meal.
> So if you could see your way
> clear, you'd be putting balm
> on sore consciences.

> RACHEL'S INNER VOICE
> Stop that, Rachel! What are
> you thinking of!

CLOSE SHOT - RACHEL

Standing outside the car, as before the fantasy began.

> RACHEL
> It's awfully nice of you and
> Angela, Willard, but it's
> Mother's bridge night and
> I always do coffee and
> sandwiches.

Stern creates a sense of simultaneity of past and present by combining
dialogue from the past with actions in the present. Rachel has been anx-

iously waiting for a phone call from Nick. Nick is the man with whom she has just had her first and only sexual experience. She is in the bathtub when he calls.

> Rachel bursts out of the bathroom and onto the landing, wrapped in a towel and dripping.

>> MOTHER
>> (surrenders phone)
>> He says it's a Dr. Timothy
>> Leary --

>> RACHEL
>> Hello?
>> (relieved)
>> Oh, hello—!

EXT: RACHEL'S HOUSE - AFTERNOON LONG SHOT - RACHEL

SHOOTING PAST Nick, who sits in his parked car, waiting as Rachel hurries toward him. NOTE: The conversation that follows is an unbroken continuation of the phone call in the preceding scene, with Nick's VOICE filtered throughout.

>> NICK'S VOICE
>> (filtered)
>> My folks are away for the
>> weekend, so I thought maybe
>> you'd like to play house.
>> We've got like six bedrooms,
>> so we can—you know—we
>> can chase each other and—
>> you know—

> She presses his hand quickly and he drives away.

>> RACHEL'S VOICE
>> Well that sounds like a very
>> interesting book. Can you get
>> it at the Public Library?

INT: NICK'S CAR - RACHEL AND NICK - AFTERNOON

SHOOTING from behind them. Her arm lies along the back of his seat.

NICK'S VOICE
(filtered)
You can't talk now, right?

RACHEL'S VOICE
Absolutely. At the moment
I'm "Venus Observed."

She smiles at him and fondles the back of his hair.

In these scenes we experience simultaneously the present and the future. This entire screenplay is a constant interchange of realities with each reality chosen to communicate the cause and progression of Rachel's growth and change—a constant blending of film form and film content.

REFERENCE

1. Pauline Kael, *The Citizen Kane Book*, Boston: Little, Brown, and Co., Inc., 1971, pp. 260–262.

---------------------------------------*4*---------------------------------------

ELEMENTS OF FILMIC SPACE

We talk about time and space as if they were separate from each other. Actually they're only different aspects of the same phenomenon. We know time as an accumulation of a series of events and their duration. What we know as space is an arrangement of the material objects of an event and our relationship to those objects. One doesn't exist without the other. One is the duration and the other is the arrangement—of the same event. The same thing is true of filmic time and filmic space. Filmic time has to do with the manipulation and progression of an *ellipsed* order of events within a given time frame. Filmic space is concerned with the arrangement of the *selected* visual and aural elements of those ellipsed events within a given area. Each is a part of the same thing.

Real time and real space and filmic time and filmic space are inseparable but what is real and what is filmic are very different. We've already examined the ways that filmic time is different from real time and now we'll look at how filmic space is different from real space.

Filmic space is illusionary. It doesn't exist in reality. It only exists on celluloid. Filmic space is created by photographing and then juxtaposing the photographed fragments of different spaces. By "cutting together" different shots from different locations film form can instantaneously take the viewer from one place to another and can create the illusion that distant places are contiguous. Within the space of less than a minute, the major capitals of the Western world can be visited; and, as a continuation of the same action, an actor can walk out of a room on a sound stage to enter a courtyard at a location many miles away. (See illustrations on the following page.)

VIEWER SPACE

A less obvious aspect of filmic space is its ability to manipulate the viewer's space. This ability to constantly and abruptly shift the viewer's space re-

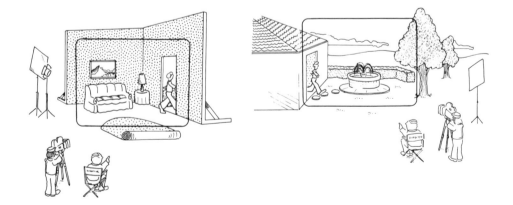

lationship with the people and objects on the screen is one of film's most unique characteristics.

In the legitimate theater house, the audience maintains a fixed position. They sit in front of the proscenium arch and watch the entire performance from one point of view.

The proscenium arch.

In the motion picture house, viewers sit in front of the screen, but their relationship to what's happening on the screen is constantly being altered.

The motion picture theatre.

Film form can put the audience on a crane to look down at a passing parade and the crowd watching it,

A crane shot.

and then, in less than a second's time, move the audience in close to see a tear on a man's face.

A close up.

118

The audience can be positioned to see the interaction between two people,

A two shot.

and then, when others enter the scene, be re-positioned to see the new action.

A medium shot.

Film form can make the audience lie down to look up at the horses legs going by.

A low angle.

It can jump the audience far back to see the entire location and action.

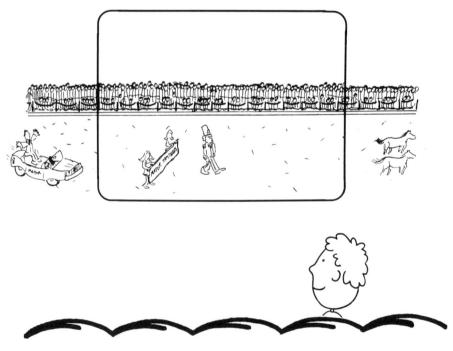

A full shot.

It can move them around in a circle to look at what's happening from all sides.

A dolly shot.

These kinds of abrupt and radical shifts in space relationships simply don't exist in the real world, and it's rare that we ever look at anything or any event from so many different and unusual points of view.

This ability to shift the viewer's space is the result of changes in the placement and movement of the camera. In a sense, the viewer becomes the camera. When the camera moves up to look down, the viewer is moved up and looks down. When the camera is placed close to the subject, the viewer is placed close to the subject.

A shift in the viewer's space can also result from the use of different lenses, but, of course, here the determining factor is the choice of lens rather than the position of the camera. As illustrated in the chapter dealing with the static image, the magnification of the long focal length lens brings us closer to the subject/object, and the wide angle lens both broadens and deepens the filmic space.

The cultural anthropologist Edward T. Hall observes the phenomenon of shifting space as a communication.

> Spatial changes give a tone to a communication, accent it, and at times even override the spoken word. The flow and shift of distance between people as they interact with each other is part and parcel of the communication process. (1)

These same observations are applicable to both the arranged filmic space within each shot and the viewer's space. A movement forward can be menacing or caring. A movement around a person or object can be exploratory. A movement away can signal withdrawal and distancing. The distance between the viewer and a person or object on the screen represents the degree of involvement. The closer the camera, the greater and more subjective the involvement. The farther away, the more objective. Low angles tend to make a subject more powerful. High angles often produce a sense of submission and helplessness. Eye level shots, being our normal view, have less tension. Close shots contain revealing detail. Long shots establish the scene or sequence. Medium shots are the way we normally see other people.

Use your viewfinder and move around, in and out, and up and down to vary your distances and angles just as you did when we were working with the static image. Only this time, you've added a new and very important ingredient—the ingredient of camera movement. Feel the impact of that movement on the emotional content of whatever you're looking at.

The determination of the camera placements, movements, and lenses to be used will be greatly affected by the exigencies of production, and current screenplay format practice eliminates these specifications from the screenplay. This does not mean, however, that you have no input about the choice of camera position, movement, and lens. The utilization of space as a means of communicating content is an important part of the process of screenwriting. It's a matter of how the information is given, not whether or not it's given.*

VIEWER POINT OF VIEW

In addition to shifting the viewer's spatial relationship to the persons and objects on the screen, the placement of the camera can also shift the viewer's point of view. The camera, and thus the viewer, can assume an objective point of view, a subjective point of view, or the point of view of each and all of the characters.

The objective point of view creates the sense that the viewer is merely watching something happening. The camera takes the detached position of an observer. Here again you can use your viewfinder to gain a better understanding and internalization of the different viewer points of view. Of course, you'll be able to understand the differences by simply reading about them but an intellectual understanding is not enough. You need to visualize and feel the differences as well.

So—go out onto the street and find something of interest happening between a group of people—people at a bus stop, an argument in process, or somebody helping another person across the street. Whatever you find, watch it through your viewfinder and you'll be experiencing an objective point of view.

The subjective point of view creates the sense that the viewer *is* the character. The camera lens becomes the eyes of the character and

---

*Methods of suggesting camera position, movement, and lens will be dealt with further in a later chapter.

the camera movements become the movements of the character. Here the viewer is very actively involved. Again, use your viewfinder and pretend you're a screenplay character walking down a street looking for someone. Notice how your viewfinder (the camera lens) moves with your eyes as you walk and examine the sights ahead of you. This is a subjective point of view.

A character's point of view creates the sense that the viewer is seeing what a character is seeing. Here the camera takes the position of the character, not to become the character, as the viewer does in the subjective point of view, but to see what the character is seeing. Use your viewfinder again, and this time arrange a man and a woman so they're standing talking to each other. Now, stand behind the man to look over his shoulder. His shoulder and the back of his head will be on one side of the frame and, on the opposite side, you'll see the woman. This is the man's point of view. Now, move in closer to exclude the man's shoulder and head so you see only what he is seeing. This is also the man's point of view. Next, move behind the woman and do the same things. The camera includes part of her body or simply stands in her position. This is her point of view—and becomes your point of view.

So, through changes in camera positions and movements and through the editing process of juxtaposing different shots, the viewer's orientation is in constant flux. We passively observe, actively participate, and figuratively stand in all of the character's shoes.

LINEAR AND LAYERED MOVEMENT

As previously discussed, the basic structure of a film is simultaneously linear and layered. Film takes us forward through time and space in a horizontal, linear fashion while we're moving inward and vertically from layer to layer. Both consist of arrangements of selected events within a filmic space, and each layer interacts with the others. Linear and layered are just other words for everything in your screenplay. They're all the information you need in order to tell your story and suggestions about where that information is to be placed. The placement, amount, kind, and interactive nature of the linear and layered information is your story. The tablet upon which you write that story is a series of motion picture frames.

In our examination of the static frame we dealt primarily with the inward, layered movement of visual form, and we developed a long list of elements used in the design of the static image to communicate content—the magnetism of the frame, the various planes within the frame, shape, color, light, texture, lenses, camera angles and distances, multiple exposures, tension/resolution, balance, and rhythm. Of course, all of these elements are as operative in a series of static frames as they are in a single static frame. However, now you will think of them in the context of the moving frame—a series of moving frames.

The moving frame, like the static frame, contains layers upon which to position information. The static frame holds layers of visual form and layers of content. With the addition of motion, the moving frame also contains the layers of movement and sound.

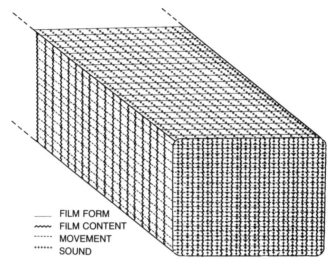

___ FILM FORM
∿∿ FILM CONTENT
------ MOVEMENT
••••••• SOUND

Simultaneous layers of content, form, movement, and sound.

All of these layers are always available for every shot, but all are not always used. One shot could use many different layers and the next use only a few.

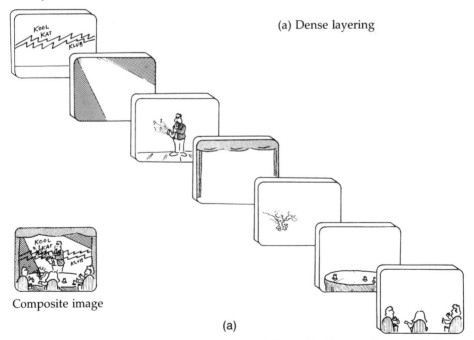

(a) Dense layering

Composite image

(a)

Information layers of composite image

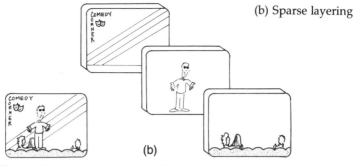

(b) Sparse layering

(b)

Composite image   Information layers of composite image

The information level of any shot may be dense or sparse. The more layers utilized, the greater the amount of information and the richer our knowledge. However, the more dense the image, the less directed may be our perception. The more things there are to look at, the less chance there is to channel concentration on any given thing. This may or may not be your intended communication so, obviously, the density or sparsity will depend upon what you want to say and how you want the viewer to respond.

Information may be placed in the foreground, middle ground, background, center, camera right, camera left, or in any of the spaces in between and around. Also, it must be remembered, as we discussed in reference to the static frame, the placement of any and all objects and/or persons within the frame produces an interaction with the frame and creates various experiences of tension, balance, and rhythm.

The horizontal film space is flat; the vertical space contains depth; and the directions of internal movement on each of these planes is different. If you think of each shot as being in the shape of a box you can clearly see how the movements differ.

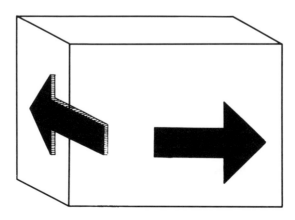

The illusion of depth is created by the placement of objects within the frame. The foreground objects are larger and closer to the bottom of the frame. As objects get farther away—depth movement—they get smaller and closer to the top of the frame. So, in this sense, the depth movement is a vertical movement.

Another type of movement can be induced by a shift in focus. The characters/objects remain stationary but the area of sharp focus changes to create a sense of movement and re-channel the viewer's attention.

Shift in focus that creates illusion of movement.

The importance of such internal movements—horizontal, vertical, or induced—primarily lies in their ability to blend and establish relationships between the multiple pieces of primary and secondary information placed on the various layers within each shot.

Primary and Secondary Information

Each story is built upon both primary and secondary information. The primary information is plot, progression, character, and theme and is chiefly communicated through actions and dialogue. Secondary information is detail, coloration, enrichment, and commentary. Often this secondary information simply creates the natural and normal ambiance of the scene. However, generally—and more importantly—in addition to this natural and normal ambiance, the screenwriter deliberately selects and integrates very significant secondary information into the scene. This information will include secondary actions and dialogue, props, color, lighting, expressive sound, off screen voices and unusual costumes, hairstyling, and makeup. Secondary information deliberately chosen to interact in some way with the primary information may range from simply providing the important details of a setting to creating visual similes.

Primary information is very easily recognized while secondary information is often simply taken for granted. In one of the opening scenes of *Beverly Hills Cop*, Petrie lists only primary information—plot actions. The secondary information is inferred from previous scenes.

ANGLE ON THE REAR TRAILER

A pile of cigarette cases begins to move; Axel emerges from underneath them. He hops out of the trailer, drawing a Smith and Wesson .38 with a two inch barrel. Swinging around the end of the trailer he sees Mirsky and shouts:

AXEL
Hold it there!

—but Mirsky has a gun too and he fires wildly. Axel dives to the pavement, then is up again and running as Mirsky hops onto the loading dock and sprints through the big double doors of the plant.

Here the action is the important element, is easily recognized as primary information, and will be performed foreground and center.

Later, after Axel gets a lead on who's responsible for his friend's murder, he returns to his apartment. The way Petrie asks Axel to enter his apartment provides primary character information. This is the purpose of the shot and no other information is included. No other layers are utilized.

INT. AXEL'S BUILDING—LANDING—NIGHT

Axel's front door bears three paper police seals. Without hesitation Axel opens his door anyway.

Then, when Axel arrives in Beverly Hills, it's the detail of the location that's important. As establishing data this is primary information. From this point on it will be secondary information.

EXT. BEVERLY HILLS STREETS—HELICOPTER SHOTS—DAY

We follow Axel past the serene, haughty Presbyterian
Church; he turns north and drives up a tree lined street of
handsome big homes incongruously packed together on
small lots. Axel turns to look at the Rolls, Mercedes, Clenets
that pass by. There are no people on the sidewalks; the
occasional gardener is the only sign of life. Axel's G-T-O
crosses Sunset—we get a great view of the Beverly Hills
Hotel -and cruises through the gentle hills north of Sunset.
Here the homes are grander, the lots bigger, the landscaping
even more lavish. Axel turns south again on Charing Cross,
and eventually comes back to Wilshire.

When secondary information is deliberately chosen and arranged to interact with primary information for the purpose of creating new or enriched meanings, it fully utilizes the poetic potential inherent in layering.

This poetry is clearly created in the scene from *Out of Africa* where Karen is watching her coffee shed and entire crop of coffee beans go up in flames. Karen has mortgaged the farm in order to plant this crop. The loss of the crop means the loss of the farm. She's in the foreground and the burning shed is in the background.

EXT/AT THE COFFEE SHED-NIGHT

Hundreds of Kikuyu stand silent, grave, in the glow of the
huge fire. Some have buckets.

The entire structure is ablaze, all hope of saving it gone.

Karen watches, detached, a spectator.

A toddler comes to her, hands at the pocket of her robe
where there might be candy. When she kneels to the child -
strangely--it has her full attention. She smiles, pokes the
child, tickling; it wriggles.

                    KAREN
          All gone.

She stands to watch the fire, her hand idle on the child as it
tries the other pocket.

Here Kurt Luedtke has created a visual simile. The candy in her pockets is all gone just as the coffee crop and the farm are all gone. The presence of the natives adds yet another interactive layer. The fire announces their relocation. Their land is all gone, too. Her words spoken to the child about candy become words spoken to all of the natives about their homeland.

In *An Officer and a Gentleman*, Stewart frequently utilizes secondary information to enrich the meaning of primary information. In a scene portraying the rigors of the physical training exercises, he places an ambulance in the background.

> On cue from Foley, they begin to P.T. Zack's class into the ground, running them up and down the stairs shouting in their tender ears until some members of the class actually start passing out.
>
> An ambulance is there with two white-smocked attendants to carry away the casualties.

The presence of the ambulance is a necessity but, more than that, it serves to intensify the constant thematic threat of physical failure.

In *An Officer and a Gentleman*, Stewart deliberately chose to play the big confrontation scene between Zack and Byron during a Blue Angels Air Show.

> The JETS ROAR close overhead and Zack has to raise his voice to be heard.

The jets overhead are secondary information but they intensify the argument by forcing Zack and Bryon to shout over the roar of the jets.

The ability to layer allows primary and secondary information to be delivered simultaneously rather than piece by piece. This not only provides a greater amount of information but also permits the interaction of the various elements and details. These interactions release energy. They create movement. They establish directions. Layering, by itself, creates a very full and rich palette—and then, with the addition of the forward movement of the linear structure, the palette becomes even fuller and richer.

The linear structure is at the same time progressive and additive. It's a series of images and sounds, one after the other, revealing and unfolding information in time and space. Information builds upon information and we experience a passage through time. The present becomes the past as we store the memories of what once was. Each shot, each scene, each sequence catapults us forward into the next as we "leap frog" our way from FADE IN to FADE OUT.

THE EXPRESSIVE POWER OF JUXTAPOSING IMAGES AND SOUNDS

The primary function of the linear movement is to move the story forward by progressively adding new information, but, also, it has another very important function. It utilizes the creative, artistic power of the juxtaposition of images and sounds. Juxtaposing images and sounds can simply move the viewer from place to place and direct the attention of the viewer to the significant action but it can also carry an emotional tone from one shot into the next. It can contrast different emotions and by so doing, strengthen each. It can establish relationships. It can make statements.

The final decisions about the juxtapositions of shots occur in the editing room, but they are the shared responsibility of the screenwriter and the film editor. The screenwriter may never enter the editing room, but his or her presence is omnipresent as embodied in the screenplay. This partnership was recognized by Pudovkin, one of the pioneers of the motion picture art form.

> The scenarist must be able to write his material on paper exactly as it will appear upon the screen, thus giving exactly the content of each shot as well as its position in sequence. . . . Editing is one of the most significant instruments of effect possessed by the film technician and, therefore, by the scenarist also. (2)

In *An Officer and a Gentleman*, Douglas Day Stewart juxtaposes a dangerous psychological scene between Zack and Paula with a dangerous physical scene in which we're forced to ride the Dilbert Dunker. Paula has fixed breakfast for Zack, creating a very domestic scene. Zack challenges her motives, they spar with each other, and then come together again.

> He takes her in his arms and they kiss. The moment turns suddenly real and Zack finds himself pulling away, afraid of the feelings that are churning his guts. Paula studies him a moment.
>
>
>
> PAULA
> Zack, when you're through
> with a girl, what do you do?
> Do you say something or do
> you just . . . disappear?
>
> ZACK
> I've never had a girl.
>
>

Their eyes stay together for a long time.

                        ZACK
                    (continuing)
                I forgot to thank you for
                breakfast.

                        PAULA
                Any time, sailor.

                                            CUT TO:

This direct cut takes us to the Dilbert Dunker and plunges us underwater, turns us upside down, traps us within a harness, and finally rescues us before we drown. The juxtapositioning of these two dangerous moments increases the feelings of danger in each.

In *Beverly Hills Cop* Daniel Petrie, Jr. portrays feelings of joy juxtaposed with an image of terror.

EXT. AXEL'S BUILDING—EVENING

Axel parks in his space in front of the fire hydrant and steps over the snowdrifts on the curb. A sudden playful thought occurs to him: he breaks through the black outer crust on the snow to the clean snow underneath, and rapidly makes three snowballs.

INT. AXEL'S BUILDING—EVENING

Axel pauses outside his door, uses his key to unlock it, gets a snowball ready to throw, and eases the door open.

                        AXEL
                Oh, Mikey!

INT. AXEL'S APARTMENT—EVENING

Axel takes a step into the apartment and stops; he drops the snowballs. Lying on the floor in front of him is the body of his friend Michael Schecter. There are great gouts of blood coagulating in several pools on the couch and floor. Schecter's hands have been cut off at the wrists.

The juxtaposition of these two opposite emotions intensifies the feeling of terror.

Kurt Luedtke does a similar thing in *Out of Africa*. He takes us from feelings of ecstasy to despair. Denys has taken Karen for a ride in his airplane. It has been what Luedtke describes as "the finest moments of her life." The plane lands.

AT THE PLANE

He GUNS it around, KILLS the engine. Both wriggle from the cockpits, Denys first; now he sees that she is streaming tears. She grins, LAUGHS, cries, TRIES TO SPEAK, can't, laughs, TRIES AGAIN, still can't, shakes her fist at the sky, SHOUTS an aargh. He laughs at her, starts to walk. She runs after him, jumps on his back like a schoolgirl.

INT/BANKER'S OFFICE-DAY

A number of polo trophies. The BANKER is 50, has a stump where his left hand should be. He hands her documents.

> BANKER
> Here, you're giving us a lien
> against your crop. We'd take
> it over should you default.

> KAREN
> I'd default only if the crop
> failed. In which case . . .
> there'd be no crop.

Ecstasy followed by despair. Spontaneity followed by rigidity.

In *An Officer and a Gentleman* Douglas Day Stewart uses the juxtaposition of different scenes to establish a relationship between Zack and Sid and Paula and Lynette before they even meet each other. We're introduced to the young ladies as they get off work and hurry to leave in Lynette's "old Falcon." This scene cuts to Zack and Sid having their hair shaved off while Foley lectures about Puget Sound Debs.

. . . poor girls who come across the Sound on the ferry every weekend for only one reason, to marry themselves a Naval aviator.

Skeptical looks from the candidates.

The hair-cutting scene cuts to a scene of the young ladies changing their clothes, putting on makeup, and boarding the ferry while Foley's voice continues talking about the Puget Sound Debs. Later, as Paula and Lynette are on their way into the Officer's Club, they see Zack and Sid doing push-ups in front of the barracks.

> LYNETTE
> Paula, look at the new
> Poopies.

> PAULA
> Yeah, I saw 'em. Poor guys.

> LYNETTE
> (calling to them)
> See you in a month when
> you get liberty!

By the juxtapositioning of these scenes the screenwriter visually establishes the relationship beween the two men and two women—and foreshadows what is to come.

The examples cited above have emphasized the juxtaposition of contrasting, contradictory, and related content, but film content alone, without the careful selection and composition of film form, does not fully utilize the potential of the medium.

COMPOSITION IN MOTION

All of the visual elements we examined in relationship to the spatial composition of the static image also apply to the composition of the moving image. The same visual elements and concepts of selection and arrangement that communicate frozen truths communicate emerging truths, only now they're continuously altered by movement and by the impact of cutting from one image to another.

A sense of confusion can be created by the movement of objects/persons within the shot.

The use of the horizontal and vertical planes contains varying and changing amounts of calm and excitement.

The associative meanings of shapes in one shot impact on the shapes in the next shot.

The lines that control the viewer's attention and eye movements in one shot are directly related to what happens in the next.

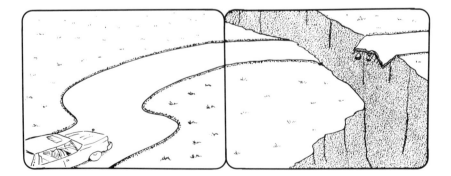

The emotional messages contained in the colors of one shot influence the colors of the shots to follow.

The affective atmosphere created by the lighting in each shot either continues or contrasts with the next and compels the viewer's attention in both.

The emotional memories evoked by textures can bind or separate the shots.

The ebb and flow of simplicity and complexity within and among the shots elicits different responses.

Tension is created by the collision of imagery—colors, lines, shapes, movements, textures, and positions.

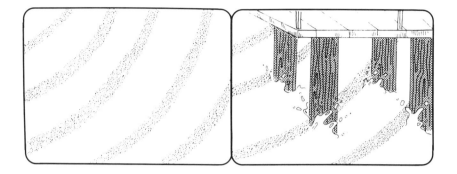

The repetition and alternating of images within and between shots creates rhythm.

It is in the selection and arrangement of visual and aural elements to create filmic space where we most especially see the power of blending film form and film content. The elements of filmic space embody many of the most unique aspects of the motion picture medium—aspects dealt with during the production and post-production of the screenplay.

And again, it needs to be emphasized that the implementation of film form is a function of the production team, with primary input from the film director, director of photography, and film editor. Their inspirations and expertise are what realize your visions. You would have no podium without them, just as they would have nothing to produce without you. And, just as the blending of film form and film content produces greater art, so, too, does collaboration between the screenwriter and production people produce a greater film. The screenwriter's contributions to the utilization of film form can only enhance the work of the production team.

REFERENCES

1. Edward T. Hall, *The Silent Language*, A Premier Book, Fawcett Publications, Inc., Greenwich, CT, 1959, p.160.
2. V. I. Pudovkin, *Film Technique and Film Acting*, Lear Publishers, Inc., New York, 1949, p. 39.

---5---

FILMIC ELEMENTS OF MOTION

Motion as an attribute of motion pictures is something we tend to take for granted. It's just there, because in reality—it's just there. Also, we infrequently think of motion as having an aesthetic or communicative value, unless, like Slavko Vorkapitch, we consciously study its expressive qualities.

> I firmly believe that there is no scene in any picture which could not be made more effective, emotionally—more intense and artistically more lasting by imparting to it the proper rhythm and devising some significant motion which would best express the given mood. (1)

Vorkapich identifies "shapes of motions" and describes them as ranging between simple to complex. He defines a simple motion as "a segment of space as it is cut out by a door opening or closing" and a complex motion as a space "traced by a newspaper dancing high in the wind." Motion, actual or implied, goes toward something—it has direction. The direction may be horizontal, vertical, diagonal, or circular and, once established, can be reversed. Motion occurs for a reason—to achieve something or as a result of something. It has intention. Every motion has energy—varied, accumulating, and alternating. Its energy may be powerful or weak. Motion has a beginning and an end. It has a duration.

As a screenwriter you need to become aware of the omnipresence of motion and experience it as a part of your daily life. It's important for you to recognize, analyze, compare, classify, and describe it. The more you understand it, the more effectively you'll be able to manipulate it to communicate your ideas.

Go motion hunting—wherever people are doing things or machinery is in operation. Watch what's happening, select a motion that intrigues you,

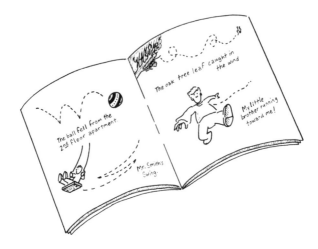

analyze it, and then diagram it. Use your Journal and start a collection of motions.

Motion is, by itself, compelling and powerful. When coupled with and used to contribute to the communication of an idea it becomes even more compelling and powerful. But, of course, the use of motion, like all things in an art form, needs to be deliberate. When used solely for its own sake, it calls attention to itself and slows the forward momentum of the story being told.

It's the responsibility of the screenwriter to create motion—the motion of actions. *Actions are your vehicles for communication.* They are the outward expression of your character's feelings and thoughts. They manifest the character's decisions and choices. This doesn't mean, however, that *all* character actions are specified in the screenplay—most are simply implied. The mandatory plot actions and the actions that reveal the essence of the characters are included. From these actions, along with dialogue, the actor or actress will develop their "business" that will interpret and give dimension to the character.*

The elements of motion most important to you as a screenwriter are natural and induced motions and motions used interpretively and structurally. Natural motions are those performed by people and objects in the normal course of everyday life and the natural motions created by camera movements. Induced motions are those created by filmic or compositional devices. Expressive and structural motions are created editorially.

---

*Actions as a means of characterization will be dealt with further in a later chapter.

NATURAL MOTIONS

Natural motions are generated in a number of different ways and serve different purposes. There are primary natural motions, secondary natural motions, and natural camera motions.

Primary Natural Motions

Primary natural motions are the actions of the principal characters and objects that advance the plot, provide information about the characters and events, and tell us what the characters are thinking and feeling.

In *An Officer and a Gentleman*, when Paula and Lynette leave work and drive to the Naval Air Force Base this is an action that primarily advances the plot. When we watch them changing into "sexy disco dresses" this is an action that describes the event and how the characters are relating to it. By this action we learn that they're radically and deliberately changing their images and they're on their way to a social occasion. When Lynette takes off her shirt and bra, giving a man in the next car "an eyeful," she "sees him and gives him a dirty look." This action tells us what Lynette's thinking and feeling.

Secondary Natural Motions

Secondary natural motions are actions that often develop into a primary action, that portray reactions to the principal action, create texture, or present counterpointal action. Secondary actions are an extremely important part of the tapestry of each shot.

In *Out of Africa*, during the funeral ceremony for Barclay, Luedtke creates a secondary action that becomes primary. Mariammo, the native wife of Barclay, attends but cannot participate in the Anglican funeral ceremony. She stands behind the cemetery fence, "proud witness to a ceremony at which she is unwelcome."

OUTSIDE THE FENCE-LATER

The Europeans disperse, go to their cars and carriages, MURMURING. As Karen passes Mariammo, she pauses just a moment, inclines her head respectfully. Mariammo, proud with grief, just looks at her.

In *Body and Soul* Polonsky uses the actions of a group of young people to show the way Charley is admired.

INT. CAR - CHARLEY IN F.G.

SHOOTING through the windshield. We see the street from
Charley's point of view: the lights from the poolroom, the
hangers-on in front, some older boys playing Johnny-ride-
the-pony under the street lamp, the dark stores, etc. Charley
starts to get out of the car. The kids at the stoop in front of
the candy store look up curiously.

> BOY
> (whispering, royalty is
> coming)
> It's Charley Davis!

Charley comes by, and the boys step back, admiration and
excitement on their faces. Charley starts up the stoop.

Then, in the sequence before the championship fight, Polonsky uses
secondary action to provide texture.

The room is jampacked, overflowing into the corridor with
reporters, observers, photographers, officials, friends, etc.
The crowd makes a way for Charley, who is followed by
Quinn. Marlowe brings up the rear with his manager, DANE.
The scene is continuously punctuated by flashlight bulbs, as
Charley stands near the doctor. In the b.g. is ROBERTS.

In *Witness* Wallace and Kelley create contrast and counterpoint with
secondary action.

EXT. COUNTRY ROADS, LANCASTER COUNTY - DAY

A few BRIEF SHOTS of a lone buggy containing the Lapp
family take us from the 18th century into the 20th from the
reassuring RATTLE OF THE CARRIAGE WHEELS on a quiet
backroad, to the ROAR OF TRAFFIC as the buggy waits
patiently for a chance to cross a busy interstate highway.

Natural Camera Motion

Along with primary and secondary natural motions there's natural camera
motion. And, like all other elements, camera motion should be used as a

channel for communication—not just camera movement for the sake of camera movement. Each movement contains it's own affective and cognitive sensations and can be used to help you tell your story.

From a fixed position, on a tripod, the camera can move horizontally, PAN, and vertically, TILT.* Use your viewfinder again and get the feel of these moves. You did some of this before when you were working with camera distances and angles, but this time direct your thoughts more specifically to what the camera movements in themselves can communicate.

Stand in one spot and look through your viewfinder. You and your viewfinder are the camera. Turn your head to the right and then to the left. This is a PAN. Notice how slowly you have to move in order to clearly see everything. If you move too rapidly, things will blur. Also note how things directly in front of you are larger than the things to your far left and right. Now, again standing in one spot, move your head up and down. This is a TILT. The PAN and TILT create a sense of looking for something or someone. There's a feeling of discovery—that something will be at the end of the movement. A slow movement produces a feeling of suspense and a rapid movement is more compelling.

From a vehicle mounted on wheels the camera can move horizontally forward, backward, and follow along with an object or subject. To get the feel of these shots, imagine that you're standing on a moveable platform of some kind, and, using your viewfinder, walk in toward an object or person and then back away. This is what a DOLLY IN and DOLLY OUT looks like. Next follow along beside or behind someone, keeping them in the same image size in your viewfinder. This gives you the feel of a TRAVEL DOLLY—or TRUCK. DOLLY shots very actively involve the viewer—the viewer moves toward, away from, or follows someone. The viewer is not just looking at someone—the viewer is actively participating.

Mounted on a mechanism that can be raised and lowered, the camera can CRANE UP and CRANE DOWN. Imagine yourself in an elevator that has a window looking outside. In your mind, ride up and down while looking through your viewfinder and you'll have the feel of a CRANE shot. The sensation of upward movement may have a sense of optimism and exploration while the downward movement can feel more like returning and approaching resolution.

Each of these moves can be executed individually or in any combination. Walk forward and at the same time PAN to the right; walk forward as you TILT DOWN; imagine TILTING UP as you CRANE down. What're the feelings you experience with the different movements? Maybe by themselves you feel little or nothing, but think of an emotional situation you'd like to portray and then examine the different camera movements that could help you communicate that situation. Do you want the viewer to be a passive observer? Do you want the viewer to have a sense of discovery?

---

*The words signifying camera movements are always capitalized in the screenplay.

Do you want the viewer to experience boredom? What camera movements would you use to enhance your communication? What camera movement—film form—would you blend with the film content?

INDUCED MOTION

One of the most obvious uniquenesses of the motion picture medium is its ability to induce and record motion. This is what we call animation. In full animation, instead of twenty-four frames of natural movement, there are twenty-four frames of different drawings of subjects and objects in slightly different positions to duplicate the natural movement. Limited animation consists of drawings that "jump" from position to position and make no attempt to absolutely duplicate natural movements. Animation is a specialized form of filmmaking and has its own procedures and conventions for the screenwriters who create their stories. For those of you particularly interested in learning about animation, references are listed.*

Another aspect of created motion occurs in the manner in which objects are arranged within the frame to deliberately direct the movements of the eye and the mind of the viewer. As previously discussed in the context of the static image, motion can be achieved through compositional elements like light, color, form, mass, line, and texture. These same compositional concepts apply to the moving image and, when used in conjunction with actual motion, enhance the compelling nature of motion.

Also, there is induced viewer's motion. Although, as we discussed earlier, viewers remain seated throughout the film, they are, in a very real sense, "on the move." The camera's angle and distance from the object or subject keep changing to bring the viewers closer or move them farther away. The camera movements fly the viewers up in the air, bring them down on their knees, dance them through a ballroom, and twirl them around in circles.

EXPRESSIVE MOTIONS

Natural and induced motions focus primarily on progressive and additive information, but motion can also function as an expressive—interpretive—device. In other words, motion can "act out" what's happening and can also express a value about what's happening.

Some motions, like camera movements, seem to have intrinsic meanings, or as Slavko Vorkapich expresses it, "different emotional values," and he

*Stan Hayward, *Scriptwriting for Animation*, Focal Press, London & New York. 1977; John Halas: (ed) *Visual Scripting*, Focal Press, London; Hastings House, New York. 1976; Kit Laybourne, *The Animation Book*, Crown, New York. 1979; Tony White, *The Animator's Workshop*,Watson-Guptill, 1986.

suggests that "a whole grammar of motions could be written, analysing the elements of the cinema language." However, he is very careful to point out that these are intended to be observations, not formulas. As he says, "The golden rule is that there is no rule." (2)

Vorkapich attributes different meanings to different movements: a movement into a scene tends to draw the audience in, involve them; movements away distance the involvement; ascending motion can "express aspiration, exaltation, freedom from matter and weight"; a circular, revolving motion can express joy and cheerfulness; a diagonal movement suggests "power, overcoming of obstacles by force"; descending motions indicate "heaviness, danger, crushing power"; a pendulum motion shows "monotony, relentlessness"; cascading motion suggests "sprightliness, lightness, elasticity"; and a spreading motion indicates "growth, scattering, explosion, broadcasting." (3)

Think back on the motions you've observed and entered into your Journal. What meanings would you attribute to some of those motions? Go out again—and this time think of the emotional response the motion triggers within you. Try to become emotionally rather than intellectually involved with what you're watching. Don't ask yourself—"what does this mean?" Just watch the motion and then become aware of your feelings. Follow the movement with your eyes—let your eyes move down with the raindrops on a windowpane; let your eyes soar with the flight of a bird; let your eyes move back and forth, back and forth with the saw cutting wood. These can be visually exciting experiences.

STRUCTURAL MOTIONS

Along with natural, induced, and expressive motion, there's structural motion that's created through the editing process—through tempo, rhythm, and pacing. Editing can be thought of as a process of reassembling a screenplay. Just as a jigsaw puzzle is a complete picture before it's cut up into separate and interlocking pieces, the screenplay is a complete picture before it becomes broken down into its separate but interrelated shots. The editing process reconstitutes the whole with the organization and sometimes re-organization of the interrelated shots.

The editing process is rarely, if ever, a process for its own sake. It functions to serve the purposes of the story as first envisioned by the screenwriter and then interpreted and executed by the production people. This requires the creative editorial skills and sensitivity of an editor who fully grasps the essential elements of the story. There's an old saying, "Don't worry about it—we'll save it in the editing room," but this rarely happens. The film editor does indeed make a major contribution to the successful realization of a screenplay. The art and craft of the film editor deals with the most filmic aspects of the medium, but he or she can only work with what has been written, enacted, and photographed. The editing process starts in the screenwriter's mind, it materializes on a sound stage or location and is completed at the editing bench. As the originator of this process it's necessary for you to think, feel, and see your stories as structured motion—as a series of juxtaposed images maintaining continuity, sometimes colliding, always revealing, and constantly communicating the dramatic thrust of the story through varying tempos, rhythms, and paces.

Tempo

The tempo of a film is determined by the length of the shots. These shots can be arranged with progressively accelerating, slowing, measured, or varied lengths. They can be juxtaposed according to a visual pattern similar to the juxtapositioning of measures in a musical composition or they can be determined by continuity and expressive arrangements of filmic time and filmic space.

The determination of tempo comes from the dominant objectives and tones embedded in each scene and sequence. A sequence designed to communicate boredom suggests the monotony of measured shot lengths or new shots that do not contain new information. A race may call for progressively shorter shots. The loss of excitement in a relationship could be emphasized by progressively longer shots. The varied and shifting moods of a group of people might be portrayed by a combination of all lengths.

Rhythm

Rhythm results from internal patterns of repetition—repetition of dramatic beats, sound, objects, and forms. The rhythm of film imagery and sound is very much like the rhythm of music. In music there are the recurrences of themes, melodies, instrumentations, beats, and intervals. In film there are the deliberate recurrences of actions; the types of shots—both distance and angle; the re-introduction of objects, props, set dressings, and vehicles; the repeated use of lighting effects, different camera speeds, lines of dialogue, sound effects, and opticals.

In *Beverly Hills Cop* the last line of the screenplay is repeated three times. The line is set up on page 38.

> LT. BOGOMIL
> Vacation or not, you should
> have checked in with the
> department as soon as you
> got to town. This is Beverly
> Hills, understand?

> AXEL
> I can't fuckin' *wait* to get
> back to Detroit.

The line is echoed on page 80.

> LT. BOGOMIL
> Keep talking like that and
> you'll wear out your welcome
> in this town.

> AXEL
> I can't fucking *wait* to get
> out of this town and back to
> Detroit.

On page 119, the last line of dialogue in the screenplay, we hear it again.

> CHIEF HUBBARD
> Yes, I imagine you'll be
> something of a hero when
> you go back to Detroit.
> (dryly)
> I hope you'll forgive me for
> hoping that'll be soon?

> AXEL
> Sir, I can't fuckin' *wait* to get
> back to Detroit.

> FADE OUT.

Petrie also creates rhythm through the repeated use of sound. The Beverly Hills police are constantly being outsmarted by Axel and the BOP DE DE BOP BOP, BOP BOP sound of his auto horn is used to taunt them. We hear this sound on the screenplay pages 41, 46, 55, and 113.

There's a recurring motif of the night sky in Stern's *Rebel Without a Cause*. The major portion of the story takes place at night, but over and above that, Stern keeps showing us the moon and the stars. The screenplay opens on a shot of the night sky; Jim's second confrontation with the Kids occurs during a Planetarium field trip while viewing a simulated night sky; the scene in which Jim decides to participate in the "chickie-run" starts with him looking up at the moon; and the beginning of the scene of Judy's major confrontation with her father starts with her looking up at the moon. Also, the "chickie-run," the flight to the mansion and the death of Plato are all specified to be illuminated by moonlight.

In *Body and Soul* Polonsky rhymes both actions and dialogue. Shorty, Charley's best friend and personal manager, discovers that Roberts has fixed Charley's championship fight. During the victory celebration Shorty confronts Charley and Roberts with this information, but Charley doesn't believe him. Shorty quits and makes his final statement before leaving.

> SHORTY
> (picking up his glass of
> champagne)
> Okay, Charley.
> (turning to Roberts)
> I christen you king of the
> king of the ring.

He flings the champagne into Roberts' face. Charley grabs Shorty's arm as Roberts wipes his face with a silk handkerchief.

Later, in the ring fighting what was to be another fixed fight, Charley discovers that he, too, has been double-crossed and he fights to win. During the fight Roberts writes a note intended to get Charley to change his mind. Charley's answer echoes Shorty's action.

CLOSE TWO SHOT - QUINN, CHARLEY

Quinn shows Charley the note. Charley's mouth is full of water. Instead of spitting into the cup, he spits towards Roberts. Some of the water hits Roberts.

CLOSE SHOT - ROBERTS

Hardmouthed, he wipes his face with a silk handkerchief.

In the beginning of the screenplay, before the fight begins, Charley announces.

>   CHARLEY
>   Got to win to be a winner,
>   Mister Roberts.

Roberts replies.

>   ROBERTS
>   Everybody dies . . . Ben . . .
>   Shorty . . . Even you'll die
>   some day . . .

Then after the fight, with Charley still the champion, the two face each other again. Roberts threatens and Charley echoes the words from before.

>   CHARLEY
>   Find yourself another boy.

>   ROBERTS
>   I will. You're a bigshot now,
>   Charley. I'll have to wait. But
>   I'll pay you off for this.

>   CHARLEY
>   (smiling)
>   Everybody dies. You gotta
>   win to be a winner.

From the very beginning of *Out of Africa* Luedtke tells us that Karen places a great deal of importance on the manner in which people are addressed.

Luedtke's first comment comes from Bror.

>   BROR (cont'd)
>   Hans says you want my title.

He has Felicity make the second comment—which Karen chooses to sidestep.

SHOT: KAREN AT THE PUNCH BOWL-LATER

Late afternoon. She's wan, exhausted, momentarily alone. A
girl, 14, FELICITY, blond, with the promise of being a
stunner, a revolver on her hip, picks over the hors d'oeuvres
dips herself champagne.

> FELICITY
> You ought to have a hat.

> KAREN
> You don't have one.

> FELICITY
> Used to it, I guess. I'm
> Felicity. D'you want me to
> call you baroness?

> KAREN
> What do you call Lord
> Delamere?

> FELICITY
> D. That's what everybody
> calls him.

> KAREN
> Are you allowed champagne,
> Felicity?

The rhyme continues in an interchange between Denys and Karen. Denys
would like Karen to be less formal, but she denies that in the beginning.

He gives her a leg up [onto her horse], taps her boot.

> DENYS (cont'd)
> They're the devil to walk in if
> you're thrown.

> KAREN
> I don't get thrown, Finch-
> Hatton.

> DENYS
> Not ever .. remarkable ..
> You wouldn't rather call me
> Denys?

Moment. She looks down at him, grave.

> KAREN
> I don't think so.

Then when Felicity comes to Karen for advice about very personal matters her directness creates a bond between them and concludes the rhyme.

> KAREN
> Try to learn something
> useful: they wouldn't do that
> for me. Then you can stand
> alone. If you care to.

> FELICITY
> D'you like being alone?

> KAREN
> (a long beat, then, direct:)
> No.

And stands to end it, walks her to her horse. Felicity infers the reprimand. At her horse:

> FELICITY
> Baroness? I didn't mean to
> pry. I've got nobody who'll be
> direct with me.

> KAREN
> (awkward herself)
> Then you'd best call me
> Karen.

Each time an action or dialogue is repeated it can gather and carry new meaning. Karen's invitation for Felicity to call her by her first name would have had relatively little meaning by itself, but following her prior insistance on formality it becomes a significant change. The repetition of Axel's horn heightened the growing tension between Axel, with his methods of criminal investigation, and the Beverly Hills police, and their methods. Also, this sound became a very funny non-verbal "running gag" about Axel's one-upmanship. The omnipresent moon and stars in *Rebel Without a Cause* create a sense of traveling through and into new and distant places. The moon and stars articulate the "passages" of the characters. The repetition of dialogue and actions in *Body and Soul* create enriched meaning. When Charley spits water in Roberts' face he echoes the same spirit of self-respect that drove Shorty away from Roberts. Roberts' response is the same for each. Polonsky's choice of these actions shows growth and change in Charley and reflects the lack of change in Roberts. Charley's dialogue before the fight was a foreshadowing. At the end it was the fulfillment.

Rhythm is film form. It is repetition, but not repetition for its own sake. It reminds us of the past in the new light of the present. It accelerates and intensifies. It comments. It enriches. It punctuates.

Pacing

Pacing has to do with the internal motion of how fast or slow a scene is played by the actors and objects. It is directly derived from the events, tone, and dramatic intention of each scene, sequence, and act. These are the elements that tell the film director and performers about how fast or how slow to play the action. This is clearly illustrated by the opening shots of two different scenes in *Witness*. The first takes place in the lobby of the train station as the homicide detectives start to investigate the murder. The pace is rapid and the tone is intense.

INT. LOBBY-MAIN TERMINAL - NIGHT

Captain TERRY DONAHUE, Chief of Homicide, strides past the crowd of journalists and TV crews, ignoring requests for interviews. He's just arrived on the scene and is issuing instructions to a uniformed officer.

> DONAHUE
> Close it all down. I want the
> crime lab vehicle in here
> *now*, and I want to talk to
> you, Captain.

He indicates Book should follow him, and they move a little
away from the crowd. Donahue turns a cold stare on Book.

> DONAHUE
> What are two undercover
> cops doing here minutes
> after this guy Zenovitch gets
> his throat cut . . .

> BOOK
> (cutting in)
> I want it, Terry.

> DONAHUE
> (continuing)
> . . . Talking to witnesses and
> generally acting as if it was
> their job!

> BOOK
> I want it.

> DONAHUE
> That's not what I asked you.

> BOOK
> I know.

> DONAHUE
> What's this about, John?

> BOOK
> I can't tell you that.

The other scene is located on the Amish farm in Eli's barn. Eli has decided
that Book is well enough to help with the chores. Here the pace is slow
and the tone is earnest but casual.

INT. BARN

as the milk herd of half dozen or so cows ambles in with
Samuel prodding them along, headed for the milking stalls.
Book looks on in the lamplight, nonplussed.

SAMUEL

Where he's pitching hay into the cow's feed-troughs.

BOOK, ELI

Where the old man is showing Book how to milk a cow by hand.

>   ELI
>   Good, firm twist and pull,
>   eh? See?
>   (and)
>   Right. Now you try it.

Book gives him a look, takes over the milking stool. The cow shoots him a rather skeptical look over her shoulder. Book bends to his task.

>   ELI
>   (continuing)
>   Didn't you hear me, Book?
>   Pull! You never had your
>   hands on a teat before?

>   BOOK
>   (grimly)
>   Not one this big.

Eli unexpectedly finds this hilarious, cackles, gives Book a comradely, man-of-the-world thump on the shoulder that jars him. Then he moves off. Book bends to his task, and . . .

SAMUEL

as he pours a pailful of milk into a large, stainless steel milk can.

EXT. BARN

as the milk herd is released back into the pasture. Book crosses into the f.g., stares O.S.

The content of a scene immediately announces the tenor of its performance, and every event represents dozens of screenwriter decisions about how the event is to be presented. Even the choice of words to describe the event needs to be carefully selected to indicate tempo, pacing, and tone. In the train station Donahue "strides," he "ignores requests for interviews," he "is issuing instructions." These are all aggressive and high action words. In the barn the milk herd "ambles," Book "looks on . . . nonplussed," Eli "moves off," "Book bends to his task," "the milk herd is released" and Book "stares O.S." All passive and slow action words.

Motion is both physical and psychological and the screenwriter creates the structure for both. The physical organization of motion determines what we "see" on the screen—how long it takes for a boat to tie up at a dock or how many things happen before the hero and heroine get around to the first kiss. The psychological organization has to do with the deliberate manipulation of the viewer's emotional responses. Here, the screenwriter is trying to create within the viewer the same feelings being experienced in the scene or sequence, or is making a comment about the event itself. Through tempo, rhythm, and/or pace the screenwriter blends *how* something is said with *what* is said to create the desired viewer's response.

Our primary focus has been on visual motion but there is audio motion, too. Sound can stand still or move very rapidly. It has direction. It can go around in circles, climb, run, jump, and even hide. Sound is music, dialogue, narration, and sound effects. Sound can be silence.*

REFERENCES

1. Slavko Vorkapich, *CINEMATICS—Some Principles Underlying Effective Cinematography*, Cinematographic Annual, 1930, Vol. I, p. 33.
2. Vorkapich, p. 32.
3. Ibid, pp. 32, 33.

*Sound is an important filmic element and we'll deal with its many aspects in a later chapter.

6

IMAGERY

We live in a world of images. We communicate with each other through images. We communicate with ourselves through images. We learn through images. We see a friend approaching and we wave; dark clouds warn us to carry an umbrella; we enter our driveway and know we're home; the classroom is dark so we turn on the lights. We see a dead fawn and feel sad. What we see tells us what's happening, what we must do, where we are, and what our feelings will be. We simultaneously experience, participate in, and observe the images around us. It is here—in our direct experiences—where our primary knowledge comes from.

Knowledge also comes to us through symbols—symbols that stand for past experiences. These symbols create vicarious experiences to relate to and to expand our direct experiences of the past. This ability to transcend the direct experience through symbology allows us to accumulate knowledge from the past to help us understand the present and predict the future.

There are word symbols and there are picture symbols.

WORD SYMBOLS

S. I. Hayakawa, one of the foremost exponents of general semantics, describes the origin of word symbology.

> . . . human beings have agreed, in the course of centuries of mutual dependency, to let the various noises that they can produce with their lungs, throats, tongues, teeth, and lips systematically stand for specified happenings in their nervous systems. We call that system of agreement *language*. . . . we have been so trained that when we are

conscious of wanting food, we make the noise 'I'm hungry.' (1)

He goes on to say, there is, ". . . *no necessary connection between the symbol and that which is symbolized.*" This creates a problem that we, as human beings and as screenwriters, need to be aware of and compensate for. Because the meanings of word symbols come from our individual experiences with these symbols and the things they symbolize, word symbols can never have precise meanings that will be understood by all people in exactly the same way.

The word *dog* means many different things to many different people. Generally speaking, this word will symbolize a four-legged domesticated mammal, but for some it will evoke feelings of fear and terror, for others it may signify annoyance, and for many it will stand for companionship and affection. The mental image of *dog* may be male or female; long tailed, or short tailed, or no tail at all; brown, black, or white, or all of the above.

In two-way, face-to-face communication we can compensate for this—we can keep checking to see if our assumptions are correct. "Do you mean—?" "Is this what you're saying—?" "Do I understand you correctly?" With the one-way communication of the written or spoken word there's no opportunity to do this. Where exact communication is essential, it's important to use the word symbols that most closely—most concretely—communicate your intended meaning: thoroughbred dachshund instead of dog; a sunny, warm day instead of a gorgeous day; or fear of assault from unknown assailants instead of feelings of terror.

PICTURE SYMBOLS

Happily, as screenwriters, you communicate with both word and picture symbols and the combination of the two gives greater concrete meaning to each. Most, but not all, picture symbols create a much more concrete vicarious experience than do word symbols. This is particularly true of the natural visual symbol, the semi-conventional visual symbol, and the correlative visual symbol. It is not true of the conventional visual symbol.

Conventional Visual Symbol

John Hospers defines the conventional visual symbol as that

> . . . which stands for its referent only by a common convention resulting from an explicit stipulation of the meaning to be attached to it. Thus a nod of the head means yes; a shake of the head, no. A red flag means danger; a white flag signifies the desire for a truce. (2)

There are comparatively few conventional visual symbols and, although their meanings are arbitarily assigned, they are quite universally understood and accepted within a given culture. In screenwriting, conventional visual symbols are most often used as an extension of word symbols: a hand outstretched and palms forward means—"Stop"; a thumb held out and pointing in a direction down a road means—"I want a ride"; a thumb held upright means—"Right on!" or "Okay."

Natural Symbol

The natural symbol very closely resembles the object it symbolizes by reproducing it. A color photograph of a bowl of red, purple, and orange zinnias is quickly recognized as a polychromatic symbol of a bowl of red, purple, and orange zinnias. We're not confused by the conventions of photography that render this to be two-dimensional and probably reduced in size. We understand perfectly what is being symbolized. The motion picture medium is the best of all means of creating natural visual symbols. It exactly reproduces the thing(s) being symbolized, including motion. This, in part, is what makes it such an outstanding communication vehicle. The communication is direct and concrete. You're showing the viewer what you want to say almost as if you're pointing to it. Polonsky wants us to know his story is taking place in New York in 1938 so he shows us a license plate that says that; Stewart wants us to know that Sid committed suicide so he shows Sid's body hanging by his necktie; Stern wants us to know that Jim feels responsible for Plato so he shows Jim going after Plato and trying to help him.

Semi-conventional Symbol

The semi-conventional symbol falls somewhere between the conventional and the natural symbol. There's some natural connection between the symbol and what's being symbolized but not enough to make it clear without a prior agreement about its meaning. Institutional symbols are generally good examples of semi-conventional symbols: the American eagle, the Royalty lions, the scales of justice, and the coiled snake of the Culpepper minute men. Because of the multiple and more subjective information, semi-conventional symbols evoke deep emotional meanings with strong nuances and overtones.

Generally speaking, visual similes and metaphors use semi-conventional symbols. Similes and metaphors developed primarily as literary devices, and corresponding visual devices are used in screenwriting.

Visual Simile

When creating a literary simile the poet paints two different word pictures connected by the words "like" or "as." Something is like something else. When creating visual similes the screenwriter juxtaposes contradictory or complementary images within the same shot or juxtaposes the different images in two different shots. A deliberate comparison is made. A literary simile is a comment made by the poet. A filmic simile is a comment from the screenwriter.

In *Rebel Without a Cause* Stern wanted to make a comment about how Jim's father is simultanously *like* a man and *like* a woman so he shows us the contradictory image of the father dressed in a business suit wearing his wife's apron while on his knees cleaning up spilled cream of celery soup. This simile visually presents the inherent contradiction between the two simultanous identities, and in the combination each gains stronger meaning. Later, after Jim leaves and his father runs after him, the simile is carried further and resolved.

OUTSIDE JIM'S HOUSE

The father bursts out into the moonlight. He runs to the middle of the pavement and stops, looks up and down the street.

FATHER
(yelling)
Jim? Stop! Jim?

Suddenly he looks down and notices that he is still wearing the apron. He rips it off and throws it down - then stares around - as if by his last gesture his son might magically return. A couple of neighbors poke their heads out. He hurries inside.

In *Body and Soul* Polonsky compares the complementary image of an unraveling bandage roll to the unraveling of Charley's life. Charley is wrapping his hand with the bandage roll while he and Roberts talk about the agreement to fix the fight. Roberts, at one point, "takes hold of the long end of the bandage and jerks it with a sudden fierceness." Then, after Roberts leaves, Charley is alone in his dressing room.

CLOSE SHOT - CHARLEY ON RUBBING TABLE

He wraps the bandage around his hand more and more slowly. He stops. Conflict, indecision, and memory touch his face. Suddenly he lies back on the table and covers his face with his hands. The bandage falls to the floor and unrolls.

> CHARLEY
> (Murmuring)
> All gone now . . . all gone
> down the drain . . .
> everything down the
> drain . . .

It's the complementary action of unraveling that makes the bandage roll a semi-conventional symbol, and, by comparing this action with Charley's action, Polonsky tells us that Charley's life is unraveling *like* the bandage is unraveling.

The classic examples of the juxtaposition of two different shots to create a visual simile are found in Eisenstein's *Ten Days That Shook the World*. We see a shot of Kerensky walking intercut with a shot of a peacock "strutting" and we see shots of Kerensky and General Kornilov intercut with statuettes of Napoleon.

Visual Metaphor
In the case of the metaphor, the artist is not comparing one object to another; instead, the object *becomes* something else. The imagery expresses the essence of the object.

> Like the savage, the artist suspends his intellectual, scientific analysis of things. He looks beyond the chemical formulae and atomic structures seeking out the soul of the world around him. It is just this that he wishes to communicate to his fellowmen. The wind God blows the clouds across the earth, and in moments of great euphoria bodies fly free of gravity as in Marc Chagall's painting "The Birthday." (3)

The visual simile makes a comment. The visual metaphor shares an experience. In *An Officer and a Gentleman* and the fight between Zack and Troy, one of the locals, Stewart specifies that Zack's kick "gathers incredible speed, until it's slamming with the force of a mule-kick into Troy's face." Zack's kick *became* the kick of a mule. In *Out of Africa* after a joyous airplane ride that Karen would remember "as the finest moments of her life," Luedtke has her express her joy by jumping "on his [Denys] back like a schoolgirl." She *becomes* a schoolgirl by this action. This action is a semi-conventional symbol that communicates her feeling.

The visual metaphor is, in many ways, analogous to Japanese haiku. Both present an experience rather than a description, evoke understanding rather than knowledge, rely on semi-conventional symbols, and express and elicit emotional responses.

> On a withered bough
> A crow alone is perching;
> Autumn evening now.
>
> *Basho*

> In the rains of spring
> An umbrella and raincoat
> Pass by, conversing.
>
> *Buson* (4)

Lewis John Carlino sees a profound similarity between the structure of film and the structure of haiku. He describes the power of haiku as being the ability to

> . . . illuminate a thought with all kinds of multiple meanings in such a reduced amount of words . . . . And more and more I'm beginning to believe that film is essentially nonverbal, that films really are behavioral rather than verbal. And I tried to evolve a style where the behavior really is what's important, and the dialogue is what releases the tension that illuminates the behavior, much as how the haiku functions. (5)

Correlative Symbol

The correlative symbol creates meaning within the immediate context, not through any prior and cultural agreement. This is achieved by the choice of expressive objects with which the character(s) can interrelate.

It's the choice of the object, the choice of the interacting action, and then the wedding of the two that creates a correlative symbol. First, the object is selected and presented as one aspect of the mise-en-scène. The selected object is generally an expressive thing in itself, containing its own cognitive and affective meaning. Then the object is acted upon by the character or event and this action expresses whatever the character or event is experiencing at that moment. The object now stands for that particular thought or feeling. Then, when this object is reintroduced in a new situation, the prior experience and its meaning is recalled and subsequently coupled with the new experience.

In *An Officer and a Gentleman* Foley's cane becomes the correlative symbol for his authority, unyielding demands, and his constant threat to force the candidates to DOR.

FOLEY
You don't say. See this cane,
Della-Serra? See these little
notches near the handle?
There's a notch for every
college puke like you, Della-
Serra, who I got to D.O.R.—
drop on request—from this
program. And the first one I
want to carve out of this
class is you, Emiliano.

He carries the cane throughout the entire film and at the end there are "newer notches clearly recognizable from the ones that predate this class."

In *Mask*, the story of a young boy, Rocky, with a grotesquely distorted head caused by a fatal disease, the screenwriter, Anna Hamilton-Phelan, links the abrogation of plans for a European trip with his recognition of his imminent death. Throughout the screenplay Rocky has plotted the route of his anticipated motorcycle trip by placing tacks in a map of Europe. The tacks represent hope and his belief that he will live to take this trip. In the end, he removes the tacks and we know he no longer has hope and he knows he will soon die.

Objects that become correlative symbols take on new meanings—meanings rich with emotional color. The recall of past feelings and thoughts in a new context involve us in the character's most revealing moments—their sacred moments of insight, decision, and acceptance. These are the moments that elicit our insight and caring. These are moments of filmic poetry.

ASSOCIATIVE IMAGES

In addition to symbolic images there are associative images. Associative images, like visual similes and metaphors, rely on similarities as the means of conveying depth and overtonal meaning. However, while the visual simile relies on content similarities, the associative image takes its meaning from the juxtaposition of visual similarities. If a dead tree trunk with its dried, rotting limbs clutching the ground is juxtaposed with a shot of a human hand clutching the handle of a cane, we have a different feeling tone than if we see only the hand. If bars of frozen icicles are juxtaposed with a shot of posts on a bed frame we have a sense of the imprisonment of frigidity.

Like symbolic images, the associative image can be a part of the mise-en-scène that is later selected for emphasis, or it can be an image totally out of context. And, like the visual simile, the associative image is a comment from the screenwriter that will influence our feelings about a character or an event. Suggestions for associative images are rarely seen in current screenplays but this does not condemn their usage.

Visual compositions that include such things as associative images are customarily thought of as being the primary domain of the director of photography, and, indeed, they are. It is his or her "artist's eye" and knowledge of the elements of visual composition that take your images from the printed page and verbal discussions to "paint" them on celluloid. Artist par excellence! The director of photography uses the elements of visual expression in production. The screenwriter uses them in creation.

MISE-EN-SCÈNE

The French term *mise-en-scène* comes to us from the legitimate theater. Its meaning was originally limited to the arrangement of actors and scenery on a stage for a theatrical production. Filmmakers have adopted this term and expanded its meaning to recognize the availability of a wider range of "scenery." The playwright was limited to a very few locations. The screenwriter has limitless possibilities. The term mise-en-scène is now used by filmmakers to include the entire spectrum of imagery—all of the arrangements of time and space, including actor and camera placement and movements; locations; sets and set dressings; props; and even costumes, hairstyles, and makeup.

A very large part of mise-en-scène is the deliberate and careful choice and creation of the environment—the setting. The setting contributes to everything that happens in the shot, and may well be the determinant of what happens. The setting can be neutral or a very active participant. The more actively it does participate, the more fully this important layer of information is being utilized. The setting is pervasive and inescapable. It can be nurturing and loving, hostile and frightening, cold and sterile, elegant and ornate, spiritual and calming—and on and on. But whatever it is, it needs to be chosen on the basis of how it contributes to the communication of the scene. The setting is not just any place to have something happen. It must relate to the content of the scene, support what the scene is trying to say. It must provide the opportunity for interactions to illuminate the characters and theme. It must contain possibilities for surprises—reversals.

The screenwriter places the characters and actions in settings that support and provide insight into what he or she wants to say. Douglas Day Stewart deliberately chose to introduce Zack in "The Honky-Tonk Sailor Town of Olongapo" which was "Known throughout the Seventh Fleet as the armpit of the Orient . . . " He wanted to contrast Zack's origins with what Zack wanted to become.

Stewart deliberately shows Paula's environment to contrast her dreams with her reality. She comes home late at night and is summoned into her parent's bedroom.

INT. JOE AND ESTHER'S BEDROOM

JOE POKRIFKI is a tough, barely-literate Polack with enough
hair on his chest to compete with some apes. Esther lies in
bed beside him. Paula enters the darkened room and Joe
suddenly snaps on the light, bathing them all in its harsh,
almost police-room glare.

Sid's suicide takes on the tacky feeling of the Tides Inn Motel.

INT. THE ROOM - DAY

The big Okie hangs by his necktie from a cluster of exposed
drainage pipes in a corner of the ceiling.

An argument between Zack and Byron is intensified by the activities and
sound of jets at the Blue Angels Air Show.

EXT. THE AIR SHOW - DAY

Six jets fly DIRECTLY AT US, jolting our senses.

The argument between Zack and his father could have been staged any
place but Stewart deliberately chose the Air Show as the most dramatic
backdrop for this scene. Also, he deliberately chose the National Paper
Mill as the setting for the final scene of the screenplay. This setting—a
tapestry portraying the unrealized dreams of hundreds of Puget Sound
Debs—was the perfect place in which to make Paula's dream come true.

PAULA CAN'T BELIEVE IT

Almost as she might have dreamed it long ago as a little girl,
she watches him take her face in his hands and kiss her in
such a romantic way that it's unlikely the women at
National Paper, or any of us will ever forget that kiss.

An environment has a life of its own that forces the characters to react
to it and contains the events that may provide ingredients for complications
and surprises. In *Out of Africa* there's the heat that makes Karen faint; the
lioness about to attack that allows Denys to protect her; the fire that destroys
Karen's coffee crop and leaves her bankrupt; the airplane that crashes and
kills Denys.

An environment is many things. It's a place with a special look about it: a court house, cemetery, hull of a boat, senior prom, or cornfield. It's a time of the year: springtime, Christmastime, harvest, or Valentine's Day. It's time of day: just before lunch, when the alarm goes off, high noon, or the witching hour. It has weather: chilly, muggy, foggy, or picture perfect. There are characters in the environment: business-like in downtown, scared in hospital waiting rooms, casual and varied at the beach, and bored in the long line at the check-out counter. The place has objects: tractors, adding machines, hat racks, and operating tables. The place has color, a color that fits the mood and communicates content: it's grey, crimson, or mauve. All of these things are operative in each scene and they change every time the scene changes.

Just as the setting is part of your vision, so are props, costumes, hair-styles, and makeup. You see these things when you see your characters. They become another one of the many pieces of the mosaic.

Foley's cane is used to spear "a pair of lacy underwear in Casey Seeger's suitcase" and "He brings his cane up suddenly, like a majorette's baton" to reveal Zack's hiding place for the polished boots and buckles he sells. Foley's cane as a prop is carefully chosen—it's not just any object—it is the object that symbolizes his authority.

Paula's and Lynette's ". . . disco dresses, satiny and suggestive even in their plastic cleaner's bags . . ." are contrasted with "prim Sunday dresses" they wear to church the morning after the Regimental Ball. The difference in the costumes clearly communicates the duplicity of their be-havior. When Jim decides to participate in the "chickie run" his decision is communicated by his change of costume. "Jim suddenly makes his de-cision and now sheds his jacket for a leather one" and he "kicked off his shoes and put on his boots." The Officers Copeland and Grant in *Beverly Hills Cop* look like "Boy Scouts." In *Witness* Book is required to wear Amish clothes when he goes into town. ". . . the pants are highwater, the hat low-rise, the jacket ill-fitting." The costume communicates a recurring theme of the screenplay—the fact that Book cannot and will never be able to fit into the Amish ways.

After Sid DORs and comes to ask Lynette to marry him he finds her with "her hair up in curlers." Her unattractive appearance sets the stage for her unattractive behavior. Axel arrives in Beverly Hills and "has not shaved or bathed all the way from Detroit" and after he showers he is "dressed in more or less clean clothes." Axel's appearance visually com-municates how foreign he is to this environment—a recurring theme throughout the screenplay on many levels.

The choices of the elements to be included as a part of the mise-en-scène are initially the screenwriter's responsibility. They will become the work of the film director, the assistant director, the production manager, the art director, the set designer, the prop master, the costume designer, and the makeup artists. All of these people will take their inspirations and instruc-tions from the screenplay. The more vividly you see the way the environment will be arranged and how the characters will look, and the more expressively you translate these images into words, the more clearly these production people will understand and be able to reproduce your vision.

A FLOW OF IMAGES

The art of film is realized in the creation of images that carry significant meaning. These images gain their power to involve, influence, and instruct by the combination of form and content. The vitality of this combination comes from the original vision—and from the endless flow of images this original vision can produce. The images then become words so the words can return to imagery. This, as stated many times, does not mean that your screenplay will include exact specifications of how the images are to be photographed, but just as the composer of music includes the notes to be played, the screenwriter includes the images to be photographed.

Images are not just shopping lists of the items to be included in each shot. They have mood, direction, tension, and emphasis. They are there to serve a purpose. They are conscious choices, choices that, along with all of the other filmic elements, utilize concepts of visual composition: light, color, line, form, texture, and motion.

REFERENCES

1. S. I. Hayakawa, *Language in Thought and Action*, 2nd edition, Harcourt, Brace & World, Inc., New York, 1964, p. 27.
2. John Hospers, *Meaning and Truth in the Arts*, Chapel Hill, NC, The University of North Carolina, 1948, p. 29.
3. William S. Mehring, *An Investigation of the Visual Symbol as a Communicative Function of the Motion Picture*, A Thesis Presented to the Faculty of the Department of Cinema, Institute of the Arts, University of Southern California, 1953. pp. 58–59.
4. Kenneth Yasuda, *The Japanese Haiku*, Charles E. Tuttle Company, Rutland, VT, 1957, pp. 184, 190.
5. William Froug, *The Screenwriter Looks at the Screenwriter*, The Macmillan Company, New York, 1972, p. 12.

7

SOUND

Visual communication reveals itself through the manipulation of space, time, motion, and imagery. Sound is known through human voices, sounds of the situation, expressive sounds, symbolic sounds, and music.

Sound, in all of its aspects, is an element of film form and, like visuals, contains multiple layers of information. All of the channels of aural communication, each carrying multiple pieces of information, can operate simultaneously AND in conjunction with all of the channels of visual communication. An awesome challenge for screenwriters!

In the beginning motion pictures were "silent" but they were rarely without sound. Spoken dialogue was implied by the use of title cards, in some cases sound effects accompanied the showing of the film, and almost always some form of music was performed. Although there were those, and perhaps there still are, who lamented the invention of the "talkies," there was never any dispute about the importance of sound. The history of the sound film has been linked to technological advancements and has moved from its early preoccupation with the realistic reproduction of dialogue to the creation of multifaceted and stunning audio experiences.

The screenwriter's major sound emphasis has been on the creation of dialogue and/or narration. The voice has been all important and, generally speaking, the only sound element written into the screenplay. Some music and sound effects have been included in some screenplays, but all too frequently these elements are composed, created, and added after the film has been shot and edited.

There is, of course, the use of motivated sounds that create the reality of the scene. A person goes to the door when the doorbell rings. There's the sound of breaking glass when a vase falls. A match is heard to strike. These sounds will be recorded automatically. You've created the action that produces the sound and it's not necessary to specify the sound effect in your screenplay. However, when you feel the importance of non-

synchronous sounds—sounds chosen for their communicative and expressive values rather than as naturalistic necessities—you do specify them
in the screenplay.

When screenwriters don't utilize the potency of the multiple layers of
sounds or when they delegate responsibility for the discovery of appropriate sounds, they yield or are denied access to these extraordinarily
powerful channels of communication. This does not mean that the screenwriter should write voluminous sets of instructions about music, situational, and expressive sounds. It does mean that wherever these sound
layers significantly contribute to and enhance the communication they
should be included in the screenplay. But first the sounds must be heard
in the mind of the screenwriter. They must be experienced and understood
as vehicles for communication.

Again, I'd like you to go out—this time into the world of sound. Go to
places where there are people, and places where there are no people. Hear
the sounds and hear the silences. Close your eyes and just listen. Separate
the many sounds around you, identify them, and think about what they
can mean in different contexts. Then combine different sounds to hear how
they might interact with each other. You may want to audiotape some of
the sounds, but certainly you'll want to write about them in your Journal.
The world of sound is a unique and exciting world—a unique and exciting
world to explore and then recreate. Enjoy.

Sound on film has, to a large extent, been used to make the reality of
the concrete image more real. People talk, we see them talking, we want
to hear what they say. A door slams, we want to hear the slam. A telephone
rings, we want to hear the ring. All very proper uses of sound, but as V.
I. Pudovkin said:

> The role which sound is to play in film is much more sig-
> nificant than a slavish imitation of naturalism . . . ; the
> first function of sound is to *augment the potential expressive-*
> *ness of the film's content.* (1)

And he goes on to say, "Unity of sound and image is realised by an
interplay of meanings . . . ." Neither stands alone and, hopefully, they
are never parallel. They are one.

There are a number of ways of combining picture and sound—of creating
the interplay of meanings: the picture can play the dominant role and be
supported by the audio; audio can be dominant and picture subordinate;
the dominant and subordinante roles can switch back and forth; picture
and sound can share a co-dominance; the two elements can switch back
and forth and share dominance. Obviously, the last approach allows for
the most flexible and effective use of all filmic elements. The choice is solely
governed by your determination of which elements, in whatever combination, most effectively communicate your meaning at any given time.

DIALOGUE

Dialogue has traditionally been the writer's forte. It's a primary method
by which the screenwriter develops theme, character, structure, and mise-
en-scène. It's the form that expresses content through what's said and how
it's said. Dialogue is never just voices talking. It's voices saying things very
deliberately. They tell us what each character is thinking, what they want,
and what they believe in. The dialogue between Peg and Charley, in *Body
and Soul*, clearly states all of these things.

> PEG
> What do you want, Charley?
>
> CHARLEY
> You understand? The only
> thing I know how to do is
> fight!
>
> PEG
> All right . . . if you want to
> fight, fight. People have to
> find their own ways of facing
> things . . . the way they feel
> . . . the way they can. You
> have to meet things the way
> they are.
>
> CHARLEY
> Then it's all right with you?
>
> PEG
> Anything you want is all
> right with me. I love you,
> Charley.

The words characters say and the way they say them can tell us where
they came from, what their social status is, something about their occu-
pation, educational background, temperament, and emotional state. Look
at the difference between what Quinn says about Marlowe—the young
contender who's taunting Charley about his age—and what Roberts, the
"king of the fight rackets," says about Marlowe.

<pre>
                    QUINN
                 (to Marlowe)
            Lay off with the propaganda.
                 (shakes hands with Dane)
            Can't you plug up Loud-
            mouth?

                    . . .

                    ROBERTS
            The kid was only putting on
            an act to make it look good,
            Charley.
</pre>

These differences in the characterizations of Marlowe and his behavior tells us a great deal about Quinn and Roberts.

In *Beverly Hills Cop*, the differences in Axel's dialogue and the dialogue of the Beverly Hills police demonstrate their very different worlds.

<pre>
                    AXEL
            I bet you think you're hot
            shit with all this computer
            stuff here. Why don't you ask
            your computers where the
            fuck you guys get off
            arresting somebody for being
            thrown out a window?
</pre>

Taggart's face reddens. He can't remember the last time a prisoner spoke to him this way, and he doesn't like it.

<pre>
                 SGT. TAGGART
            We have six witnesses that
            say you broke in and started
            shooting up the place, then
            jumped out the window
            when the guards took your
            gun away.
</pre>

In addition to portraying your characters, dialogue has other functions. It compresses and extends action, presents facts from the past and information about things that happen beyond the scene. When Peg and Charley are reunited after Charley's first road trip, four lines of dialogue tells it all.

> PEG
> It's been a long year, Charley
> . . .

> CHARLEY
> Yeah . . . twenty-one fights
> . . . nineteen knockouts, two
> decisions . . .

> PEG
> A lonely year . . .

> CHARLEY
> Missed you, too.

Dialogue can intensify what's happening visually. In the scene where Ben dies as a result of Roberts' badgering we're fearful for Ben's life. Ben is allowing himself to become extraordinarily excited and we know that Roberts' dialogue will exacerbate the problem, perhaps precipitate Ben's death—as it does.

> BEN
> (yelling in sudden fury)
> You killed me four years ago
> with a doublecross. I can't
> scare any more.

His voice sounds in the quiet air, and the camp people start coming towards the ring from the shadows. Quinn comes up.

> ROBERTS
> You're punchy, Ben. Your
> head's soft. I let you stay on
> Charley's pension list.

> CHARLEY
> Let him alone, Roberts . . .
> Don't get him excited. He's
> sick.

Charley starts pushing Ben away, but Ben tears away from him and faces up to Roberts.

>   BEN
>   (screaming)
>   You don't tell me how to live!
>
>   ROBERTS
>   (coldly)
>   No, but I'll tell you how to
>   die.

CLOSEUP - BEN

A pulse beats in his temple, his eyes glaze, and his voice strangles inarticulately.

>   BEN
>   Huh . . .
>   (strangling)
>   Huh . . . Charley . . . no . . .
>   it's the old . . . like I said
>   . . . Charley . . .
>
>   ROBERTS
>   (exploding to Drummer)
>   Get this crazy punch-drunk
>   wreck out of here!

Ben shrieks in agony suddenly, quivers, covers his head with his hands, and starts to cave in. Charley grabs him.

It's rare to have dialogue precipitate death as it does in this interchange between Roberts and Ben, but it will always intensify an emotionally charged scene, precipitate some form of action, and drive the story forward.

As previously discussed and illustrated, dialogue contributes to editorial motion through rhythm, tempo, and pacing. Dialogue has rhythm in its repetition of words, ideas, and manner of speech. It develops tempo through the length of speech patterns. It creates pacing by the speed of delivery.

One of the best ways to learn about dialogue is to listen to the ways people talk. Learn to spot highly emotional charged events occurring around you and focus your attention on the verbal interchanges. Audiotaping and studying different dialogue patterns can be a very fruitful activity. You must, however, be aware of the important fact that much of what people say in everyday life doesn't qualify as screenplay dialogue. Dialogue is *selected* information, while everyday conversation includes much random and extraneous information. Another excellent way to study dialogue is to read screenplays. Here you can see *what* the screenwriter has selected to be said as well as the *way* it is to be said. Another blending of form and content.

In learning to use dialogue there are two major problems to avoid. There's the problem of letting it become redundant and the problem of allowing it to become expository.

Once information has been "said," either verbally or visually, it need not—should not—be "said" again, unless accompanied by new information and delivered in a new context. Dialogue is there to move the story forward—not repeat known information. You're "selecting" dialogue to communicate information to the readers/viewers who are participating in the unfolding of your story. You're not "selecting" dialogue to communicate information to the other players in the story.

In *An Officer and a Gentleman*, we've seen Sid commit suicide, so Zack doesn't have to carry the news. Foley simply says "Mayo, the rest of your class knows about candidate Worley, and we're all sorry." His dialogue communicates a reaction—not redundant information about the suicide.

In *Out of Africa*, we saw Denys's plane explode so no one had to "tell" Karen about it. Luedkte shows us reactions to that fact. He does not restate the fact.

EXT/THE FARM-DAY

The last of the rummage sale, most items gone. Karen's taking money from a shopper, looks to the terrace.

HER POV

Farah, hands behind his back, staring at the sky. Now he looks to Karen, sees her watching, turns away, guilty.

ON HER

She knows.

Although you're selecting information for the readers/viewers, you don't want to talk directly to them. The moment the readers/viewers sense that they're being "talked at," the dialogue becomes expository and the magic of "being there" is lost. The medium then becomes a device rather than an experience. The more obliquely information is revealed, the more believable and the more effective it becomes. It does the job of communicating necessary information and, at the same time, communicates depth and breadth character information.

In *Witness,* Book expresses his contempt for Deputy Chief Schaeffer by indirection rather than by direct accusations. This gives us information about Schaeffer while giving us information about Book.

> BOOK
> Lost the meaning did you,
> Paul?

> SCHAEFFER
> What?

> BOOK
> Isn't that what you used to
> say about dirty cops?
> Somewhere along the way
> they lost the meaning.

In *Beverly Hills Cop,* Axel's personality is revealed by the tone of his dialogue as well as by its content. Axel has left the police station and he sees that Taggart and Siddons are tailing him.

EXT. BEVERLY DRIVE AT OLYMPIC BLVD. -- NIGHT

Axel stops at a red light. The Plymouth pulls in behind him. Axel gets out of his car and walks back to the cops.

> AXEL
> I'm going to 611 South El
> Camino.

> SGT. TAGGART
> So?

> AXEL
> So maybe you want to drive
> there, and I'll follow you for
> a while.

Dialogue revealing necessary information often needs to be disguised. It needs to be well motivated. It needs to be embedded in situations that demand its expression. It has to have the appearance of being information the characters *must* hear or say. It *must not* be recognized as expository information intended for the reader/viewer.

Volatile scenes of anger, intimate scenes of love, and scenes of relentless questioning are situations that motivate and disguise necessary information. *An Officer and a Gentleman* has excellent examples of all three of these situations.

During the Angels Air Show, Zack and Byron argue about Zack's mother. Prodded by his anger Zack tells us facts about his mother's and father's relationship and reveals his feelings for his mother.

> BYRON
> (beat)
> Okay, I wrote those things
> . . . and yeah, I had big
> thoughts of getting together
> with your mom . . . but then
> she hit me with being
> pregnant. I saw who she
> was. I'd had quiff lay that
> shit on me before!

> ZACK
> (suddenly livid)
> What did you call her? What
> did I hear you call her, you
> son of a bitch?

Both men rise angrily to their feet, but a split second later the Angels are making another pass over the stands and everyone is standing and applauding, making their argument less public.

> ZACK
> (continuing; screaming
> above the noise)
> She loved you, you bastard!
> And she believed you when
> you said you loved her: She
> never gave up thinking you'd
> come back.
> (beat)
> Don't you ever talk about her
> like that again or I'll kill you,
> Byron!

Zack pushes toward the exit, shaking with anger.

In a scene with Paula and after a shared moment of intimacy, Zack is compelled to reveal the very important fact that he has never had a close relationship.

> He takes her in his arms and they kiss. The moment turns suddenly real and Zack finds himself pulling away, afraid of the feelings that are churning his guts. Paula studies him a moment.

>   PAULA
>   Zack, when you're through
>   with a girl, what do you do?
>   Do you say something or do
>   you just . . . disappear?

>   ZACK
>   I've never had a girl.

> Their eyes stay together for a long time.

In the scene where Foley tries his utmost to get Zack to DOR, Zack's strength is pitted against Foley's physical commands and psychological badgering. Toward the end, when Zack is stripped of his defenses, he finally reveals his drive to succeed.

> Foley puts his lips close to Zack's ear and whispers:

>   FOLEY
>   (continuing)
>   Let's get down to it. Why
>   would a slick little hustler
>   like you sign up for this kind
>   of abuse?

> Zack's legs are shaking wildly with the effort to keep them aloft.

>   ZACK
>   I want to fly, sir!

>   FOLEY
>   That's no reason. Every-
>   body wants to fly. My
>   grandmother wants to fly.

                    FOLEY (continued)

You going after a job with
one of the airlines?

                    ZACK
I want to fly jets, sir!

                    FOLEY
Why? Because you can do it
alone?

                    ZACK
No, sir!

                    FOLEY
What is it, the kicks? Is that
it?

                    ZACK
I don't want to do something
anybody can do.

                    FOLEY
Pity you don't have the
character.

                    ZACK
That's not true, sir! I've
changed a lot since I've been
here! And I'm gonna make it,
sir!

                    FOLEY
Not a fucking chance,
asshole!

Zack bolts up suddenly, meeting his eyes.

                    ZACK
                 (defiantly)
I got nothing else to fall back
on, Sir! This is it for me . . .
and I'm gonna do it!

Foley studies him with squinty eyes.

                         FOLEY
                 All right, Mayo. Get on your
                 feet.

Both men get up and start walking back toward the base.

   When the situation and its environment motivate the content of the
dialogue to advance the story, the readers/viewers feel as if they are a part
of what they are watching.

NARRATION

Dialogue is people saying something to each other or themselves. Narration
is people saying something to the world at large but to no one in particular.
When we think of narration, we generally think of a voice on the sound
track explaining or telling us about the significance of an idea or an event.
But narration doesn't have to be limited to that. It can be poetry, internal
monologue, out-of-sync dialogue or a combination of all these things. It
can be descriptive, instructive, humorous, and rhetorical as well as expository. Narration is used in the beginning and end of Luedkte's screenplay *Out of Africa.* In the beginning it is the voice of the character, Karen
Dinesen.

                       HER VOICE
                 I had a farm in Africa, at the
                 foot of the Ngong hills.

   She describes the unique characteristics of her place in Africa and how
it affected her. At the end the screenplay specifies that the actress who
plays the part of Karen Dinesen " . . . in blue jeans, strolls, talks directly
to us."

                       THE ACTRESS
                 These are the hills where she
                 lived. Denys is buried down
                 there, and her house was
                 over there.

   The narration goes on to tell about Isak Dinesen's life after she left Africa
and ends on a report that a lion and a lioness often meet and lie together
on Denys's grave.

SITUATIONAL SOUND

Situational sound is descriptive. These are the sounds of nature and the non-verbal sounds that people and objects make.

Situational sounds tell us where we are. The sound of waves and gulls are the ocean. Dried leaves are a forest or autumn just before the first snowfall. One automobile passing by is an empty street. Many fast cars are a freeway. A calliope takes us to an amusement park. Crickets are country on a summer night. Many flags flapping are the Washington Monument on a windy day. Applause is a performance. Really loud applause is a very good performance.

Situational sound tells us who is around us or coming and going. A doorbell announces an arrival. A honking horn says to get out of the way. A barking dog warns of an intruder. Closing doors say someone is gone.

They tell us about the time of day, the time of the year, what year it is, and something about the weather. Alarm clocks are early morning and curfew sirens are early night. Birds singing say it's day and birds not singing say it's night—unless it's a mockingbird! Sleigh bells say it's Christmas and fireworks are the Fourth of July. Bodies splashing into a swimming pool make it summer and geese honking on their way south announce autumn.

There are old cylinder recordings: the first automobile horns, music for each year of any decade and century, and the sound of propeller airplanes.

Hard wind through barren branches is cold. Soft breezes are warm. Icicles crack. Waves crash. Snow crunches.

In *Rebel Without a Cause* "the silent tone of a bell is HEARD sounding the strokes of midnight," there are the ever-present "siren wails", and when the Kids discover Plato and chase him into the empty swimming pool, "the only sounds are the stamping of their boots as they try to distract him from side to side, and the animalistic grunts they make to scare him."

EXPRESSIVE SOUND

Natural sounds can be used expressively. They can create a mood. Set a tone. Intensify. They can evoke emotional responses. Provide texture and depth to all situations.

Relentlessly approaching footsteps are frightening; dripping water is nerve racking; laughter is joy; the cry of an infant produces anxiety; jackhammers are intrusive; a gentle breeze is soothing; and the beat of a metronome becomes irritating.

In *Body and Soul* "Far off a train whistle in a distant river valley SOUNDS a note of melancholy hysteria," " . . . a farm dog hysterically barks at the moon," and " . . . SOUND of the crowd stomping overhead" and then "Suddenly the stomping of feet stops. There is dead silence from the crowd."

There is silence before and after sound that intensifies what will be and what has been— the silence before birth and the silence after death. There is the silence where sound should be—the soundless scream; the silent thud; the quiet rage. There is silence that anticipates the coming of sound— the alarm about to go off; the tree about to fall; the expression of love about to be said.

The contrapuntal use of sound is an extremely expressive and effective method of intensifying, contradicting, or raising issues. Here the images and sound are in opposition and it's this opposition that creates the meaning. An automobile careening out of control down a mountain road, accompanied by pastoral sounds, makes the plight of the automobile even more frightening. Images of police brutality juxtaposed with sounds of religious rituals contradicts the spirituality of human behavior. Visuals of nuclear plants being built, colliding with the sounds of grade school lessons on safety, raise an issue of adult wisdom.

As stated before, motion pictures are very concrete, very objective channels of communication. A picture of a thing with its accompanying sound and motion is the closest possible symbol of the thing. Concrete visual communication deals with the present, giving objective information about a world of reality. Sound is a more subjective channel of communication that can reveal memories of past experiences and add emotional tones to the present. The deliberate manipulation and blending of these two channels engages the whole mind of the viewer—the subjective and the objective parts.

In *An Officer and a Gentleman*, Douglas Day Stewart shows his awareness of the subjective contributions of sound when he emphasizes "screaming" in his short description of the near drowning of one of the candidates. ". . . he goes under already screaming that silent little scream of the mind that drowning people hear." As the Dunker turns him over and over, "The silent scream is louder." When a diver goes down to rescue him and himself gets tangled in the harness, "The scream now becomes the scream of two drowning men." This is a suggestion for sound to be used either expressively or as a part of the musical score.

SYMBOLIC SOUND

Just as you can create visual similes, metaphors, correlative and associative symbols, so can you create the same effects and meanings with sound.

Imagine a rough and ill-tempered man performing a very gentle action. And imagine, along side of him, a calico kitten playing with a brightly colored feather. Imagine the soft meows of the kitten at play. The sounds of the kitten say that the man is really just *like* a pussycat. A simile.

Now hear the voice of the same man shouting demanding orders as his voice blends with and becomes the noise of a dog barking at an approaching visitor. Here the man *becomes* a barking dog. A metaphor.

Suppose this same man has had a life-long battle of trying to overcome his shyness and fear of being discovered as a "softy." In an attempt to portray an image of "toughness" he has taken up the habit of carrying a metal cane, and when confronted with situations demanding his "toughness," he unconsciously, but rhythmically, taps his cane against whatever is close at hand. This becomes a repeated behavior pattern. The tapping stands for his need to summon courage. A correlative symbol.

If the natural sound of the cane tapping became a hollow echo of the tapping, it would add depth and overtonal meaning. It would speak of the hollowness of the man's emotional crutch. An associative symbol.

Situational and expressive sounds tend to be more general and most frequently are an integral part of your story, but the use of symbolic sounds—similes, metaphors, correlative and associative—are deliberate and provide specific layers of meaning designed to play a substantial role in the communication of your ideas.

MUSIC

Music as a companion of motion pictures originated with silent films. In the early "motion picture houses" nothing separated the projector from the viewing audience. Its loud clanking noise was both disenchanting and a constant reminder of the mechanical nature of the medium. Music solved the problem and became a practice that ranged from an improvising pianist to a full orchestral score. Only rarely would a picture be shown without some musical accompaniment. Most of the conventions of how to combine music and film were firmly established by the time the capability of sound on film was invented.

There was the musical motif for the principal characters. This was introduced with the character and then repeated when he or she reappeared or somehow exerted influence in the story. Very frequently there was a musical theme associated with the film. The theme would contain a recognizable melody and its own structural identity—a musical preparation and resolution. Music was primarily used to mirror and duplicate what the picture was doing. A love scene had to be lyrical, a fight frenzied, and suspense needed ominous chords. Many of these cliches were highly developed and served as "shorthand" to foreshadow, predict, recall, and illustrate. Above all, it was believed, the best kind of musical score was the kind that didn't call attention to itself. It was there, but the audience wasn't supposed to be aware of it.

More recent approaches acknowledge the special contributions music can make as a valuable layer of communication. Also, there is the greater realization that motion picture music is a very unique musical form with particular requirements mandated by each particular screenplay.

As a writer, it's not necessary for you to be able to compose music any more than it's necessary for you to be able to do the job of the director of photography. It is necessary for you to know what music can do to enhance and support your visions. When music and images are wed, together they create a unity of expression. They must be bound together, but need not say the same things.

Music contains motion. It is motion. The step from one note to the next, like the step from one shot to the next, creates movement. It creates forward movement with rhythm, tempo, and pacing and can, on its own, carry things forward when other sound or visual elements slack off. Music can create the illusion of images speeding up or slowing down. It can stimulate and invite motion. It can foreshadow, predict, recall, and illustrate. It can bridge, sustain, modify, intensify, and enhance.

The very essence of storytelling is continuing questions with delayed answers, suspense about what will happen next, and uncertainty about resolutions. Music can accomodate these uncertainties and ambiguities. The discords and lack of resolution in modern music create questions. The harmony and predictability of more traditional music create answers.

Just as the juxtaposition of the meaning of shot A with the meaning of shot B creates a new third meaning C, so does the simultaneous combining of pictures and sounds create new ideas that would not exist if heard and viewed separately. Picture in your mind a well-dressed, middle-aged man wearing a striped bow tie, seated in a rocking chair. Watch him as he very rhythmically moves back and forth, back and forth. What do you think is going on in his mind? What are his thoughts and his emotional state?

Now, keeping this image in your mind, hear a passage of atonal, un-resolved music—something of Prokofiev or Hindemith. What does this tell you about the man's state of mind? Next, try something by Beethoven or Bach. Does this change your perception of what the man is thinking? By combining image and music—and different types of music—you have entirely different impressions of this man than if you simply saw the image of him sitting in a chair, rocking.

It's important to remember that our minds store and retrieve information in clusters. These clusters contain the major sensory elements of each experience and the significant visual and aural relationships. A parade clusters the images of marching people and the viewing crowd along with the marching music and situational sound. Given any one of these ele-ments, all will be recalled. This is a phenonemon you can use. Show a parade and the audience will hear parade music. Play parade music and the audience will see a parade.

There needs to be a meaningful relationship, a purposeful unity, between the picture and music. This unity grows out of the dramatic needs of your screenplay—not out of a restatement of the obvious. To use music to restate and duplicate motion is meaningless. To use music as ornamentation and padding is a costly waste.

It is the belief of Hanns Eisler, composer and writer, that

> The insertion of music should be planned along with the writing of the script, and the question whether the spectator should be aware of the music is a matter to be decided in each case according to the dramatic requirements of the script. (2)

This would be a startling departure from current procedures and may or may not echo the wishes of other composers, but it underscores the need for the conscious awareness of music as a functional rather than oramental and auxiliary art. The bottom line for you is the realization that the more you know about the communicative potential of music, the more effectively you'll be able to hear it and use it.

This is true of all of the sound elements. The more you know about each potential layer for sound information, the more skillfully will you orchestrate each of them according to their individual and very powerful capabilities.

REFERENCES

1. V.I. Pudovkin, *Film Technique and Film Acting*, Lear Publishers, Inc., New York, 1949, pp. 155, 156.
2. Hanns Eisler, *Composing for the Films*, Oxford University Press, New York, 1947, p. 11.

CHARACTERIZATION

Since the time of Aristotle, some twenty-four hundred years ago, people have been arguing about which aspect of storytelling is the most important—plot, character, or theme—and which comes first. These are, in my opinion, fruitless arguments. It's my view that all three perform important functions, are inexorably linked together, and are developed concurrently. Characters must be developed in a context and that context is plot. Plot is conflict and plot and character are designed to communicate theme. Theme emerges from character change and growth. Change and growth results from characters in conflict. None exists without the others and none can exist without the art form that contains them all. This is the context in which we will examine the nature of structuring characterizations.

UNIQUE ASPECTS OF FILMIC CHARACTERIZATIONS

Characterization portrayed through film form is very different than characterization portrayed through print literature and the verbal performing arts. In novels and short stories, *the author tells us* what the characters are doing and what they're thinking and feeling. In stageplays, the playwright gives the characters broad actions and has *the characters tell us* what they're thinking and feeling. The same thing is true for opera. In screenplays, the screenwriter has *the characters SHOW us* what they're thinking and feeling.

Characterizations portrayed through film form are, in the opinion of many, the most challenging and most difficult of all characterizations to achieve successfully. There are a number of reasons for this.

First, screenplay characters must be developed in a very short amount of screen time. Their character traits have to be compressed and condensed. All non-essential character traits must be eliminated and then compacted—layered—into a denser form.

Second, the external non-verbal behaviors screenwriters use to communicate the essential qualities of their characters tend to be both specific and unambiguous. This specificity and preciseness is finite and does not challenge or involve the reader/viewer's associative imagination in the same way or to the same extent as abstract verbal symbols.

Third, film form portrays the objective world—it shows the world as it is—and screenplay characterizations emerge from the portrayal of subjective feelings and thoughts. In other words, the screenwriter must find ways to externalize subjective content within an objective context.

So, the task of the screenwriter is to create multi-faceted characters within a very short amount of screen time through specific external behavior that communicates subjective feelings and thoughts. Not a simple task!

Screenplay characters are revealed obliquely. The reader/viewer is like a "Peeping Tom" looking through a window to vicariously experience other people's lives. The players are rarely, if ever, aware of the reader/viewer. They don't feel obligated to explain their thoughts, their feelings or past experiences. They simply live the moment. The "Peeping Tom" identifies with—becomes—the character to feel the same emotions, share the same thoughts, and struggle toward the same goals. Any obviously expository material breaks the illusion of "being there"—the illusion that makes it possible to vicariously experience what the character is experiencing.

All of the performing art forms, including film, use dialogue and actions according to the conventions of their medium. Actions performed on a stage must necessarily be both limited and broad. Limited because all of the action takes place under the same proscenium arch. Broad because small actions would not be visible to those seated toward the back of the theater. Motion pictures have no such limitations. Screenwriters work with the broad plot actions, but also, and most importantly, they work with the tiny actions that reveal a character's unspoken and innermost secrets.

The playwright has the soliloquy, the librettist has the aria, and the screenwriter has actions.

ACTIONS

The essense of character is action. Actions are the windows into the character's mind, heart, and soul. The character's change/growth is precipitated by actions and revealed through actions.

Actions are decisions acted out—thought processes externalized. The purchase of an engagement ring is the decision to wed. A new hairstyle is a decision to look different. Opening the refrigerator is a decision to find food. Making a phone call is the decision to contact someone.

Actions are feelings and thoughts acted out—internal behavior externalized. "I'm sad" is shown by tears; "I'm tired" by lying down and closing one's eyes; "I don't want anything to do with you" by walking away; and "I don't want you to know my feelings" by holding back the tears.

Actions are visual. They move. They occupy time/space. They generate sounds. Actions are filmic.

There are basically two kinds of screenplay actions. There are the plot actions and characterization actions. The plot actions move an event from one moment in time to the next. Characterization actions tell us what the character is thinking and feeling. These characterization actions occur on at least two levels. There are the thoughts and feelings the character wants other people to see and respond to and there are those the character wants to conceal from others—and often from himself or herself. The thoughts and feelings the character wants to hide are sometimes referred to as the subtext. They are the loci of the character's inner conflicts, insecurities, and fears. The discovery and creation of these actions are your greatest challenge and greatest resource.

Although the plot actions and characterization actions are different, the two usually occur in tandem. Except for habitual actions, we rarely ever do anything without having some feelings and thoughts about what we are doing. The two go together.

In real life we often conceal our feelings and thoughts. We have the sense that we'll become vulnerable if we show what we really think and feel. However, in drama—and especially in motion pictures—the external overt expression of feelings and thoughts is essential. Screenplay characters often seek to conceal their feelings and thoughts, but ultimately they must reveal what they're thinking and feeling.

To again use Susanne Langer's words, every work of art is "the outward showing of inward nature, an objective presentation of subjective reality." It is through these private and often carefully guarded thoughts and feelings expressed through actions that we learn the most important aspects of our characters and the essential quality of what the screenwriter wants to say. It is through these actions that the screenwriter creates the most expressive images.

Pudovkin speaks of these expressive images as the "plastic material" of the scenarist.

> The scenarist must know how to find and to use plastic (visually expressive) material: that is to say, he must know how to discover and how to select, from the limitless mass of material provided by life and its observation, those forms and movements that shall most clearly and vividly express in images the WHOLE CONTENT of his idea. (1)

In *An Officer and a Gentleman*, Stewart's use of a tattoo becomes "plastic material." As a boy in Olongapo, "the armpit of the Orient," Zack enters a tattoo parlor.

HIS POV - THE TATTOO PARLOR

A sailor is getting an elaborate tattoo of a naked girl on his
belly. Zack's POV shifts to a display of tattoos on the wall,
one of them an eagle with intricately detailed wings.

Here, simultaneously, we see the seeds of Zack's interest in flying and
his wish to live a different life than that of his father. From the environment
of Olongapo and an occupational trait of "U.S. sailorboys," Stewart chose
the plastic material that characterized Zack and expressed the "whole content" of the scene.

Then, when we see Zack entering the gates of Port Ranier Naval Air
Station, he "covers his eagle tattoo with a band-aid." Now Zack wants to
conceal the tattoo. Another characterization. He's ashamed.

Later, when lined up to meet Foley, Stewart uses the tattoo again—this
time to characterize Foley.

Foley suddenly tears the Band-Aid off his arm, revealing the
eagle tattoo. Foley leans close to inspect it.

                    FOLEY
          Where'd you get this, Mayo?
          This is really wonderful
          work.

                    ZACK
          Subic Bay, sir. In the
          Philippines.

                    FOLEY
          I thought I recognized the
          work.
               (stares him in the eye)
          Be proud of those wings.
          They're the only ones you're
          gonna leave here with, Mayo-
          naise.

Through Foley's behavior in relationship to Zack's tattoo we see that
nothing can be hidden from this man, that he censures Zack's shame, and
that the two are immediately locked in conflict.

Stewart's selection of the tattoo as an expressive object clearly illustrates the value and importance of discovering objects that are, within themselves, expressive images. All objects carry their own unique meanings. Smooth pigskin leather says one thing and nubby wool says another. A wooden rocking horse says motion, while a china doll represents a frozen moment. The Star of David communicates one thing and a Christian cross another. A pen represents permanence and assurance; a pencil with an eraser represents change and uncertainty.

An object itself carries a communication. When coupled with how the character *acts upon it*, a third meaning emerges. This is similar to what happens when two shots are juxtaposed to produce a meaning that is not simply the sum of the parts. The relationship between the object and the character's action communicates the character's thoughts and feelings about what is currently happening to him or her and also, in a larger sense, tells us about the character's values.

The pleasure or displeasure of nursing a sick person can be seen in the simple action of offering and administering a spoon of cough medicine. The spoon can be slowly and gently or quickly and roughly thrust into the patient's mouth. Even the way a few spilled drops of the medicine are cleaned off the patient's nightgown can clearly express the content of the scene and a dominant personality trait.

In the first few scenes of his untitled screenplay, Tony Gayton establishes his character's sense of fairness and responsibility.

> In a squalid bedroom littered with beer cans we see SUNNY
> MORALES wake up. Lying next to him in bed is a woman
> that he doesn't know. He looks at his watch and realizes that
> he is late. . . . Sunny dresses quietly so that he will not
> awaken the snoring woman. As he is leaving the room he
> spots a wad of money on the dresser, hesitantly he takes it.
> In the living room he is greeted by a cute little girl
> (presumably the daughter of the woman), who is playing
> with a doll. She says hello and smiles at Sunny, who, in turn
> asks her what her name is. He bends over and strokes her
> hair then returns to the bedroom and replaces the money
> and adding a twenty of his own. He returns to take ten of it
> back, says goodby to the girl, then leaves. (2)

There are those who say that the discovery of subtext actions is the responsibility and prerogative of the actor. The actor does indeed make major contributions to the discovery of ways to portray a character through appropriate and convincing behavior, but the actor is interpreting—not creating the character. It is through the actions and words that screenwriters give to their characters that actors learn about the person they are to interpret. Sunny's interaction with the little girl and the money gives the actor—and the reader/viewer—a great deal of information about Sunny. It is precisely for this reason that Gayton has given his character those actions. He is describing Sunny by externalizing his feelings and thoughts. Words are important, too, but screenplay characters rarely tell what they're thinking and feeling, they rarely announce their decisions—they act them out. Sunny's feelings, thoughts, and decisions about the little girl and the money would never have been verbalized. When the actor learns who the character is and the reasons behind his or her behavior, then the actor can discover and contribute other actions that reinforce and embellish the character they have come to know and understand.*

Now, for you to have an immediate experience with discovering and selecting expressive—"plastic"—material, imagine you're writing a screenplay about a young lady, Cathy, who is struggling with a decision about her future. She really wants to be a screenwriter but her family, particularly her father, wants her to major in business administration and prepare to take over the family manufacturing business. Cathy is filled with anger toward her father for placing her in this situation, but at the same time, she loves her father and is proud to be regarded as capable of stepping into his position. Imagine that Cathy must make a final decision. She can no longer straddle the issue. She must face the struggle within herself and allow one side to win. She has been accepted into universities that could qualify her for either profession. Picture her in her room, at her desk, surrounded by seventeen years of memories and possessions: high school trophies from sports, debate and writing contests, family pictures, gold earrings and bracelet, tapes for her stereo, a large orange piggy bank, a computer, stacks of dog-eared screenplays, pencil marks on the closet door to show her growth from year to year, a pair of very old slippers in the shapes of dog faces—and any other objects you may want to place there.

Your writing task is to communicate her feelings and thoughts and her final decision—the subtext and text. Choose an object(s) for her to interact with and then structure the scene. Take your time and build a scene utilizing Cathy's interaction with an object(s) to externalize her inner struggle. Portray her emotions—not the event. Give the scene a beginning, a middle, and an end. Do not use dialogue or written symbols. Find the actions that will carry the whole content.

Now, having created your scene, set it aside to give it some distance—to give yourself some objectivity—and later in this chapter we'll come back to it.

---

*I strongly recommend that you read Constantin Stanislavski's book, *An Actor Prepares*. This classic book will give you valuable insights into the work of the actor. And, even more importantly, you can use many of the same methods to discover your character's subtexts.

MEETING YOUR SCREENPLAY CHARACTERS

Creating and structuring your screenplay characters is, at the same time, a most enjoyable and most challenging task. It's like meeting a new person. At first there's the glimpse of someone you'd like to know. There's something about the person that interests you that you want to know more about. Then there are the first questions—and the answers that lead to more questions, until finally you have a "handle" on who you're interacting with.

At first it's the questions that ask for very concrete information. What's your name? Where do you come from? What do you do for a living? Are you married? Children? Where are you in school?

Then come attitude questions. Do you like your work? Do you believe there's a God? Who are you voting for? What do you think about capital punishment? Is it okay to cheat on your income tax?

Next come shared experiences—responses and behavior that express feelings. Situations that produce anger, jealousy, joy, boredom, love—and all the rest.

Then, and only then—after all the questions, the answers, and the shared experiences—do you begin to know that person. It doesn't happen easily and it doesn't happen quickly, but it's always an adventure and always demanding.

Creating and structuring a character is an awesome task—one often reserved for the gods. It's not a discovery of who someone is and where they come from—it's the discovery of where someone *MUST* come from in order to be who you want them to be. It's not looking at the end result— it's creating the causes that can produce the character who will best tell your story. Creating and structuring a character is finding a point of view, a way of looking at the world. It's discovering a set of attitudes, a group of opinions, a number of interests, a collection of needs, a cluster of behavior patterns, and a series of responses. It's amalgamating years of individual experiences within both private and shared cultures.

"GOOD" SCREENPLAY CHARACTERS

Creating a screenplay character is "like" meeting a new person, but a screenplay character is *never like* a real-life person. A screenplay character is always larger than life, more fascinating and more compelling than anyone in real life could ever be. Charley Davis is not your ordinary, run-of-the-mill boxer. He's a "sensational" boxer. He's not just proud, he's proud to a fault. He's not just capable of anger, he's capable of rage.

A "good" character—such as Charley, Zack, Karen, Jim, Book, and Axel— is a unique individual. Each has his or her own public and hidden worlds, strengths and weaknesses, successes and failures, fears and hopes, and the times and places when needs have been fulfilled and denied. Good characters grow out of these special and different worlds. Human behavior is never accidental. Each character has a past they carry with them that determines their present and future behavior. Characters are believable when their present responses reflect their past and when every action can be justified as the outgrowth of previous experiences.

Charley carries the depression experience with him in everything he does and every decision he makes. His need for financial security influences all of his choices—until his need for self-respect becomes more important than his need for money. His need for self-respect is rooted in the Jewish culture, in his family values, and in his personal pride. Zack achieves his commission because of his determination to live differently than his father, and he is able to love Paula because of his mother's affection. He is able to take care of himself because his past experiences have forced him to learn how.

Good characters have room to grow. They start in one place and end up in another. Every character must have within him or her the potential— the seeds—for growth, and each must live out the direction in which these "seeds" will take them. Good characters learn from the screenplay experiences of "trial by fire," "sink or swim," "put up or shut up," and "do or die." They move from decision to decision and with each decision they become different. Character change is the essence of storytelling.

Good characters have universal qualities and worthwhile goals. They personify the qualities and goals of our culture. Who they are and what they want is common to all of us. Their needs are our needs; their fears we share; their joys we've known. Like Charley, none of us wants to live in poverty, all of us want to be loyal to our friends, and each of us would be enraged by a double cross.

Good characters live worthwhile lives, have worthwhile goals—but are not perfect. They embody the negative human characteristics as well as the positive ones. They portray both sides of the human coin. They can hate, steal, covet, lie and destroy at the same time they love, protect, respect and nourish. They have weaknesses and ambivalences—flaws—to overcome; weaknesses and ambivalences that make it difficult for them to achieve their goals; weaknesses and ambivalences that are very often the essence of the story to be told.

Good characters must be indomitable. They must have an enormous amount of stamina and determination in order to bounce back from the many obstacles and difficulties they must confront. Their commitment to achieve their goals and force the struggle to its outer limits must be extraordinarily strong. Stories evolve from characters capable of engaging in and sustaining conflict. Good characters are never passive. They must *actively* strive to achieve the goals they set for themselves. They are decisive and willful—always demanding control of their own lives. Foley could not defeat Zack. Roberts could not control Charley. The Beverly Hills Police were no match for Axel.

Good characters have dominant characteristics and at the same time are multi-faceted. There is a core quality that drives them and that core quality is surrounded by congruent attributes. Good characters always act from their core quality but respond in different ways to different situations. They're continually interacting in varied and special ways with other characters, with themselves and with the environment. Book talks to Samuel one way, to his partner in another way and to Rachel in yet another way. He denies his love for Rachel in one setting and affirms it in another. He controls his temper in one situation and loses it in another.

Good characters are simultaneously dealing with an inner, psychological struggle and an outer, physical struggle—an inner goal and an outer goal. The outer goal is the plot goal and the inner goal is a personal goal. These two goals contain conflicting emotions—emotions that cannot both be gratified at the same time. A character can be driven to achieve one goal while being simultaneously compelled to seek a very different and conflicting goal. IT IS THIS WARRING BETWEEN THE EXTERNAL AND INTERNAL GOALS THAT IS THE ESSENCE OF GREAT DRAMA. Charley's external conflict is with Roberts, and his plot goal is to become financially secure. His internal conflict is between his need for fame and fortune and his need to maintain his sense of self-esteem. He cannot have both at the same time. It's one or the other. This inner struggle coupled with the outer struggle pushes Charley to a greater awareness of his value system. These struggles force his final decision and reveal the depths of his commitment to those values. And, what the character finally values reveals what the screenwriter values—what he or she wants the reader/viewer to value. The theme.

A good character has compelling personal goals. These personal goals spring from very deep emotional needs, deprivations, and scars. The need for self-respect; for self-actualization. The need to be loved; to be respected. The need to be productive and creative. The need to know. The need to avenge, revenge, control, destroy, and possess. The need to prove something to one's self or to others. People never climb a mountain just to climb the mountain. They climb it to prove something. People never sacrifice themselves for the sake of self-sacrifice. They sacrifice themselves because it stands for something. People don't win races to win races. They win to win something else. It's the character's personal goals that provide the necessary energy to climb the mountains, perform the self-sacrifices, and run the races. The personal goals are the yeast that cause plot events to ferment. They're the driving force that powers the plot's forward movement.

Good characters maintain an air of mystery until the end. They keep us guessing by doing unexpected but logical things. Their final behavior is never predictable, but always understandable. There's always the sense that more information will be revealed, that there are inner resources yet to be plumbed, and strengths yet to be hewn. We have the feeling that Charley won't throw the fight—but we don't know for sure. We have the sense that Zack won't DOR—but there's the chance he might. We knew that Jim would have to go to help Plato—but we didn't know if he would survive.

CHARACTER FUNCTIONS

Screenplay characters are in the screenplay to serve a purpose. They are there as the vehicles to communicate your theme and as structural elements that push your story forward toward a resolution. They are deliberately chosen and created to fulfill these functions. Each character has been given his or her physical plot goal and inner personal goal. Each character performs a unique function and each character makes a unique contribution. John Howard Lawson sums this up and ends his chapter on characterization with these words:

> . . . the characters can have neither depth nor progression except insofar as they make and carry out decisions which have a definite place in the system of events and which drive toward the root-action [theme] which unifies the system.(3)

Protagonist

We call the main character the protagonist. This is the person who undergoes the most change—progression; the one who most actively strives to achieve his or her goal and forces the story to move forward; the one the reader/viewer identifies with; the one the reader/viewer knows the most about. The protagonist is active, never passive, and has a great deal at stake. An important part of the protagonist's life will be destroyed if he or she fails to achieve his or her goals. Protagonists are driven and compelled to set goals, to find strategies, and to struggle to achieve their goals. They must have the strength and resilience to overcome obstacle after obstacle.

Charley is the protagonist in *Body and Soul*. He changes from acceptance and complicity in a criminal act to rejection of that criminal act. His self-respect will be destroyed unless he does this. Charley is compelled to actively seek fame and fortune AND self-esteem. We know the most about Charley. We identify with him. His decisions and choices push the story forward. Zack is the protagonist in *An Officer and a Gentleman*, Jim in *Rebel Without a Cause*, John in *Witness*, Karen in *Out of Africa*, and Axel in *Beverly Hills Cop*.

The progression within the protagonist is the medium through which you communicate your theme—that which you value. It is the decisions and choices the protagonist makes, the obstacles he or she overcomes, and the resultant character change and growth that show us what the character values; what you, the screenwriter, value; and what you want the reader/ viewer to value.

Modifier

Since character change and growth, as the means of communicating the theme, is the function of the protagonist, there must then be a character whose function it is to force and promote that change and growth. This character I call the modifier. Generally, the modifier enters and is a new element in the life of the protagonist—a new element that introduces new issues and causes new things to happen. Like the protagonist, the modifier is strong and resilient. He or she is compelled to set goals, determine strategies, and struggle to achieve his or her goals. However, unlike the protagonist, the modifier does not necessarily undergo a character change. Modifiers may have a change in their situation but, generally speaking, not a character change. Modifiers are essentially the same at the end of the screenplay as they were at the beginning. The goals of the protagonist and the modifier are both related to the plot action, but they are different and generally antithetical to each other. They are headed in the same direction but the different paths they travel will collide. And, when they do, the drama—"the dance"—begins.

"The Dance"

The protagonist and the modifier each want to keep moving in the direction of their goals but neither one can, because their opposing goals stand in each other's way. It's not a matter of simply going around each other— they HAVE to come to some resolution. Once the encounter occurs they MUST continue to confront each other and struggle with different aspects of the issue until the protagonist gains the strength to force a resolution. But because they're equally matched, this doesn't happen easily. Neither will relinquish their goals. They each must continue the encounters until something new and different tips the scale—until something new and different forces the change/growth within the protagonist to make a resolution possible.

In order for the protagonist to change/grow, he or she must be confronted with new and difficult situations. There must be barriers to dismantle, resistances to neutralize, objections to counteract, skeptics to convince, bridges to build, and pitfalls to avoid. THESE OBSTACLES FORCE THE PROTAGONIST TO MAKE NEW DECISIONS AND CHOICES THAT LEAD TO NEW BEHAVIOR. THE NEW BEHAVIOR LEADS TO THE DISCOVERY OF PREVIOUSLY UNKNOWN RESOURCES AND INSIGHTS. THE DISCOVERY OF THESE UNKNOWN RESOURCES AND INSIGHTS LEADS TO CHANGE AND GROWTH.

Foley is the modifier in *An Officer and a Gentleman*. His plot goal is to discover and shape officers capable of being "other-centered" and able to assume a military command. Zack's plot goal is to demonstrate his capabilities and gain his officer's commission. They each have the same end goal but the means and criteria for getting there are very different. Foley can't reach his goal unless Zack changes and Zack can't reach his goal unless he changes Foley—or changes himself. One or the other has to give and, since it's not the function of the modifier to change, Zack must change. He does and then reaches his goal, albeit by different means and with different criteria. Foley modifies Zack by his relentless but fair demands for excellence.

Ben is the modifier in *Body and Soul*. His plot goal is to keep Charley from selling out and throwing the fight. Charley's plot goal is to guarantee himself financial security. The two goals are related but antithetical. Ben, in one way or another, keeps forcing Charley to face the consequences of throwing the fight. Because of Ben's insistence, Charley realizes that he, like Ben, has been double crossed. This is what causes Charley to make his final climactic choice. He fights to win—and wins.

Plato is the modifier in *Rebel Without a Cause*. His emotional needs force Jim to become an independent adult and forever leave behind his adolescent dependence upon his father.

Opponents

Modifiers confront the protagonist with obstacles to overcome, but they're not the only characters who do this. There are others—opponents—who also confront the protagonist. Opponents initiate plot events that create conflict and result in success or failure, dominance or submission, and life or death. These conflict situations are additional obstacles—additional trials—that the protagonist must encounter and overcome. They become a part of the process of change/growth because they create new situations that call for new decisions and new behavior but their obstacles are more related to plot issues than character issues.

Roberts is an opponent. He wants Charley to throw the fight; Charley doesn't want to. The Kids are opponents. They want to revenge Buzz's accidental death; Jim, Judy, and Plato have to escape them. Deputy Chief Schaeffer is an opponent. He wants to kill Book; Book fights to live.

The distinction between the modifier and the opponent lies in the result. The struggle between the modifier and the protagonist results in *character change/growth* and, generally, becomes a win-win situation. The struggle between opponents and the protagonist results in a *situation change* and, generally, becomes a win-lose situation. Both are important and, generally, each functions at the same time to make their unique contribution to the screenplay.

There are some screenplays that primarily utilize the functions of opponents and in which the protagonist is almost solely engaged in a win-lose situation. *Beverly Hills Cop* is an example of this type of screenplay. Axel comes into the story as an unorthodox and incorruptible cop who prefers to work in Detroit, and at the end of the screenplay he is still unorthodox, incorruptible, and preferring Detroit. He has, however, encountered and overcome many opponents before he solves the murder and catches the killer. The theme of *Beverly Hills Cop* is articulated by the absence of change.

It's important to make this distinction between the modifier and the opponents. They are very different kinds of characters who serve very different functions and achieve very different results. As you recognize and identify these differences you'll be better able to structure your characters accordingly.

Catalyst

Another important character with a different function is the one who introduces a new situation or new information that demands a response from the protagonist, but who does not enter into face-to-face conflict with the protagonist. This character is often times referred to as a catalyst.

Sid's suicide in *An Officer and a Gentleman* is a catalytic act. Zack has to respond to the action but not to Sid. In *Out of Africa* when Felicity asks Denys to take her on a camera trip, she precipitates a separation between Karen and Denys. Karen responds to the situation but not to Felicity. The social worker in *Body and Soul* presents Charley with the information that his mother has asked for welfare assistance. This pushes Charley into the fighting ring in spite of his mother's objections. Frequently it is the catalyst, a character not involved in the main action, who will introduce new situations—new difficulties—and thus new directions.

Thematic Spokesperson

A character can also personify the thematic issue and become the thematic spokesperson. In *Body and Soul*, Shorty, Charley's childhood friend and promoter, discovers that the fight between Charley and Ben had been fixed. He quits, refusing to play that kind of a game. Then there's the grocer whose words represent an ethnic pride, " . . . In Europe today they're killing people like us just because they're Jewish. But here Charley Davis is the champeen . . ."

Supporting

Other characters function as vehicles to illuminate and "color in" the main characters. They're people from the characters' past, people the characters are interacting with in the present, and people who are involved in the characters' futures. Although often referred to as supporting or secondary characters, they perform very major functions, have their own plot and personal goals, and their decisions and choices affect the forward movement of the story. The people from the past help fill in the character's backstory and explain some of their present behavior.

Charley's mother, Anna, in *Body and Soul* helps us to understand Charley's childhood and his initial set of values. Peg, Charley's first girlfriend, communicates information from his past but also about the present and future. Through Charley's interaction with Peg in the past we learn about his basic personality. Through their interaction in the present we experience his turmoil and inner struggle and, finally, with Peg we look at their future together. Charley's interaction with Alice, a different girlfriend, creates a different picture of his present life.

Supporting characters often function as a contrast. The contrast between two characters sharpens the qualities of each. Alice is a very different person than Peg. The kind of person Alice is and the way Charley responds to her is in sharp contrast to Peg and Charley's relationship with her. In *An Officer and a Gentleman*, Lynette is very different than Paula. Lynette is capable of deceit and manipulation in a way that is impossible for Paula. Lynette's deceitfulness makes Paula's honesty more honest!

Just as there are supporting characters who illuminate and color-in characters, there are supporting characters who illuminate and color-in the situation—define the atmosphere. Quinn, Charley's manager, creates the atmosphere of the boxing world. Casey, Perryman, and Della-Serra, other officer candidates in *An Officer and a Gentleman*, create the atmosphere of the Naval Air Station. "The Kids" in *Rebel Without a Cause* strengthen and generalize the sense of young people in search of meaning and purpose. Farah, the native who manages Karen's house, in *Out of Africa*, gives us a glimpse of African native life. Chief Hubbard, in *Beverly Hills Cop*, epitomizes the difference between Beverly Hills and Detroit.

Lesser Roles

Then there are others with lesser roles and more limited functions who contribute to the reality of the situations and provide necessary plot information. We see this in characters like Paula's parents, in *An Officer and a Gentleman*, who act out the role Paula wants to escape; and the Amish clergy, in *Witness*, who decide if Book must leave or stay.

And, of course, there are the very minor characters who add color to the tapestry—the "bit" parts and extras who contribute to the ambiance of the plot events.

Being able to identify the functions of your characters is the first step to creating them and it's essential that you develop your sensitivity to this aspect of characterization. Also, you need to become acutely aware of the ways in which these functions interplay—interact—to create your total screenplay.

Character Orchestration

The next time you read a screenplay or see a film, take time to identify and label the characters in terms of their function. Think about how each one contributes to the telling of the story and the communication of the theme. Then think of the characters as different voices in a composition—like the musical instruments in a symphony. See how they each carry the melody at different times, how they interrupt and overlap, how they conflict, when there's dissonance and when there's harmony, how they contrast and compliment each other. See how each one has his or her own special place in the composition.

Doing this will help you understand the importance of choosing and creating your characters—orchestrating them—*because* of their function and their interrelationships. As has been said so many times, the essence of storytelling is struggle and conflict. This demands uncompromising characters who must struggle and who *will* conflict *because of* their differences. If the principle characters have the same function, approach life in the same way, and have the same goals, it will be difficult, if not impossible, to generate conflict between them.

This analysis of your characters as players in a chess game, with each having a name and unique moves, may create the impression that characterization is a mechanical and contrived process. Nothing could be further from the truth! The learning process is somewhat mechanical and contrived, but the end goal is not. To repeat the metaphor—just as when you learned to drive an automobile you had to identify and master each function and action, as you learn characterization you need to identify and master each function and interaction. With practice, the selection and creation of characters with different functions and interactions will ultimately become a part of your being—a part of the process that flows from an internalized and integrated sense of storytelling.

PERSONALITY DEVELOPMENT

In order to create well-motivated, dynamic, and multi-faceted characters who will serve your dramatic purposes, it is helpful for you to know something about personality development. Many different theories have been formulated to explain how and why one person takes one road while another chooses a totally different one. Although I strongly recommend more than just a casual reading of some of the psychological literature that deals with personality, it isn't necessary for you to thoroughly study the many volumes of thought and research that are available on this subject. It's sufficient for you to know the generally accepted theories of personality development that range from those who claim heredity as the most important factor to those who believe that environment is the major determinant. And, for the screenwriter, it is most profitable to look at those theories that take ideas from both extremes and advance the notion that there's an important relationship between the environment a person is born into and the physical characteristics he or she arrives with.

Gaining a knowledge about personality development and the psychology of human behavior will provide you with many insights into your own development and behaviors. You will unlock doors to places within yourself you have not known before. This can be a very constructive experience, and it can sometimes be quite painful. Often these kinds of insights—especially the painful ones—can mark the beginning of self-exploration and increased self-awareness. Happily you live in a time and place where there's access to psychological help and the search for self-awareness is applauded rather than ridiculed. Actually, as a screenwriter, self-awareness is a necessity. Who you are and what your experiences have been is what you write about. The greater your access to all of this information, the greater your capacity to create believable characters and structure believable stories. Self-awareness ought not to be the special privilege of people who have problems that need treatment. Self-awareness belongs to everyone—especially screenwriters!

The screenwriter is not nearly as much concerned with the genesis of "healthy" personalities as with the causes for compensatory behavior and with the development of defense mechanisms that allow us to cope with problems and adjust to given circumstances. The "healthy," perfectly adjusted personality is not the best dramatic character, but neither is the other extreme, the psychotic. It's the everyday, run-of-the-mill neurotic behavior that screenwriters work with. It's the everyday, run-of-the-mill neurotic behavior we all engage in from time to time that stories are written about.

Screenwriters work with the characters who refuse to admit to the truths that are staring them in the face; those who direct their hostility toward a non-threatening person rather than the source of their hostility; those who use humor to hide behind; the ones who avoid feelings by engaging in predominantly intellectual concerns; those who accuse others of the behavior they dislike in themselves; the persons who deny their feelings, continuously excuse their own unacceptable behavior, over-achieve, under-achieve, live in fantasy worlds, repress anxiety-producing feelings and thoughts, and adopt and imitate the behavior of other people rather than develop their own. Screenwriters people their screenplays with these kinds of characters because they are reflections of parts of themselves and the people they love and live with; and because these kinds of characters do the things that stories are made of. And in order to create these kinds of characters, you need to know something about where their behavior comes from.

Personality development is a gradual and sequential process that starts with infancy and continues into and through our adult years. According to many psychologists there are progressive stages of development and each presents a central problem that must be dealt with and solved if the person is to successfully move forward into the next stage.

The first, and perhaps the most important, stage occurs within our first year of life. This is when we acquire our sense of trust—or distrust. It's during this first year when we're totally dependent upon others that we develop our dominant view of the kind of world we live in. Is it a world we can trust? Is it a world where we know we'll be fed when we're hungry, made warm when we're cold, dry when we're wet, played with when we're bored, and comforted when we hurt? Or is it a lonely world full of pain, hunger, and neglect—a world that doesn't meet our needs? Those unloved and uncared for in infancy may carry a dominant distrust of others and find it very difficult to develop a sense of responsibility toward the people in their world.

Then come the years when we learn about ourselves, when we learn we're independent and separate beings with a mind and a will of our own. This is the time of muscular maturation—a time of toilet training, beginning to walk, talk, and play with things. A time when we start to form our opinions about ourselves. If we're allowed to make choices, allowed to make mistakes, and lovingly are guided to channel this sense of autonomy in acceptable and productive ways, we grow with a sense of the necessary boundaries and a sense of self-esteem. If we're robbed of our opportunities of free choice, confronted with rigid and negative training, we can emerge from this stage of our development with feelings of doubt, shame, guilt, and excessive rebellion.

It's at this point when our attitudes about ourselves are developing and we begin to shape our self-images in the "mirrors" of how people treat us. Mother says, "Stop bothering me, Peggy. What's the matter with you? Can't you see I'm taking care of brother!" Peggy hears and sees herself— "I bother Mom. She prefers my brother. There's something wrong with me." A grown man waves a paper airplane in front of the child, "You call that an airplane? Look, guys, it's an airplane!" The little boy hears and sees himself—"What I do isn't very good. People laugh at me." Or, in a happy playful situation—"People like to play with me; they like to have me around. I'm a nice person."

This process continues and accelerates in the next period when we're four and five years old and when we're discovering who we are and what we can do. This is our period of rapid learning, creativity, imagined fantasies, and the beginning of a conscience. There are many things we want to do that we can't do and shouldn't do, but many things we can and should do. We need the opportunities to experiment. We need encouragement for the appropriate things we do. We need gentleness in learning and accepting what we can't do. If the supervision is overly restrictive and punitive, our activities and initiative can become greatly constricted at this early age and follow us into adulthood.

These three stages, experienced within the first six years of our lives, are of prime importance for personality development. The quality of our sense of trust, autonomy, and initiative are the basis for our dominant world and self views. This is why there's the common belief that a person's personality is pretty well set by age six. This is why it's important for you, as the creator of characters, to develop the early childhood experiences that will produce the personalities your screenplay requires.

The stage of development that ranges between ages six to eleven or twelve involves us in learning how to do things and do them well. We acquire knowledge and skills and begin to learn the rules of cooperation and fair play. We continue to see ourselves in the "mirrors" of other people's responses to us and we can come out of this period with a sense of accomplishment and worthwhileness or, depending upon what the "mirrors" tell us, with a sense of inadequacy, inferiority, and discouragement. "Gary's a crybaby, crybaby, crybaby." "I don't want Betty on my team—she's no good!" "You kids are all alike—ya all steal an' lie—all the time!" Or, "You're my best buddy—forever!"

The next period is adolescence and the time when we establish our adult identity—decide who we are and what we will become. All along we've been developing this sense of who we are, but now it becomes of paramount importance and determines much of the direction of our future. This is a very stressful time of physiological changes and a preoccupation with the necessity for peer approval. The task of adolescence is the discovery of a knowable future with a definite and positive role to play. Serious personality problems can arise when the answers to these issues are not found. When we don't know who we are, what we want to do, or what we want out of life, it becomes very difficult to happily face the responsibilities of adult life.

With adult life and some sense of identity comes the desire for intimacy. This is different from the "buddies" of our earlier days and isn't limited to sexual intimacy. It expresses itself in different ways—close friendships with either sex, love relationships, and a communion with previously undiscovered aspects of ourselves. However, if we haven't yet found ourselves, we'll avoid close relationships with others and with ourselves; our interactions will be more formal and stereotypical, without the warmth and spontaneity that attracts and creates intimacy.

With the gratifications of intimacy comes the need and wish to be creative—either through parenthood or the creation of material objects and/ or art forms. It's the desire to create, nourish, and be responsible for a being or thing outside of one's self. It can only be achieved when we can value giving as much as receiving, and loving as much as being loved.

The final stage of personality development comes with a sense of integrity—when we accept ourselves and the people within the scope of our lives as being important and worthwhile. This brings an acceptance of responsibility for our own lives, a sense of communion with all people in all times and all places, and the ability to defend the dignity of our own lives against any external threats. When we don't have this sense of integrity we live lives of despair and malcontent. We feel defeated and contemptuous about life and the way we've been treated.

Although the fortunes or misfortunes in this developmental sequence sculpt the personality, it is entirely possible for the adult to shed the shapes of past conditioning. Children are captives. They cannot escape their environments to find a better place. But adults can—and often do. New sources of trust can be discovered. New circumstances can help the person feel autonomous. The ability to achieve and a sense of initiative can be created through adult responsibilities and activities. Adults can come to know who they are, take pride in what they can do and finally emerge with a sense of intimacy and integrity.

People can change and grow. *Characters change and grow.* Screenwriters discover who their characters are, the events that have shaped them, and the events that can create their change and growth.

This is, of course, a very narrow and simplified look at personality development. It is not the purpose of this chapter to explore with you the depth and breadth of this very complex and important science. It is my intent to give you a sense of personality as a developmental process and to stress the importance of creating environments out of which your principal characters will emerge as believable and dynamic human beings. It is my intent to suggest the questions you will need to ask and the nature of the answers you must seek. Also, in addition to asking questions and answers, I hope you'll SEE your characters as they emerge and move from one phase to the next. Words alone are not enough. Words tend to carry cognitive information. Images contain affective information. You need both.

CHARACTER DEVELOPMENT

Just as there's no formula for writing a screenplay, there's no formula for creating a character. There are many different ways to approach this task.

It may be that the original inspiration for your screenplay is a person—someone you know, have read about, or a piece of yourself. Here you already know the kind of a character you're dealing with. If this is your starting place, you'll be focusing on discovering the experiences in the character's background that will complement, "flesh out," and explain what you already know about the character. In this situation you start out with a fairly substantial amount of knowledge about the character.

If your inspiration has come from an event, you'll be looking for and creating the kind of character who will most convincingly portray a similar incident. Chances are you've observed that event and already know the general types of characters who normally become—or don't become—involved in the incident you want to portray. Here you'll be working back and forth between the event and the character—matching the two and discovering the qualities within the character that will push the plot events in the directions you want them to go to say what you want them to say.

If you've started with a theme you want to communicate, then you'll be searching for the characters who can personify this theme. You'll be starting with what the character will become at the end—the change/growth that will occur—and then you'll work backwards to construct the events that will cause this change/growth. You'll determine the kind of a person who is the appropriate vehicle for your theme and then you'll create that person.

Although the inspirations and approaches in all three of these situations are different, the end results will be the same. In all three you will end up with a comprehensive look at your principal character's PHYSICAL TRAITS, LIFE HISTORY, DOMINANT VIEWS OF WORLD AND SELF, VALUES, DOMINANT EMOTIONAL TRAITS, and GENERAL TEMPERAMENT.

You'll start with some general ideas about your character's dominant physical traits: AGE, SEX, RACE, HEIGHT, WEIGHT, and COLORING. Each of these characteristics carries its cultural roles and an almost inevitable bias toward all issues. A teenager views life differently than a person sixty years old; a woman lives in a much different world than a man; black people see the world through a different set of eyes than whites, Orientals, or Native Americans. Height and weight determine many of the things that a person can and cannot do, and the color of a person's hair, eyes, and skin can have an effect on their view of the world and themselves. These physical characteristics are givens and even before birth begin to exert their influence. Sight unseen, someone may be saying, "I hope it's a girl," and another may say, "He's got to be just like you."

As previously stated, it is the adult and cultural expectations and environment into which people are born and live the first years of their lives that establish the core of their being. So, obviously, you need to know and weave the pattern of your character's CHILDHOOD experiences. You need to know about the character's BIRTHPLACE and CHILDHOOD HOME.

What country?
What region of the country?
Was it a rural or urban environment?
What was the character of the neighborhood?
What kind of a house?
What was the character's room like?

You need to know a great deal about the character's PARENTS AND/OR GUARDIANS. You need to know about their EDUCATIONAL STATUS, ECONOMIC STATUS, SOCIAL STATUS, POLITICAL AND RELIGIOUS BELIEFS.

What was their level of schooling?
What kind of work did they do?
What was their income?
What were the conditions under which they worked?
Did they work long hours?
Was their work stressful?
Did they contribute to the activities of the community?
What was their standing in the community?

Were they politically active?
What was their political affiliation?
Were they active in an organized church, temple, or mosque?

You need to know the VALUES of your character's parents or guardians.

What did they believe in?
What were the most important things in their lives?
What were the principles by which they lived and which they taught
to their children?

You need to know about the character's SIBLINGS and the FAMILY
LIFESTYLE.

How many were there?
What were their sexes and ages?
Where did your character fit among them?
How did the adults respond to the siblings?
How did the siblings respond to each other?
Were there extended members of the family living in the home?
Did the family act as a unit or go their separate ways?
Who was your character's favorite sibling?
What are the things they did together?

The answers to these questions will lead you to other and more important
questions.

Were the infant physical dependency needs of the character met?
As an infant, was the character played with?
Did he or she have fun time?
Was he or she frequently held?
Was your character a planned and wanted child?
Was there stability or turmoil in the character's childhood?

And then you can ask *the most important questions*.

How, as a child, did your character view the world and himself or
herself?
Was it a world to feel comfortable in?
Was it a capricious world full of anxiety and distrust?
Was it a world to be manipulated?
A world to escape?
Did your character feel lovable?
Worthwhile?
A burden?
A disappointment?
Worthless?

Can your character move forward into the next stages of his or her life with a sense of worth and trust?

It is here that you find the seeds of your character's strengths and weaknesses—and the images that will portray each. It is here that your character's DOMINANT VIEWS OF THE WORLD and DOMINANT VIEWS OF HIMSELF OR HERSELF are formed.

Imagine a fifteen-year-old character who is riddled with fears and reluctant to enter into even the most normal teenage activities. We'll call him "Jimmy." When Jimmy was a child he wasn't taught to do things. He was just told not to do them. When he tried to climb and reach for things, his mother said, "No, Jimmy, you'll fall and bump your head." When he reached out to pet the neighbor's dog, his mother screamed, "Get back!! He'll bite you!" When he went close to the edge of the ocean and felt the water tickling his toes, his father yelled, "No! Jimmy, get back!" When he climbed up in the tree in the backyard his father yelled again, "You'll fall!" When he started to climb a hill, his father called, "Come down this minute." Jimmy wanted to learn how to hammer nails and they took the hammer away. He wanted to ride a bike and they took the bike away. He wanted to help with the barbecue and they took the tongs away. He wanted to help pull the garage door down and his father stopped him.

Now Jimmy's in high school and he doesn't do many of the things the other boys his age are doing—playing basketball, surfing, managing a paper route, or even dating. His parents are puzzled and don't understand why Jimmy is so different from the other boys. Jimmy doesn't understand it, either. All he knows is that many things make him very uncomfortable and always afraid. His world is a very frightening place and he feels totally incapable of dealing with it.

Fear, anxiety, and a sense of inadequacy are Jimmy's core qualities—his core characteristics. They're the result of the **repetition** of his parent's anxieties and fears and their inability to allow him to explore, experience, and learn. Jimmy undoubtedly had many positive things happen to him as well as these negative things, but in Jimmy's case, the negatives outweighed the positives. It's when the same thing happens many times and we learn the same thing over and over again that it becomes a habit—and a core characteristic of our personality. These are the characteristics that influence all of a person's behavior. They're like the hub of a wheel, from which all the spokes radiate. They're the attitudes and behavior from which life-long traits and behavior are born.

Jimmy's fears, anxieties, and sense of inadequacy will influence all aspects of his life. How do you think these characteristics could effect the type of work he chooses? Recreational patterns? Social activities? Educational pursuits? How will they influence his approach to marriage and children? What kind of woman might he marry? Will his sexual practices and attitudes reflect these characteristics? How will he respond in situations where physical courage is highly valued? What kind of religious beliefs will he choose?

There are many possible scenarios for Jimmy, but whichever is chosen must emanate in some way from his dominant view of himself and his world. *It is the necessities created by core characteristics that generate a consistent, but varied, character.*

If your characters are born into and grow up in "good" situations, they'll learn more direct and more constructive ways of coping. They'll be open to experience. They'll be able to fully feel and see their world without having to shut it out of awareness. They'll show faster intellectual development. All of their energies can be devoted to receiving rather than defending. They won't need to live in fantasy worlds, deny or shape reality, or assume someone else's identity. This doesn't mean that these characters will be allowed a life of "peaches and cream." Life's not like that for anyone. However, they'll approach life's tasks with more originality, a wider range of alternative behaviors, more confidence in their own abilities, and a tendency to fully live each moment. For these kinds of characters, their struggle is less with themselves and their inner problems and more with the obstacles of life itself.

The childhood experiences establish the fundamental direction of the character's life but the ADOLESCENT YEARS and entrance into ADULT-HOOD also exert significant influences. You'll continue to ask questions about how your characters interact with their parents and/or guardians, and you'll search to discover what happens to them as they move out into the neighborhood and the larger communities of town, county, state, and nation.

How do they relate to their schoolmates?
Are they "popular?"
Are they a part of the "in" group or are they "wallflowers?"
Do they have the approval of their teachers?
What are their scholastic achievements?
Are they leaders or followers in school?
Do they follow the rules of the school or do they rebel?
Do they participate in extra-curricular activities?
Do they enjoy competitive activities?
Are they members of a clique?
Are they identifying with the sex roles of their culture?
At what age are they attracted to the opposite sex?
If they date, do they "play the field" or "go steady?"
Do they use drugs?
Are they preparing to go on to higher education?
What are the classes they excel in?
What are their goals for their futures?
At what ages do they leave their parental home and where do they
   go?

What are their special interests and achievements?
Who are their special friends and how deep are their relationships?

The answers to these questions will give you many very specific images of your characters. Now you can see and hear them. You can describe exactly WHAT THEY LOOK LIKE and can give them their names.

Are their names commonly used or unusual?
Are they attractive?
Unattractive?
Any disfiguring marks?
Physical handicaps?
How do they dress?
Neat and clean?
Sloppy?
Dirty?
Fashionable?
How do they talk?
Do they use proper English?
Have an accent?
Speak very softly or hesitantly?
How do they walk, sit, and gesture?
What is their body language?
Do they have any unique mannerisms?
Quirks?
Pick their teeth?
Twirl a hat?
Carry a walking stick?

You know where your characters come from, their dominant views of the world and themselves; you know what they look like and now you can easily discover what they've become—their CURRENT ECONOMIC, POLITICAL, EDUCATIONAL, SOCIAL, RELIGIOUS, and FAMILY STATUS.

How do they earn their livings?
Professional?
Blue collar?
Unskilled labor?
How much do they make?
Do they enjoy what they do?
What are their working conditions like?
What are their political affiliations?
Are they politically active?
Are they still in school?
Graduated?
Did they enjoy learning?

Who are their friends?
What do they do for entertainment?
What are their hobbies?
Musical preferences?
Sports activities?
Do they belong to any religious groups?
Who do they live with?
What kinds of places do they live in?
Are they married?
Children?
What are their current relationships with their parents?
What are their family lifestyles?
What are their sexual practices?
Attitudes?
What kinds of people are they attracted to?
Do they have pets?
What kinds of automobiles do they drive?
What are their most prized possessions?

You'll want to think about your characters' VALUE SYSTEMS.

What are the "rules" they live by?
What are their philosophies of life?
What are the most important things in their lives?
What is right and what is wrong?
How do they treat other people?
How do they want to be treated themselves?
Of all of the things in this world, what do they want most of all?
What are their conflicting values?
What are the private little wars that go on within them?

You'll need to know a great deal about their EMOTIONAL RESPONSES.

How do they handle their positive and negative emotions?
What makes them angry?
What makes them cry?
What do they fear?
How do they deal with failure?
Success?
What are their vices?
Are they jealous?
Do they enjoy life?
Can they love?
Who do they love most?
Are they giving?
Vindictive?
Spiteful?

You need to know about their TEMPERAMENTS.

Is the character easygoing, open and sharing?
Secretive and self-centered?
Is this a dominant person or submissive?
Is the character enthusiastic and active?
A conservative or a radical?
How controlled?
Willing to take chances?
Needing reassurances and approval?
Self-sufficient?
Responsible?
Reliable?
Suspicious?
Sensitive?
Awkward?
Cowardly?
Shrewd?

You want to discover the characters' SECRETS and explore their intimate, private moments.

What do they try to hide from others—and from themselves?
What are the things they do they wouldn't want anyone to see?
What silly little mannerisms do they hide?
What's their "little girl" and "little boy" behavior that's reserved for the immediate family?

These are only a few of the questions that demonstrate the wide ranges of human behavior—each a different color on your characterization palette. These are the kinds of questions you need to work with—questions that carry you from your character's birth to the opening scenes of your screenplay; questions that instruct you to look at each stage of your character's development; questions that involve you in their transitions from one stage to another; questions that evoke expressive images; questions that force you to "become" the character you're creating. These are the kinds of questions that demonstrate the truth of the Native American proverb that tells us we must walk in another man's moccasins in order to understand him.

In working with these questions it's important to find the kinds of answers that create images. You aren't going for sterile yes or no answers—you want answers that are rich with vivid detail—so vivid that you SEE your characters in the times and places you're investigating. This is important because it brings your characters to life and accelerates your process of getting to know them, but it also will help when you create your screenplay images. Remember the image of little Jimmy at the beach? Remember, he went close to the ocean, and as he felt the water tickling his toes, his father yelled, "No! Jimmy, get back!" Of course, Jimmy responded to the fear in his father's voice and pulled his feet away from the tickling water—and the new sensation. This very same image can be used to show the adolescent Jimmy standing at the edge of the beach, wanting to join his friends in the ocean, but unable to get past his fear of the water that tickles his toes. BECAUSE THIS IS THE WAY HE RESPONDS IN THE PRESENT, WE KNOW HE HAS RESPONDED THIS WAY IN HIS PAST—*and if he has responded this way in the past, we can predict that he will do so in the future.* The discovery of these behavioral images, as your characters move through and from one phase to the next, provides extraordinarily rich and honest imagery.

BACK TO CATHY

Now let's go back to Cathy. Hopefully by now there's some distance between you and your Cathy assignment. It's very hard, if not impossible, to have any objectivity about your work immediately after you've completed it. This is why you need feedback.

Now, before you re-read what you've written, think about the objects in Cathy's room and the possible meanings each object contains. Also, think about symbols—similes, metaphors, and correlative symbols. Any one of the objects in Cathy's room could stand for something else and could assume symbolic contextual meanings to become a vehicle for externalizing her feelings and thoughts. For example, the gold earrings and bracelet clasp could represent a gift from her parents or the security and wealth of the family business; the piggy bank is a symbol of a future and saving; the trophies symbolize Cathy's identity and capabilities; the computer represents a writing tool—to be turned on or off; the slippers and the marks on the closet door are things of her past—to be clung to or discarded, erased or cherished. The "dog-earedness" of the screenplays could be utilized. Each dog-ear contains something to be remembered, something of particular interest; the action of dog-earring demonstrates active involvement; "un"dog-earring shows that the memory is no longer important. Of all of the objects in her room, the family pictures are the least imaginative. They are the most obvious and therefore predictable. By choosing something less obvious you will engage the reader/viewer in the discovery of its symbology—you will INVOLVE the reader/viewer with Cathy's discovery of her feelings and thoughts in relationship to that object.

Now read your Cathy scene. Remember that your assignment was to develop her emotion—not the situation. Think about the object you chose and how Cathy related to it to show her emotion. Become aware of the power of using a single object. Contrast the power of a single object with the fragmentation of multiple objects. Think of how emotions deepen as a character deals with different aspects of the single object in relationship to different aspects of his or her emotion. Picture in your mind how shifting from object to object moves the emotion horizontally rather than vertically. The horizontal movement is linear and moves from one "place" to another. Vertical movement is circular and "walks around" the emotion to look at its many aspects. Think about the differences between developing Cathy's emotion horizontally and vertically. And then think about a different object you might have used and how you could have developed a different emotion. The more you think about these things—the more you practice—the easier it will become to find the expressive images that give your characters definition and depth.

Next, look at how you built the scene. Did Cathy start with one state of mind, move through a struggle to reach her decision, and then arrive at a different state of mind? Were we unsure about what her decision would be until the very end? What were the incremental steps that carried her to a decision? What were the sizes of the steps? Were there bridges connecting the steps? What was the factor that finally pushed her to a decision? Did Cathy's struggle occupy enough time and space appropriate to the magnitude of this decision? Did you unfold her emotion or did you focus more on the unfolding of events? Did you develop Cathy's emotion in depth through a single object?

Think about these things. Develop your skills of self-analysis. Rewrite based on your analysis. Find a friend who has a knowledge of dramaturgy and who can give you constructive comments. Ask for feedback and then rewrite as it is indicated. Rewriting is practice and the more you practice, the faster you'll become the screenwriter you want to be.

STRUCTURING CHARACTERS IS A PROCESS

You must know as much as you possibly can about your characters. Your screenplay will contain only a very small portion of the information you accumulate, but the believable and multi-faceted behavior of your characters will unconsciously flow from the aggregate of this information. The time will come when you will know your characters so well that they will assume control over their own lives. They will decide what to do and when and how to do it. You will simply follow their instructions. They will become alive and capable of making their own decisions. But this doesn't happen magically. *It happens because of you and the process of character development you engage in.* Through this process you give them life; you give them knowledge; you give them feelings; you give them goals. You create them out of your images of their pasts.

Structuring your characters is a process that functions both consciously and unconsciously. It's a process you learn; a process you deliberately enter into; a process you practice. There is nothing mysterious or miraculous about it.

At first your characterization palette may be very small, but each time you make contact with a different behavioral trait—in others and within yourself—it becomes larger and larger. You can deliberately enlarge your palette—your knowledge of human behavior—by studying psychological theory and research—and I strongly recommend this. But also, I recommend and urge you to do your own research and collect your own characterization data.

PEOPLE NOTEBOOK

You can very easily and very pleasurably do this by keeping a People Notebook. This is like your Journal, only more specifically directed toward notes about people you meet and observe. These can be people that would make viable screenplay characters or just simply people you find interesting. They might be people you'd like to know better, people you can't fathom but want to understand, or people you don't like and don't want to be around. Jot down notes about their appearances, snatches of their dialogue, their mannerisms, and, most of all, record their actions that seem inappropriate or funny—or tragic. Draw sketches—crude caricatures—that emphasize their outstanding characteristics. This will help you preserve their images. Your People Notebook, like your Journal, is a valuable lifetime resource. Treat it and prepare it as such. Write your notes in enough detail so your observations are clear and fully drawn. A single word about a character may serve to jog your memory within the next few days or weeks but will be meaningless within the next months and years. Be sure to write enough to retrieve the total memory of the people and the circumstances of meeting or observing them.

CHARACTER PROFILE

The first step in the process of structuring a character is the creation of a character profile. This profile is drawn from your answers to all of the questions that describe your character from infancy to the first pages of your screenplay—the questions I've suggested and many others you will think of. This is your next assignment—the creation of a character profile.

Go out into the street and watch people going by until you see someone who interests you—preferably a middle-aged person. Watch that person for as long as you can. Then write down his or her physical traits and begin to ask yourself the questions that will build a character profile.

Don't just think the answers—write your answers down. By the time you get to the questions about his or her adult lives you'll have more information than you can easily remember, and from time to time you'll want to go back to refer to some of your first ideas. Also, at some future time you may want to put this character in one of your screenplays. Character profile work is like putting money in your savings account—everytime you create a character you're developing an asset. Take your time. You have many things to think about and you'll need a minimum of two or three hours to devote to this. Really get to know your character and then, when you're through, come back and we'll do some more things to help you know him or her even better.

CHARACTER SITUATIONS

I hope you did stop reading and that you now have a person you've created. If you haven't yet—why not now? You'll learn so much more from what we'll do next if you've done a character profile.

After you've created your characters you'll be able to put them into a number of different situations—give them specific things to react to. By doing this your characters will come to life—they'll breathe, talk, and gesture—and you'll discover many more things about them.

What did you decide was your character's greatest fear? Was it the loss of a family member? A bodily disfigurement? Being involved in an automobile accident? Whatever—put your character in the situation he or she fears the most. I know this is a terrible thing to do to your new friend but remember—it's only a hypothetical situation! Create the situation and then visualize it. Do this same thing for at least two or three more situations. Discover what your character does on a vacation, when confronted with betrayal, when granted his or her most cherished wish, or whatever situation you want to choose.

Watch how your character responds differently to different people and in different situations. Have the character present the same gift to a child, to a parent, a teacher, and a spouse. Watch how differently he or she takes criticism from a boss, a spouse, a friend, or a stranger. Watch the different ways your character behaves when alone, when in a crowd, and when in a family situation.

Imagine your character's behavior during the course of an entire day—watch everything he or she does from awakening in the morning to going to sleep at night. Take your character to lunch—let your character choose the restaurant, order the food, and then ask you to pay for it. Engage in conversation with your character—discuss current events, your personal problems, and your plans for your future. Challenge your character—try to change an opinion or force him or her into a new and distasteful relationship. Bring several characters together and see how they get along.

Take walks with your character, sleep with, eat with, and become your character. Speak for him or her. Ask questions and listen to the replies. Give him or her active sentences that start with "I want," "I need," "I will," and "I won't."

You, in a very real sense, will be engaging in the same process an actor goes through to discover the character he or she is to portray. I urge you to enroll in acting classes—particularly those that work with the methods developed by Constantin Stanislavski. At the very least, as previously suggested, you will want to read Stanislavski's book, *An Actor Prepares*. As you're reading this book, simply substitute the word screenwriter for actor and you'll learn many very valuable procedures for knowing and understanding your characters.

CHARACTERIZATION THROUGH THE USE OF FILMIC ELEMENTS

First, you create your character. Next, you find the actions and expressive material that will externalize the character's inner thoughts and feelings. Then you look for the filmic elements and multiple layers that will add depth and intensify the core qualities of your character.

The most obvious filmic elements to help you structure your characterizations are the persona images you create: the costumes—their style, texture and color, the hairstyles, and the makeup you may suggest. These things create an immediate impression and identification of the characters.

The environment—the mise-en-scène—that the characters place themselves in tells us a great deal about them. The living spaces, work spaces, play spaces, and the objects surrounding your characters all speak loudly about how they think and feel—what they value.

The ways your characters move their bodies communicate things. Movements toward the camera can create the sense of a menacing person, or loving; movements away can characterize the person as remote and unfriendly; sitting down tells us one thing about the character and standing up says something else. A person with broad, expansive gestures is different than a person with limited and controlled gestures.

Color, textures, and lighting can be used to emphasize the moods and core qualities of the character. Lens distortions can give us information about a character. Dominant character traits can be emphasized by contrasting traits. Placement within the frame can make the character a dominant or passive person. A character embedded in a crowded frame is different from a character surrounded by negative space. A high-angle shot gives a character a more diminutive sense than a low-angle shot. Static shots create character confinement, while moving shots expand and open things up. Situational sounds and music can voice the moods of the characters and mirror the changes. The way dialogue is spoken may reveal more about characters than the words themselves.

Now—let's practice some of these ideas. Go back to your Cathy scene. You've already found the expressive objects and behavior to externalize her thoughts and feelings. The next step is to work with the filmic elements and SEE how your ideas will LOOK within a frame. You can do this by sketching your images of each shot.

Idea Sketching

Very often, prior to the actual shooting of a film, storyboards will be drawn to show the key elements in the shots for some or all of the scenes. Storyboarding is done by graphic artists and often carries a great deal of very realistic detail. I AM NOT asking you to do that! I am asking that you begin to translate the images in your mind onto paper—sketch your ideas—so you can more accurately assess how they will work on film.

You want to discover the impact of juxtaposing your shots, the placement of your characters and objects on the various planes and layers within the frame, the character and camera movements, the size of your characters and/or objects, and the effectiveness of the camera angle. You can do this very quickly and easily by using geometric figures and symbols.

Do not work with detail. It's relationships of people and objects within the frame and camera positions and movements that you're concerned

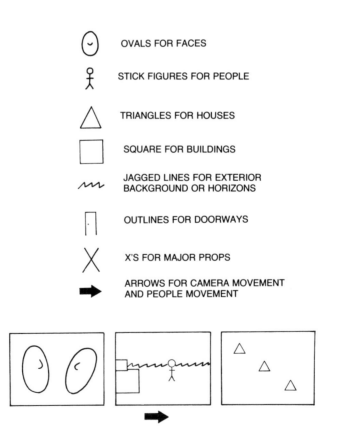

OVALS FOR FACES

STICK FIGURES FOR PEOPLE

TRIANGLES FOR HOUSES

SQUARE FOR BUILDINGS

JAGGED LINES FOR EXTERIOR BACKGROUND OR HORIZONS

OUTLINES FOR DOORWAYS

X'S FOR MAJOR PROPS

ARROWS FOR CAMERA MOVEMENT AND PEOPLE MOVEMENT

with. It will take you a little time to get used to doing this, but as with everything else, the more you do it, the easier it becomes. It's my hope that sketching—blocking out—your ideas will become a regular habit. And, that just like you'll work with your Journal and People Notebook, you'll also create and work with a Sketch book.

The more you THINK images and SKETCH those images, the more clearly and effectively you'll WRITE images.

Any looseleaf or bound notebook and a template with the standard 3:4 frame size will help you quickly create a Sketch Book. You'll find such a template in the Appendix. Also, you'll find a list of the filmic elements we've dealt with throughout this book. You can duplicate this list to include in a Sketch Book or place above your computer or typewriter. You can use this list like a help menu in a word processing program.

When you've finished sketching your Cathy scene, turn to the Appendix and look at an example of a similar assignment, but don't do that until you've completed your sketches. If you look at what someone else has sketched before you've done your own, you'll minimize your learning. You need to grapple with the problems on your own in order to find and internalize the answers for yourself. Then, if you want to, you can go back and incorporate some of the new learning into what you've previously done.

As so often stated, the details of your characters' actions and persona are rarely included in the screenplay in the form of "instructions"—but are frequently suggested in the poetry of shot descriptions.

In *Out of Africa*, Kurt Luedtke writes exactly what Karen is to do at the end of Denys' funeral.

> She bends to take a handful of earth to drop into the grave. Her lips move: we cannot make it out. She may have said: I love you.
>
> But she cannot drop the earth; the gesture is too final. It trickles away through her hand.

In *Body and Soul*, Abraham Polonsky writes exactly what Charley does to show his feelings about Peg.

> . . . Charley walks into the bedroom to the dresser and picks up the silver-handled brush.
>
> CLOSE SHOT - BRUSH
>
> which is inscribed: "TO PEG FROM CHARLEY." There are a few strands of hair in it which he fingers, removes, and then

he brushes the brush against the palm of his hand in a
caress.

In *Witness*, Earl Wallace and William Kelley specify exactly what Samuel
is to do to show his embarrassment with how different he and his mother
look in their Amish clothes.

SAMUEL

He's uncomfortably aware of the shy looks and giggles of a
little girl about his own age, standing in line with her
parents at the next counter.

He edges away from his mother . . .

It is these kinds of details that tell the reader/viewer what the character
is thinking and feeling and that give the film director and actors the information they need in order to interpret the characters the screenwriter
has created.

REFERENCES

1. V.I. Pudovkin, *Film Technique and Film Acting*, Lear Publishers, Inc., New York, 1949, pp. 27, 28.
2. Tony Gayton, revised screenplay outline, University of Southern California, Division of Cinema, TV 415, class project.
3. John Howard Lawson, *Theory and Technique of Playwriting*, A Dramabook, Hill and Wang, New York, 1960, pp. 286, 287.

9

THEME

Discussions about theme will almost inevitably arouse controversy. There are many different and opposing approaches to this topic. There are those who say that writers should never start writing until they've formed a clear and concise statement of their theme. Others contend that writers never really know their theme—until someone in an audience tells them what it is. Some say that screenplays are for entertainment and messages are for telegrams. Still others say that screenplays must serve a political purpose.

It's my view that screenwriters *may not* immediately know their theme, but before their final rewrite they MUST know it very well. Your theme— the thing within you that's demanding expression—may emerge and be discovered in the process of writing. It doesn't matter when it happens— just so it happens. Also, it's my view that screenplays can simultaneously entertain and communicate a theme. Most importantly, it is my strong conviction that screenwriters must concern themselves with theme. Theme is the reason for telling stories. Theme is the work of the artist.

DEFINITIONS

The word *theme* can be defined in different ways: what it is the screenwriter wants to say; what the screenwriter is trying to prove; where the screenwriter is going; what the screenwriter values; the screenwriter's purpose; or, to quote Webster's Collegiate Dictionary, a subject or topic of artistic representation. Also, there are many different words that have been used to symbolize these meanings: premise, root-idea, spine, direction, point, message, through line, and communication. I have chosen to use the word *theme*.

I define the word *theme* as that which is in your head and heart that you want to get into the head and heart of the reader/viewer. What you want to communicate on a cognitive, but especially, on an affective level. In my opinion, theme dictates the total artistic form of the screenplay. It is what the entire work stands for. Theme isn't something appended or extracted. It IS the screenplay. It IS the Art experience. We may pick scenes apart, analyze individual motivations, savor performances, and comment on progression, but each of these aspects will always remain embedded in its total, artistic structure. It is in this context that I use the word-symbol *theme.*

The idea in your head that you want to get into the head and heart of the reader/viewer is very different from plot. As has been said many times, plot is the vehicle for theme. Plot is events. Theme is the glue that holds all of the events together—the principle by which all things are related to each other. Theme is the unifying force. Theme is what the plot events stand for—what they communicate. In *Body and Soul,* the plot revolves around prize fighting, but the theme has to do with self-respect. *Beverly Hills Cop* is about a murder, but it's *really* about chutzpah. The plot in *Rebel Without a Cause* deals with a "chickie-run," and the theme deals with responsibility.

Plot and theme go hand in hand, cannot be separated, but are different. They illuminate different parts of the same experience. The theme tells us what the protagonist needs and yearns for—the theme goal. The plot shows us what the protagonist will do to achieve what he or she needs—the plot goal.

It is critical that you understand and internalize these dual but connected goals. You need to work simultaneously with both—the inner forces and needs that drive the character and the character's visible goal and visible behavior. In any screenplay of significance, both must be present. A theme without a plot is not a story. A plot without a theme is an empty series of events that may distract but not involve the reader/viewer.

A screenplay is a living form—it has an organic structure. It is ever-changing, expresses the rhythms of life, and all of its elements are interrelated. It is theme that governs the direction of the changes, that determines the patterns of repetition, and that discovers the connections that relate all of the elements.

THEME STATEMENTS

Screenplay themes make statements—statements communicated through emotional content; statements that make us smile—and cry, that teach us things about fear—and joy, that remind us of our dreams and give direction to our lives. The screenwriter experiences, understands, and then gives shape to human emotions to create an expressive art form. In this way, the screenwriter communicates inner, emotional experiences, evokes insights and self-understanding, and deals, on some level, with human issues. This is the work of the screenwriter.

Some themes express a value. A theme may take sides on an issue, expound the virtue of specific traits, and/or demonstrate the importance of particular choices and behavior. *Body and Soul* makes a strong statement in favor of self-esteem. *An Officer and a Gentlemen* values concern for the well-being of others. *Rebel Without a Cause* declares the importance of taking responsibility for one's actions.

Other statements emerge from fully knowing another person. By knowing Karen, in *Out of Africa*, we learn about the importance of fully experiencing life and the prices to be paid and gained for refusal to compromise beliefs. By knowing Axel, in *Beverly Hills Cop*, we learned about the importance of self-confidence and having the know-how of experience and intelligence.

There are the statements that grow out of knowing different and new situations. By experiencing the contrast between life in an Amish community and life in a modern urban community in *Witness*, we learn about a different set of cultural values and examine some of our own.

THEME ARTICULATIONS

A theme emerges from the combination of all of the filmic and dramatic elements—both linear and non-linear. It is none of the individual elements but the amalgamation of all. It emerges as the end result of the many threads woven in a particular manner to communicate a particular statement. It is what the completed tapestry says.

The theme becomes known when the story arrives somewhere—when the protagonist changes; when there is a solution to an articulated and documented problem; when a situation changes; when there is a sense of completion—unity.

As has been noted many times, it's the *climax* of the theatrical screenplay that reveals the screenwriter's theme. The screenwriter gives the protagonist a goal and involves him or her in a struggle to achieve that goal. Then, by vicariously experiencing the protagonist's struggle, change/growth, and climactic choice, the reader/viewer comes to know and understand what the screenwriter is saying—what the screenwriter values. *The theme is articulated in the climax.*

A *situation change* also reveals the theme. Here the screenwriter focuses on the cause/effect relationship between the way things were and what they become. The readers/viewers experience the situation before the change, during the change, and after the change. They know what has happened and why it happened. *The theme is articulated in the reasons for the change.*

The *sense of completion*—of unity achieved—unveils the theme. The end of a road, the bottom of a well, the kiss and makeup after a fight cause us to reflect on where we have come from and what the journey has taught us. This may be the full knowing of a person, an action, a situation, or a concept. It may be the experience of a complete cycle of an action or some natural phenomenon. It may be a question raised that can be put to rest. Whatever, there will always be some compelling connection between each of the parts that make up the whole. *It is the completion of the connection that articulates the theme.*

GUIDING PRINCIPLES

In all of these different ways of communicating theme there are two important guiding principles: the presence of passion and the absence of announcement.

The screenwriter, whether through characters, situations, reasons, solutions, or connections, must be aggressively passionate. It is through your passion that we separate the absolutely necessary goals from the ordinary "so-so" ones—and thus we discover your theme.

Almost any theme can be announced in a relatively few sentences—but that is not the function of screenplays. It is the function of screenwriters to seduce, to influence, to affect—to gain understanding and acceptance of their themes through vicarious and emotional experiences. The screenwriter reaches the reader/viewer's mind but only after entering through his or her emotions. It is the domain of the journalist to "state the facts" and expound logic. It is the domain of the screenwriter to create a journey that elicits feelings and personal insights. The reader/viewer can announce the theme after experiencing the screenplay—but the screenwriter never does.

THEME SOURCES

Where do themes come from? Where do you get them? They come from you—from your experiences, your needs, your questions—your feelings. They are the things within you that demand exploration and expression. Everybody has needs, questions, feelings, and unique life experience, but it's the artist who is driven to investigate, arrange, and organize them. This is the creative act. Themes come from things that may be troubling you, that you're compelled to understand; from new and different things in your life you want to learn about and to possess; from emotions you need to express; from insights you need to share and experiences you need to integrate. Whatever—something consciously or unconsciously attracts you to a particular theme while other things will go unnoticed. Your selection of a theme is not a random event. It's something that's important to you—something you MUST know more about. And, in the process of learning what you must know, you create a shape and form—a screenplay. Storytelling is a process of discovery—the discovery of theme.

Rarely, if ever, will you say, "I am going to write a screenplay that expounds the virtues of motherhood." Rather, you will ask things like,

"What is the experience of motherhood? What are my thoughts and feelings about motherhood? Why is it important to have children? What do I value the most about my own mother? How can I best tell someone about motherhood?"

If your screenplay does not emerge from your inner need to know; to express; to share; and to integrate, it will lack vitality and significance. It will lack authenticity. A theme must be something you believe and something your characters believe—then the audience will believe.

Theme is an abstraction that is expressed through the integration of sound, imagery, motion, filmic time, filmic space, plot, and characterization. Theme is expressed through plot—through storytelling.

STORYTELLING IS THEME TELLING

The ancient practice of storytelling had little to do with entertainment. Storytelling was an instrument of survival. Our ancestors created magic, rituals, and stories to control tribal behavior; to explain and control the forces of nature; to develop explanations about life, illness, and death; to train the young in the ways of survival; and to perpetuate and explain the traditions of the community.

The practices of magic gave the magic-maker power over all things—natural and supernatural. Ritual ceremonies celebrated and preserved the beliefs and events that formed the patterns of life. Fables used inanimate objects, plants, and animals to teach practical everyday "truths." Parables, made up of everyday life stories, taught moral and religious "truths." Allegories used symbolic fictional figures as vehicles for "truths" about human existence. Myths created deities and heros to explain and to codify the laws of life, nature and human behavior. Fairytales involved supernatural forces and beings to fulfill human fantasies. Epics use national heroes to teach national and cultural values.

Storytelling isn't too much different today. The tribes are different; we transmit our stories through mechanical media, and science explains the forces of nature, but our stories continue to be the voices that attempt to explain life, illness, and death; educate our young in the ways of survival; perpetuate and explain the traditions of our communities; and attempt to control the people, events, and forces that control us.

And, according to Vincent Robert, a young screenwriter and twentieth century citizen, "Stories are how we heal ourselves. We tell stories because we *need* to. To work out something that we may not be able to work out in any other way." (1)

Stories are the vehicles through which storytellers in all times have communicated their themes—the ideas in their heads and hearts that they needed and wanted to get into the heads and hearts of the people of their time.

SHAPES OF STORIES

Generally speaking, the shapes of stories have been and continue to be very much the same:

ONCE UPON A TIME	(a time)
THERE WAS	(a person[s])
IN	(a place)
DOING	(a set of circumstances)
THAT CAUSES	(initial action)
A STRUGGLE TO ACHIEVE	(difficulty achieving)
SUCCESS OR FAILURE	(change in character & circumstance)
THAT SAYS SOMETHING	(theme)

All going toward something. All saying something at the end. All having a unifying idea. All expressing a theme.

> Once upon a time in days of yore there lived a hungry fox who stole into a vineyard to get some grapes. He jumped and jumped and jumped but the grapes were out of his reach on high trellises. He failed to get even one grape and left in anger saying, "WHO WANTS SOUR GRAPES ANY-WAY!"*

> Once upon a time a boy in a land of happiness and plenty came to a wall and a door in the wall. The door was guarded by spirits named Indolence, Selfishness, and Timidity and Ignorance. The boy repeatedly asked, "Shall I knock at the door?" and repeatedly each in his/her turn advised him not to enter this world where he would have to work, where people would ask him to do things for them, and where life and death exist. But the boy did not heed their warnings. He knocked and DESTINY OPENED THE DOOR.**

> Once upon a time the daughter of a Tribal Chief fell through a hole in the sky into water and onto the backs of two swans. The swans called a meeting of all swimming animals to find a way to save the woman and make her a home. They decided to dive and bring up dirt from tree roots. Otter tried and failed. Muskrat and Beaver tried and both

* Based upon an Aesop fable.

** Based on a Ninteenth Century Parable.

failed. Then Toad tried and, to the surprise of all, succeeded in bringing up a few grains of sand that she spread
around the edge of Big Turtle's shell. This caused an island
to grow and it BECAME THE WORLD for the woman to
live on. Then Little Turtle gathered lightning to CREATE
THE SUN AND THE MOON. Soon the woman gave birth
to twin boys. ONE WAS KIND and THE OTHER CRUEL.
The good one made all good things for the coming of people
and the bad one made all difficult things like rocks and
thorns and fierce animals. The cruel twin died. The good
twin survived and, as a final act, CREATED PEOPLE—the
Wyandot Indians—who to this day REVERE THE TOAD
who succeeded in bringing up the grains of sand that created the world.*

Once upon a time there was a Prince named Siegfried.
Siegfried came from a long line of heros and he dreamed
of doing heroic deeds to match those of his ancestors. Siegfried was sent to the smithy of Mimir, the Master Smith.
There he was to learn the art of the blacksmith. By and by,
Mimir was challenged by another blacksmith, Amilias, to
make a sword that would sever a suit of armour. If Mimir
could not do this, he would lose his title of Master Smith.
Mimir failed to create such a sword and called upon his
apprentices to make one for him. All failed until Siegfried
declared that he would produce such a sword. He tried
once, twice, and with the third attempt he succeeded. The
sword did sever the armour of Amilias. Siegfried had
achieved a very heroic deed. But, Mimir took all the credit
and all the praise. Siegfried felt very badly that everyone
was giving Mimir the glory that belonged to him. He wanted
the praise. Then the thought came to him that HE KNEW
HE HAD MADE THE SWORD, that he had performed this
heroic deed. That was enough. IT DIDN'T MATTER WHO
GOT THE CREDIT.**

Once upon a time there was a selfish young man who
wanted to live a better life than his ancestors did. So he
set out into the world and went to a place that could teach
him to do important things and how to become a leader
among men and women. But the young man had many
things to learn and he had many shadows from his past

* Based on a Wyandot Indian Myth of creation.

** Based on the Epic tale of Siegfried.

to deal with before he could become the person he wanted to be. He had to prove himself to many people and give up many of his selfish desires. But time after time he put his needs before the needs of others until one time HE LEARNED HE RECEIVED GOOD THINGS WHEN HE GAVE GOOD THINGS. He began to like himself and to dismiss the shadows from the past so he could love others and become the person he wanted to be.*

Each story sets up a problem:

Sate hunger.
Make a decision.
Create a habitable world.
Perform a heroic deed.
Find a different life style

Each story involves a struggle:

Repeated jumps to reach grapes
Repeated questions
Difficult and multiple creation events
Repeated attempts to create sword
Overcome psychological handicaps of past

Each story involves an end to the struggle:

Failure to reach grapes
Failure to heed warnings
Final successful total creation
Successful heroic deed
Successful emergence of a whole, capable person

Each story involves a theme—SAYS SOMETHING OVER AND ABOVE THE EVENTS THEMSELVES:

Often we reject what we cannot have.
Often fate rules our lives.
The world contains good and evil and the creator is to be revered.

---

* Based on the screenplay, *An Officer and a Gentleman.*

Self-esteem comes from within.
Self-respect is earned by concern for others.

But, just because something says something, it doesn't become a story.

NON-STORIES

An editorial is not a story. An editorial expresses someone's opinion about a topic of interest. The editorial may present opposing views, but there is no encounter—no struggle—between the opposing views. There usually is a strong point of view that gives it a sense of unity, but the point of view—theme—is stated rather than emergent. The editorial is predominately cognitive rather than affective. The writer may passionately want to persuade the reader to his or her point of view, but the reader is not passionately and vicariously involved in the achievement of that point of view—goal.

A joke—a "one-liner"—is not a story. A "one-liner" says something and it may contain somewhat of a struggle, but the theme and struggle are stated—not incremental, not rising or growing, and not emerging from cause to effect. The "teller" is commenting, but not involving the audience in "choosing up sides" and participating. The audience is curious about the outcome of the joke, but is not stimulated to ask "why" this is happening.

A lecture, or printed article, is not a story. Lectures and articles are structured to teach information. They may take a point of view, but usually present *different* points of view rather than *opposing* points of view. Generally they involve the cognitive part of the audience/reader, but not the affective part. There is a linear presentation of information, and the unity of the material comes from the scope and nature of the material being presented rather than from the struggle to achieve a goal. The ideas to be communicated are stated. They do not emerge as a result of the interaction of events.

A newspaper or television news report is not a story. News reports present the happening of events *as they happened*—this happened and then this happened and then this happened. There is a sense of curiosity about what will happen next, but there is nothing in the report to make us really care about "why" these things have happened. News reports present happenings but don't draw conclusions. The happenings in reports do not have goals—objectives. The happenings may contain a potential for conflict, a potential for a theme, a potential for cause-and-effect rising action, a potential for vicarious involvement, but until these ingredients are introduced and arranged, it is not a story.

A slice-of-life experience is not a story. A slice of life portrays the events of everyday life. Unless introduced and arranged there is no conflict, no apparent contradictions, no cause-and-effect relationships between events, no goals, no direction, no expectations of something about to happen, no involvement, no questioning of "why," and no unified and emerging theme.

The basic difference is quite simple. *Zack Mayo received a commission in the United States Navy,* says nothing about human values. *Zack Mayo, with great difficulty, learned how to become an officer and how to love,* immediately involves us in human struggles and human aspirations—theme.

REFERENCE

1.   Vincent Robert, personal letter.

10

DESIGNING THE PAGE

The end product of your creating process is a screenplay consisting of a finite number of pages. Here is where you translate your images into words so that others can read them, "see" them in their heads, and then recreate them. Your objective is to choose the words and present them in a manner that will accurately transmit the images you have created. Presenting these images is not just a simple matter of putting words on pages. There's a traditional format to be followed; the pages must be easy to read; the important elements of each scene must be emphasized; the words you use and the way they're arranged on the page must be chosen and designed to evoke your intended images and emotions.

Your screenplay is the intermediary between you and the finished motion picture. Initially it is the means by which you excite and involve producers, directors and actors, and then it becomes the blueprint for each of its production phases. It is your spokesperson and "out there" it stands alone without you to explain or defend it.

When you submit your screenplay to agents, development people, or targeted producers, directors, or actors, it will find itself in the company of dozens—nay, hundreds—of other scripts. At that point, the way it looks and the way it reads becomes nearly as important as its filmic form and content.

Almost without exception, the first person to turn the first page of your screenplay will be a reader—someone hired to read and choose the screenplays to be read by others. The reader will have two piles. One pile for "nays" and a smaller pile for "maybes." The pile of "nays" will be sent back to the screenwriter and the pile of "maybes" will be given to a person who will say, "looks good" or "not what we're looking for." If the response is, "looks good," your screenplay will be passed on to a person who can say "yea" or "nay." If that person says "yea" then it will be shown to someone who can say "make a deal." In other words, your screenplay meets a lot of different people and passes a lot of inspections before it gets to the person who makes a final positive decision. So, before you send your screenplay "out there," you want to dress it in its "Sunday Best" and polish all of its buttons.

Designing the page is one of the last things you'll do before sending your screenplay "to market." It's your final act of creation. It's the thing you do after you're satisfied with your final draft. Designing the page calls upon an entirely different thought process and it shouldn't enter into your work with film content and film form. It does involve the blending of form and content but form and content of a page kind—not a film kind.

The first thing the readers—story analysts—will do is look to see how many pages there are. Then they'll leaf through the pages from back to front to check the overall length of the speeches and see if you've followed the standard format. These things will tell them if they're dealing with a professional or an amateur. Of course, they'll go on to read at least your first ten pages, but their first impression is an evaluative one and can't help but influence all subsequent opinions.

TRADITIONAL SCREENPLAY FORMAT

The traditional screenplay format has evolved from its original function as a production blueprint. Throughout the years there have been some variations—depending on the individual screenwriter and the production practices of a given period—but certain elements have remained constant.

Originally the screenplay was called a scenario, or continuity script, and consisted of a list of scenes that described the silent action and camera angles. These first screenplays evolved from the economic necessity to pre-plan rather than rely on costly extemporaneous scene development on the set. Later, when sound on film was invented, words, sound effects and music were added to combine the visual and audio elements. During the years of the studio system with their dominant producer–studio heads and contract screenwriters, screenplays included very explicit production instructions and were often rubber-stamped, "Shoot as written."

In our present era of independent production, with our free-lance screenwriters and emphasis on the film director, the current practice is to minimize the appearance of production instructions. Nonetheless, the tradition prevails and it remains the responsibility of the screenwriter to somehow, in some manner, indicate where, when, how, and what is to be included in each scene.

Throughout this book you've seen many scene descriptions from different screenplays and you've undoubtedly noted that they all have certain elements more or less in common. They all include information about whether a scene is to be interior or exterior, what the specific location is, the time of day, the camera angle, and what is to be photographed. Most of this information will be included in the scene heading—the slug line— or immediately follow in the scene description. The information is there and placed in a specified order and location so every member of the production crew knows exactly where to look for the information their job calls for.

The instructions governing the placement of this information—the margins, abbreviations, capitalizations, precise placements, order, inclusions, and exclusions—can be found in manuals devoted exclusively to format.* At first glance it may seem to you that you can "wing it" by looking at the examples shown in this book or published screenplays. Wrong! You need much more information than you'll find in this book's cited examples and most published screenplays do not duplicate the standard screenplay format.

Generally speaking, there are one hundred twenty pages in a full-length theatrical screenplay, with each page representing approximately one minute of screen time. Thirty pages of your screenplay represent thirty minutes. At page sixty, the film is half over.

The unfolding of your stories can be likened to the petal-by-petal blossoming of a rose, or a snowball gathering more snow and more speed as it rolls down a hill. All of these things—the unfolding story, blossoming rose, and rolling snowball—happen WITHIN A TIME FRAME. Words like bud, opening, full blown, small, medium, and large tell us where the rose and the snowball are within their time frame. The page numbers of your screenplay serve the same purpose. The position of your story at any given moment within its time frame is COMMUNICATED BY THE PAGE NUMBER.

The structuring of a story within a given time is the business of the screenwriter. Each scene you create has a time frame and you need to know approximately, if not exactly, how long that scene will play on the screen— its screen time. You need to become skilled in "seeing" the scene in your mind and deciding just how long it will take. Then you will choose and arrange your words to approximate one page per one minute of screen time. In other words, if a character is to be on the screen for thirty seconds, you'll use just one half a page to describe his or her actions and dialogue. The elimination of detail will compress the scene description and the addition of detail will stretch it.

It's easy to time dialogue pages. All you have to do is read the dialogue aloud and time it. With action you need to "walk" your characters through everything they do. Actually "see" them in your mind as they enter the kitchen, walk past a table, stumble over the rug, go to the sink and wash their hands. At first you may want to use your watch as you mentally watch them perform their actions, but as you become more experienced you'll develop an unconscious sense of timing.

---

*The manual which I have found most useful is "The Complete Guide to Standard Script Formats," compiled and written by Judith H. Haag and Hillis R. Cole, Jr. It is available through CMC Publishing, 7516 Sunset Blvd., Hollywood, CA 90046.

Along with the use of the standard format and the page-a-minute requirement, the absence of long speeches is an immediate sign of professionalism. Long unbroken speeches, unless they are well motivated within the context of the plot, are rarely used in motion pictures. Soliloquies are used in stage plays and arias are used in operas, but in motion pictures the characters do not talk to themselves or the audience. They either talk to others within the story or act out their thoughts.

PAGE DESIGN

Page design is important for basically three reasons: ease of reading, emphasis of important information, and the representation of emotional content.

The screenplay page can be thought of and designed in much the same way as a graphic artist designs a print advertisement. Pick up a magazine and look at the ads to see how information is arranged within their "frames." Notice how much "white space" surrounds the print and pictures/drawings. Notice that the most important information is placed in the center of the ad, or at least in one of the most conspicuous places. Also, notice how the sizes and shapes of the letters vary and utilize marks of emphasis. Notice how the design of the ad is similar to what is being advertised—a beautiful dress on a beautiful woman, an exciting place pictured with exciting colors, a dynamic item presented with dynamic lines and shapes. These same concerns, and ways of dealing with them, are employed in the design of the screenplay page.

The more "white space" on a page, the easier that page is to read. Long paragraphs filling a large portion of a page will scare off the most dedicated of all readers. It is just too much to read and digest easily and rapidly— and readers make their money by reading easily and rapidly! If a lot of information must be included, you simply break long paragraphs into shorter ones.

EXT. THE HONKY-TONK SAILOR TOWN OF OLONGAPO - DAY

Known throughout the Seventh Fleet as the armpit of the
Orient, Olongapo is one, long rain-rutted street of gaudy bars
and rattan-walled whorehouses.

Countless jeepneys careen past with their silly fringe
awnings and chrome accoutrements, many filled with U.S.
sailorboys and officers on liberty.

Zack and Byron's jeepney ENTERS SHOT and stops in front
of the noisiest and raunchiest bar on the strip.

Slug lines can "open up" your page and give it "white space."

ANGLE - PAULA AND ZACK

As they move onto the dance floor, the handsome pilot,
Donny, approaches Paula.

                    DONNY
            Hey, Paula. How about a
            dance later on.

                    PAULA
            Well . . . I'm kinda with
            someone.

She continues on with Zack.

NEW ANGLE - PAULA AND ZACK

Paula puts her arms tight around his neck and nestles her
lips close to his ear.

                    PAULA
            Think you'll make it all the
            way to getting your wings?

Unusually long, but well-motivated, sections of dialogue can be broken up by inserting actor cues or stage directions.

> FOLEY
> No you're not. You're failing
> the big one, baby, and I don't
> just mean in here. I mean in
> life. I've watched you, Mayo,
> and you don't mesh. You
> grab-ass and joke around but
> you don't make friends, not
> the way the others do . . .
> because it would mean giving
> something you don't have
> any more . . . . something
> that was beaten out of you a
> long time ago.

Zack says nothing but Foley's getting to him in ways nobody has in years, if ever.

> FOLEY (CONT'D)
> Want to know why I'm not
> an officer, Mayo? Because I
> have a servile mentality from
> growing up poor . . . from
> always being the kid on the
> windy side of the baker's
> window. That's your problem,
> Mayo. That's why you don't
> mesh. Because deep down in
> that bitter little heart of
> yours, you know these other
> boys and girls are better
> than you.

Watch your sentence structuring. Long and complicated sentences are difficult to read. As a general rule, short concise sentences serve you the best.

If at all possible, the important elements of the screenplay should be placed in one of the most prominent and conspicuous places on the page. In most cases this will be the center of the page.

WE STAY LIKE THAT, OUTSIDE HIS DOOR

The SOUND of the TV going on, loud. Some game show. The passage of about twenty seconds. Then the SOUND of Zack's MOTORCYCLE approaching, stopping.

> ZACK (O.S.)
> He's here. She said he just
> came in.

The SOUND of FOOTSTEPS ascending to the second floor, running toward us. Zack PUSHES INTO SHOT and knocks on the door.

> ZACK
> (continuing)
> Sid, it's Zack. Open up.

No reply, then from inside some SOUNDS are heard, a CHAIR FALLING, a sudden, dull SNAPPING NOISE, abrupt and final. Zack throws his weight against the door and it splinters open.

> ZACK
> (continuing)
> Sid?

Then he looks up and pales.

> ZACK
> (continuing)
> Oh, God . . .

Paula steps into the doorway and utters a little gasp as she sees what poor Sid has done to himself.

INT. THE ROOM - DAY

The big Okie hangs by his necktie from a cluster of exposed drainage pipes in a corner of the ceiling.

ZACK'S FACE IS STRETCHED WITH PAIN

Tears flood his eyes. He shakes his head in disbelief.

> ZACK
> Oh, God . . . why? Why, Sid?

Zack cuts him down and cradles his friend's body in his arms.

Notice that Stewart placed Zack's response to Sid's suicide in the center on the page. This is the most important and dramatic element of the scene. Our worst suspicions are confirmed by his reaction. Its position in the most compelling section of the page commands our attention and emphasizes its importance. Also, note the amount of white space around that reaction. It "pops out" at us because it stands somewhat isolated.

Stewart's use of sound and the capitalization of the sound cues lead us into Zack's response. Sound cues are always capitalized to facilitate the work of the sound crew, but Stewart has deliberately chosen to use sound effects and the way capitalizations stand out on the page to emphasize the event and build tension in the reader/viewer. Note, too, how he has capitalized "PUSHES INTO SHOT." This is not standard practice. He has intentionally capitalized these words and by doing so gives added force to an already forceful action. In addition to capitalization you can use underlining as a means of emphasis, and the traditional use of exclamation marks will add strength and importance.

Remember—readers, development people, producers, and directors are not going to be reading your screenplay word for word. At first reading they'll be scanning. Whatever is "buried" in dense clusters of words will be lost. If critical actions and details are not "seen," the whole sense of a sequence, or even story, could be lost.

THE WORDS

Screenplays are a combination of prose and poetry. They contain the ordinary language of prose and the emotional and visual language of poetry. Their purpose is to provide specific instructions and, at the same time, elicit emotional responses and images. Although not commonly acclaimed as such, screenplays are, in themselves, a unique and distinct art form. They are, in their structure, format, and tone, expressive of the images they are describing.

We're CLOSE ON THEM as they dance. A sense of their pain, their acceptance of it, and of great love. In time, tears on his cheeks. Not hers. [Out of Africa]

THE WOMEN ON THE NAPKIN LINE

send up a buzz of gossipy excitement as he strides past them. So clean. So handsome. So perfect. Every deb's fantasy. [An Officer and a Gentleman]

Charley looks into the headlights facing him across the chasm of Shorty's death. The CAMERA MOVES IN through the headlights. [Body and Soul]

Now two big police Chevys accelerate alongside each other, ramming the gate almost at the same instant. The gate bends, it buckles, then with a tremendous CRASH it's torn loose and carried away. [Beverly Hills Cop]

HIGH ANGLE CLOSEUP PLATO

lying as they left him, but his eyes are open and he is crying. CAMERA BOOMS UP as Plato throws off the blanket and looks after them. CAMERA BOOMS HIGHER until he is revealed as a small and lonely figure sitting by himself. The pool echoes his weeping. [Rebel Without a Cause]

Notice how, in each of these scene descriptions, the screenwriter has identified the expressive image—the closeness of a dance, the perfection of a fantasy, the blinding light of death, the force of entry, and emptiness of aloneness. And then, they have discovered the essence of the images—acceptance, escape, a separation, power, and sadness.

Notice the words that are used to describe these images—active verbs, strong nouns, and only a few but very emotional adjectives and adverbs. Pain, love, tears. Clean, handsome, perfect. Looks into, across. Ramming, bends, buckles, torn loose, carried away. Crying, small, lonely, weeping. All words and images that evoke emotional responses and tap into the readers' experiences. Notice the economy of words. Notice how only a few nouns and verbs can create a full expressive picture in your mind.

The unique screenplay art form will reveal itself to you as you read and study as many screenplays as you can get your hands on. Each one will be different and some will be more effective than others, but all will teach you something.

The screenwriter is "writing" images but is also writing words—words that people say and words that will retrieve the reader's emotional experiences. This is not a skill you're born with—it's a learned skill. It's a skill you acquire by reading—especially by reading short stories, novels, and poetry. It's a skill you acquire by exploring words—discovering their dictionary meanings, their synonyms, and their antonyms. It's a skill you acquire by expanding your vocabulary and discovering the affective and cognitive responses different words can evoke.

The effectiveness of your screenplays and your success as a screenwriter will be determined by your abilities to manipulate BOTH words and images.

The screenwriter must have MANY MANY skills!

Another skill is the ability to communicate your ideas in such a way as to help people interpret your visions as you have created them and still involve the reader in vicarious experiencing.

PRODUCTION INSTRUCTIONS TO BE INCLUDED— AND EXCLUDED

Screenplays that include specific instructions about camera placement and movement and detailed descriptions of the sets and/or locations DO precisely indicate the proper interpretation.

It is, however, the current notion that that kind of specificity infringes upon the jurisdictions of some of the production people—in particular, the film director. Because of this notion, there are those who warn you against including camera instructions and details. I really question the validity of that notion. It is my view that film directors—those whose sense of self-esteem does not rest on the absence or presence of specific instructions— will welcome all of the screenwriter's visions. This is demonstrated repeatedly by many film directors who are not threatened by the screenplay's visual contributions, who work very closely with the screenwriter, and who publicly attest to the efficacy of collaboration.

In my opinion, the possible frailty of some film directors is not sufficient reason for the elimination of specific instructions, BUT *I do believe there are valid reasons to do so*. An abundance of specific production detail diminishes the ease with which a screenplay can be read—and, as already stressed, this is an important concern. However, there is another reason that, in my view, is even more compelling.

Reading the screenplay is a total "living" experience. This demands the reader's immersion in the continuous creation of mental images of layered and progressive plot and characterization events. This experience needs to be "lived"—just as the viewing of the film needs to be "lived." If excessive camera placements and movements and set and/or location details are present IN THE FORM of instructions, the reader is pulled away from the "living" experience. This, in my view, is a valid reason to minimize *the appearance* of instructions.

The manner in which instructions can be given without making the reader aware of them as instructions can be easily seen in the murder scene from *Witness* on pages 70–73. Reread that scene and look at how it specifically requires certain camera positions and movements without actually stating them. There has to be a low-angle shot for Samuel to "see their feet under the edge of the door." There has to be a close shot of Samuel as he "tries to make the latch work, but it's warped and won't fall closed." There has to be an over-the-shoulder shot of Samuel as he opens the stall door and we see his reflection in the "blood-smeared mirror." Wallace and Kelley selected the way the shots would be executed by what the characters did and how they responded. They did not have to state the obvious for the production people and they involved the reader in a continuous flow of mental images that could produce a vicarious experience.

In *An Officer and a Gentleman*, Stewart's description of Zack's fight with one of the "local boys" suggests a camera speed.

> . . . Before his assailant can recover, Zack delivers a strange, roundhouse kind of kick that seems to come out of him in slow motion, then gathers incredible speed, until it's slamming with the force of a mulekick into Troy's face.

In the opening bedroom scene from *Out of Africa*—reproduced on pages 44–48—Luedtke sets the entire bedroom environment by "Above the rumpled bed, mosquito netting tied in a ball." It was not necessary for him to include a list of all of the items needed to decorate the set. Those details would have destroyed the sense of "being there" that the screenplay creates.

However, when Petrie wanted to emphasize the shock effect of Axel's being thrown out of the second story window of Fleming's office, he went so far as to specify the cut.

> AXEL
>
> really goes wild now: his knee catches another guy in the balls, another in the face, and it looks for a second like he's going to break free, but then his thrashing legs are pinned and—we're not certain if it's on purpose or not—the men all heave at once.
>
> SHOCK CUT TO:
>
> EXT. BEVERLY BANK BUILDING—DAY

When Luedtke wants to assume an objective and omnipotent view of Denys and Karen dancing their final dance, he specifies the camera movement and angle.

CRANE SHOT-MOVING TO A HIGH ANGLE

As he waltzes her off the terrace and out across the broad
lawn till we almost lose them in the dark.

    In other words, when you have an image that's not implied by the action, or one that you believe would substantially contribute to what you want to communicate, the explicit instructions MUST be included. This is the screenwriter's obligation. The screenwriter's raison d'être.

    The pages of your screenplay are the surface upon which you place your thoughts, but they can be much more than that. Just as the elements of film form can be blended with content *as expressions of content,* so too can the page, through its design, communicate content. Designing the page is the frosting on your screenplay. It's the sweetening. The decoration. The pride.

THE CREATING PROCESS

The creating process is, for many, mercurial, mysterious, and predetermined. In my view it emerges out of a person's life experiences, follows predictable patterns, requires practice, and is accessible to all. It is in this context that we will examine how our minds organize life's experiences, the stages of the creating process, and how to practice, stimulate, and facilitate the process.

YOUR "STORYHOUSE"

Your life experiences are the raw materials of your screenplays. Whether you recognize it or not, everything you write is the result of what has happened to you, around you, and within you. The aggregate of your life experiences and how they have affected you is your warehouse of story materials—your "storyhouse." A lawyer's materials are laws and previous judgments that have set precedents. An accountant's materials are forms, figures, and procedures. A cameraperson's materials are cameras, lights, and film. A screenwriter's materials are experiences.

There are different kinds of experiences—actual, observed, or vicarious. If you've been in a street fight—got hit and fell to the ground—you've had an actual experience. If you've watched a fight—seen the expression on a guy's face when he got hit and heard him hit the ground—you've had an observed experience. If you've viewed this same scene on a stage or screen—identified with the character being hit, felt your heart beat faster, and perhaps even ducked to avoid the blow—you've had a vicarious experience.

When writing a scene about a street fight, you'll draw on any one of, or combination of, these experiences. If you've never experienced a street fight in any way, you'll have difficulty writing the scene. You certainly don't have to go get into an honest-to-goodness fight, but you do need to look for one to observe, find a street fight in the arts, or talk to a person who has seen one. The more street fights you've experienced in a variety of ways, the more convincingly you'll be able to write about one. The best kinds of experiences are first-hand actual ones, then direct observation, and finally those that are vicarious. The more you write from your own experiences, the more convincing your work will be.

As a screenwriter you need to deliberately "collect" experiences. It's not enough to simply live and encounter whatever comes your way. You need to actively go after new and different adventures and develop ways to fully understand them. The ability to do this is enhanced by knowing how your mind works: how it takes information in, stores it, and then remembers it. Or, to use the current computer terms, how it processes information, stores it, and retrieves it.

The study of how our minds operate and how we communicate is a relatively new one. It wasn't until around the turn of the century that scientists became more interested in the workings of the human mind, and it wasn't until after World War II that communications theory and research came into its own. Now there's a large volume of literature that deals with the theories and research about how we communicate with each other, with groups, and within ourselves. It's the last of these, how we communicate with ourselves, that's especially important for you to understand. Knowing how your mind works shows you how to use the process more deliberately and more effectively.

There are many different approaches and theories that seek to explain these complex communication events. The work that has greatly influenced my thoughts was done by Richard C. Atkinson and Richard M. Shiffrin. (1) I've been attracted to this study because it sheds some very bright lights on concepts of information processing most consistent with the needs of the screenwriter.

Information Processing

The process starts with a stimulus. You see and hear something happening—maybe a street fight—and the experience enters your mind. But, it's not just a simple entry. It has to go through a number of "gates"—screens.

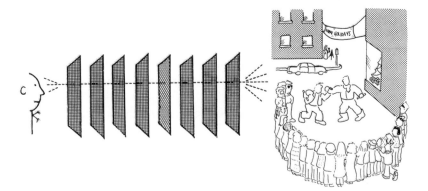

You're not just sensing and processing one thing. There are always a number of different things you're simultaneously dealing with—multiple processing. Maybe, in addition to watching the fight, you're aware of the weather, notice Christmas decorations, feel someone bump into your arm, see a Salvation Army lady ringing a bell, and hear music blasting from a passing automobile.

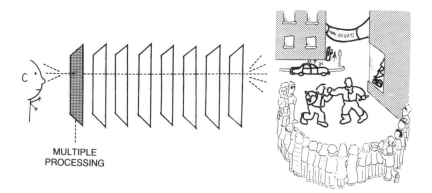

MULTIPLE
PROCESSING

Your mind may keep switching from one thought to another. Perhaps in one second you're thinking about the fight and in the next you're thinking about where you were going and what else you should be doing.

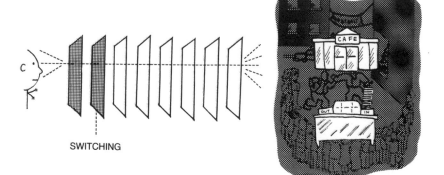

SWITCHING

In any experience, you never sense all there is to sense. Sensory abstracting occurs. You don't have to see, hear, taste, touch, or smell the whole thing in order to know what's happening. You may not see all of the people watching the fight, every blow that's exchanged, or someone leaving to call the police.

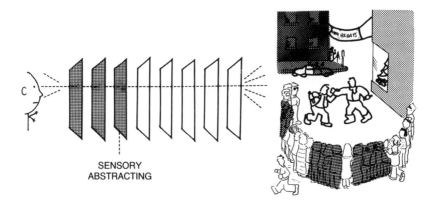

SENSORY
ABSTRACTING

Also, your mind is involved in symbolic abstracting. You respond to the experience on the basis of how you define the symbols used to describe it. If you define street fights as disgusting and degrading, you'll respond differently than if you define them as exciting and colorful.

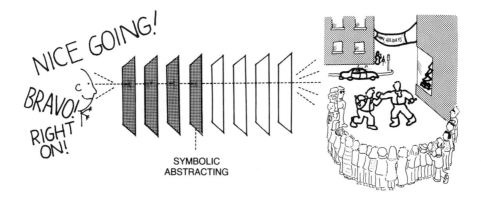

SYMBOLIC
ABSTRACTING

Just like your characters, you have dominant traits—core qualities that filter your perceptions. Your core quality may be an all-consuming need to be self-sufficient, a pervasive fear of the unknown or a passionate need for approval. If you're seeing the street fight through a self-sufficiency filter, you might applaud the fight; if you're seeing it with a pervasive fear of the unknown, you could be very anxious about the outcome; if you're preoccupied with gaining approval, you might find the fight distressing, since our culture doesn't approve of street fights. Your particular set of filters picks out what's important to you and discards or minimizes the rest.

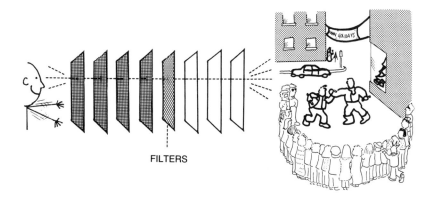

FILTERS

In every situation your mind decides on the most important part of the experience, and how these things rank on your lists of priorities and hierarchies. A cameraperson would be looking for photographic possibilities—camera placement, lighting, and lens selection. You'd be watching for expressive actions and reactions and be aware of tempo and pace. Also, if you're involved in some personal trauma or compelling life circumstance, that will be your priority and demand the major portion of your attention.

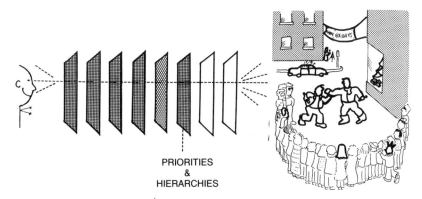

PRIORITIES
&
HIERARCHIES

In communication jargon, anything that interferes with the transmission and reception of a message is called noise. In addition to the selective and limiting factors mentioned above, noise includes internal physical factors like a sick stomach, too little sleep, or not enough food, and external physical factors, like loud sounds, excessive heat, or an offensive odor.

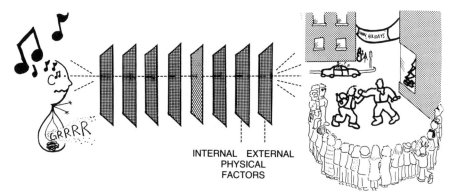

INTERNAL EXTERNAL
PHYSICAL
FACTORS

All of these factors—"screens"—are present at each moment of perception and they instantaneously and simultaneously shape the information you receive.

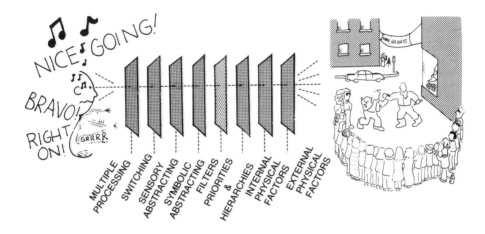

Try it out. Look around you—in a classroom, on the street, or in your home. Experience an event and watch your thought processes. Become aware of the "screens" in your mind.

Now, you may be wondering why you need to know about these things. Some of the reasons will be obvious to you. Others may not be. You've undoubtedly recognized why it's so difficult to precisely communicate what's in your head and heart to the head and heart of your readers/viewers. Also, I'm sure you've already figured out that some of these phenomena can severely limit the quantity and quality of your own perceptions. This is particularly true of symbolic abstracting, filters, priorities and hierarchies, and internal and external physical factors.

Screenwriters need to guard against dangers inherent in symbolic abstracting. Language is a system of categories symbolized by words, and most of these categories are established on the basis of similarities. To use the familiar example, the word *dog* refers to a category of four-legged, domesticated mammals. These are characteristics that all dogs have in common—but they also have a lot of differences. If you only respond to the similarities of the category, you'll limit your "collection" by a great deal. As a screenwriter you must train yourself to look for the differences between people, events, and things as well as being aware of the similarities. It's the differences that make stories, not the similarities. It's because Axel isn't a conventional cop that we have *Beverly Hills Cop*. It's because Karen has different needs than most women of her time that we have *Out of Africa*. It's because most men with Zack's background don't go to officer training schools that we have *An Officer and a Gentleman*.

Filters, as important as they are, can also limit your "collection." Filters represent your core qualities and, as such, help define who you are. They're not something to eliminate or denigrate. However, as a screenwriter, you need to recognize that they do keep you from "seeing" a lot of information. First of all, you need to identify your filters. Know them—know yourself. Then you can neutralize the phenomenon by temporarily setting your filters aside to "see" things through another person's eyes—another person's filters. Walk in another person's moccasins.

The same thing is true with your priorities and hierarchies. They're there to help you deal with given situations, and they're very useful, but they can keep you from "seeing" things of less, but significant, importance. Here again, as a screenwriter, you need to identify them and learn to temporarily substitute other priorities and hierarchies to expand your "storyhouse."

It's often difficult, if not impossible, to control the internal and external physical factors that interfere with your perceptions, but the awareness of their influence can alert you to the limitations they present.

I cannot emphasize too strongly the importance of recognizing that each of us wears a set of "blinders" that determines what we "see" and how we "see" it. Also, you need to recognize that most of us tend to believe that everyone else wears the same set of "blinders"—that we all see the world in exactly the same way. A "one-liner" about Max illustrates this.

Max, a student in a big Eastern university, was suffering with severe headaches. Max thought the headaches would just go away, but when they didn't he went to the infirmary, took a battery of tests, and saw a number of doctors. His headaches persisted but no one could find anything wrong with him. Finally, one of the doctors who was determined to find the cause of Max's headaches said to him, "Tell me exactly everything you do from the moment you get up in the morning until you go to bed at night." Max asked, "Everything?" "Yes, everything," the Doctor replied. "Okay," Max said, "I hear my alarm, I jump out of bed, walk over to the dresser, and turn off the alarm. I stretch, rub my eyes, and go into the bathroom. I brush my teeth, throw up, shave, and then I start. . . ." "Wait a minute," the Doctor interrupted, "you do what?" "I hear my alarm, jump out of bed, turn off the alarm, go to the bathroom, brush my teeth, throw up, shave. . . ." "You throw up?" the Doctor interrupted again, "Are you saying you throw up every morning!" "Sure," responded Max, "Doesn't everyone??"

It's this "doesn't everyone" tendency we all have that you have to guard against. This is the tendency to see everything through our own experiences rather than through the experiences of others. This can severely narrow and limit the quality and quantity of your perceptions. You must do a wide variety of things and think a wide variety of thoughts so your characters can do a wide variety of things and think a wide variety of thoughts.

Now, having passed through all of these screens, the "screened" stimulus—an information image—enters your conscious mind—your temporary working memory.

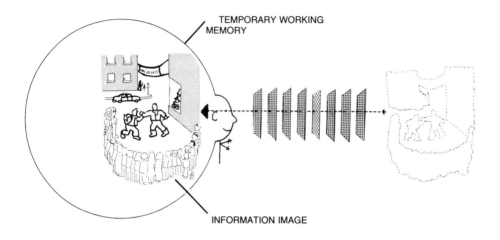

TEMPORARY WORKING MEMORY

INFORMATION IMAGE

Here's where your mind works on these thoughts and decides what to do with the new information. Here's where decisions are made, problems solved, and the destination of the new information determined. Here's where you have conscious control of your thoughts. It's here where you decide if you want to stay and watch the fight or leave. It's here you examine different ways to stop the fight—if that's what you decide to do. It's here you decide where this information will be stored.

The "shape" of an information image is quite different from the complete sentences we write and speak and the linear and abstracted ways we talk and write. It's a conglomerate of all the "screened" information—a grouping, a cluster of information. When these information images—thoughts—enter your temporary working memory, they're joined by information images similar to the one just received—your memories of other actual, observed, or vicarious street fights. These images are carried by something called a *search set* and they come from your unconscious mind—your permanent memory. (See illustration at top of next page.)

The search set—your memories of past experiences—helps you decide what to do. If you've had bad experiences with fights, you'll probably leave as quickly as possible. If you've stopped fights in the past, and ended up being a hero, you'll probably intervene in the same way. Then, after doing whatever you decided to do, the new information image—now a part of the "street fight" search set—goes into your permanent memory for storage. (See illustration at bottom of next page.)

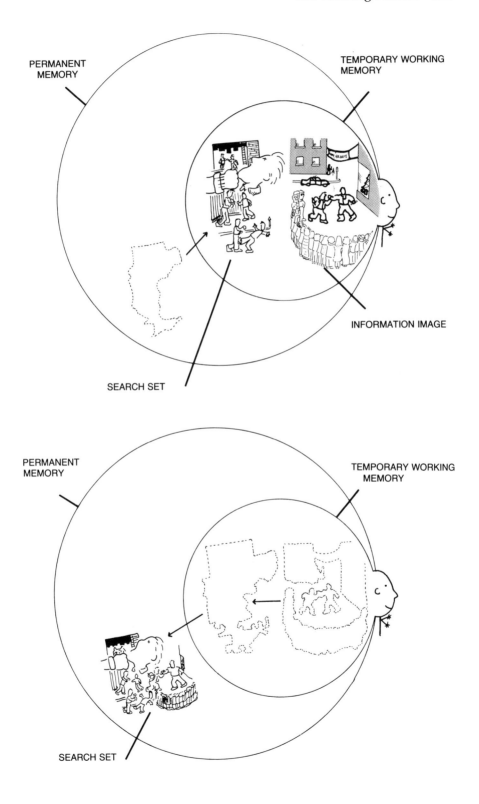

PERMANENT
MEMORY

TEMPORARY WORKING
MEMORY

INFORMATION IMAGE

SEARCH SET

PERMANENT
MEMORY

TEMPORARY WORKING
MEMORY

SEARCH SET

Information Storage and Retrieval

Your permanent memory is something like a library. Similar information images are grouped together in search sets, like similar books are grouped together under similar numbers. These search sets are catalogued by information probes. When your conscious mind puts in a request for street fight experiences, the information probe finds it and delivers it. However, as you've learned, it's not just a matter of getting individual pieces of information. You'll receive the entire image: the expression on the guy's face when he gets hit, the way it sounds when he hits the ground, the weather, the Salvation Army lady ringing her bell, someone bumping your arm, the music blasting from a passing auto, *AND* all of the feelings you experienced while watching the fight.

Because information on any one subject may be stored in a number of different search sets, we have a system of cross-referencing—free association. For example, you may be doing a screenplay that takes place around Christmas time. One of your scenes includes a Salvation Army lady and you've decided to use her to make some kind of a visual comment about the irony of simultaneous fighting and giving. In order to find the image you're looking for, you put in a request for Salvation Army ladies at Christmas time. This information probe will find and deliver a search set that contains your experiences with Salvation Army ladies, but may not immediately find the search set "labeled" street fights. Still, you have the nagging feeling that somewhere, associated with Salvation Army ladies, you've experienced this simultaneity of fighting and giving. So you let your mind wander wherever it takes you—you free associate. You think about Salvation Army ladies, about Christmas weather, and about crowds that bump and jostle during Christmas shopping. Then, chances are, you'll remember the fight—and up comes the search set and information image you want. The primary reference was street fights, not Salvation Army ladies, but by free associating—cross-referencing—you found what you were looking for.

Free association is an extremely important part of the creating process—an important part of the art of screenwriting. It's your way of gaining access to the emotional and intellectual information stored in your "storyhouse."

You'll remember that some of the images in our illustration of the information image were stronger than others and some were only a faint outline. The stronger, bolder, images come from the parts of the experience that command the most attention. The weaker, fainter, images enter your temporary memory but receive relatively little consideration. It's the stronger images that contain the most information and provide the most accessible information probes. Obviously, as a screenwriter, the stronger your information images, the greater your resources. Fortunately, there are things you can do to create strong images. Strong images are not just a matter of chance.

You've had the experience of being given a telephone number to remember until you can get to the phone. In order to remember the number you keep repeating it over and over: six nine four two zero five five, six nine four two zero five five, six nine four two zero five five. This repetition keeps the information in your temporary working memory *and* strengthens the image. It may be that you'll have no more use for this particular phone number and "forget it"—not transfer it into the permanent memory for recall. However, if you do need to keep the number, "memorizing it"—repetition—will strengthen the image for retrieval. The important thing to remember is that the longer you keep information in the temporary working memory and the more you work with it, the less apt it is to become lost or forgotten.

Of course, you aren't going to want to hang onto every piece of information you perceive. You'll be selective about how long you keep information in your conscious mind and how long you work with it. But when you see something unusual, something with a strong emotional impact, or something new, you'll want to keep it and be sure you can retrieve it. You'll achieve this by deliberately and repetitively noting all the components of the stimulus event at least two or three times. Then, when that information image is transferred into your permanent memory, it will have a bolder imprint with more information and be easier to retrieve.

You can experiment with this right now. You're probably seated reading this book. Put the book in your lap, slowly turn your head from left to right, and then close your eyes. Keep your eyes closed and mentally list the things you saw as your eyes moved to the right.

Now, open your eyes and do this again, but this time linger with each object or person. Let your eyes see the many physical details of each object or person; see where things are in relationship to each other; note how the objects are alike and not alike; think about what they are used for. Again, close your eyes and mentally list the things. This list will undoubtedly be longer, richer with detail, and easier to recall.

"Treasure Hunting"

Deliberately collecting story material for your "storyhouse" should become a regular part of your life—something you routinely practice as a part of your craft. It's a "treasure hunt"—a way of increasing your assets.

So, what do you look for when you go collecting story material? You look at the environment: its colors, shapes, textures, lines, and masses. You see the movements of people and objects, the directions of movement, and how they interrelate. You experience the weather, the temperature, brightness, and moisture. You look for the extraordinary and unusual, the incongruous, inappropriate, and startling. You watch for struggles—struggles to win and achieve, to dominate and control, to withstand and maintain. You watch the people—looking for behavior and appearances that interest you. You sensitize yourself to the expression of emotions: anger, sadness, joy, jealousy, and love. All of these things are out there; all you have to do is look for them.

Look for story material wherever you are. Your antennas are always on duty. Make excursions to the places where people congregate—beaches, airports, parks, busy intersections, playgrounds, auditoriums, and civic centers. Search out interesting people—people who are different from you, your family, and friends. Talk to them. Listen to their stories. Learn who they are, where they've come from, and what they want to become. Listen to their words and the ways they say them. Always be AWARE.

Discover your story material and then make notes to remind you of what you've experienced. Carry your Journal with you—or write on bits and pieces of paper that can be pasted into your Journal.

If you become aware of the many stories that constantly surround you and if you're alert to the presence of filmic material in all of your encounters, this heightened absorption of life experiences will become almost automatic. This will, without question, expand your capabilities as a screenwriter—and the quality of your life!

THE CREATING PROCESS

The creative process has been described by many people—theoreticians, researchers, and the creating people themselves. These descriptions contain variations, but, generally speaking, all include the same phenomena as major stages in the creating process.

Your creating process begins when you perceive *something of interest*. This can be something new, something unusual, or something shocking—but always, it's something that arouses your curiosity.

SOMETHING
OF INTEREST
PERCEIVED

Then your mind begins a *conscious random and anxious search* to relate this perception to "something else"—to find the "right" direction, the structure that "fits." This is the most difficult and most dangerous stage of the creative process. It's here you'll probably experience feelings of uncertainty. You're not standing on solid ground. You don't have an answer—and you may question whether or not you ever will. This is the stage that demands your unswerving faith in your ability to ultimately find what you seek.

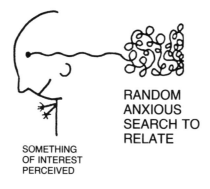

RANDOM
ANXIOUS
SEARCH TO
RELATE

SOMETHING
OF INTEREST
PERCEIVED

Next comes your *unconscious sifting* to relate the perception to "something else." This is a phase that may go on for a long time, and you're seemingly unable to do anything to help or hinder its progress. You may even think you've forgotten about it or put it on a back burner, but, off and on during the day you find it popping into your mind or at night, appearing in your dreams.

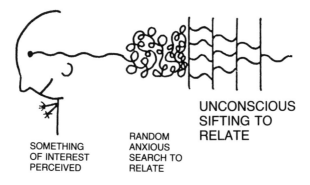

UNCONSCIOUS
SIFTING TO
RANDOM   RELATE
SOMETHING   ANXIOUS
OF INTEREST   SEARCH TO
PERCEIVED   RELATE

Then comes your first *conscious insight* into the relationship between the "something of interest" and "something else." This insight seems to be sudden—"out of the blue." Generally it appears to be extraordinarily simple and presents itself with great clarity. It's the solution to your problem. The answer to your questions. It often emerges when you're thinking about something else, in the night or first thing in the morning.

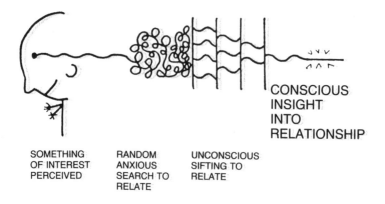

SOMETHING   RANDOM   UNCONSCIOUS
OF INTEREST   ANXIOUS   SIFTING TO
PERCEIVED   SEARCH TO   RELATE
                   RELATE

CONSCIOUS
INSIGHT
INTO
RELATIONSHIP

Next you'll make a *conscious critical choice* about whether or not to accept the initial insight or search further to discover other relationships and other insights. Here you're deciding if this is the "best" solution, the most complete solution, the most effective, most convincing—most filmic. This is the second most critical phase in the process. If you accept your first answer as your "best" answer, you deny yourself a look at alternatives. Your first "best" solution may be the most obvious rather than the most effective.

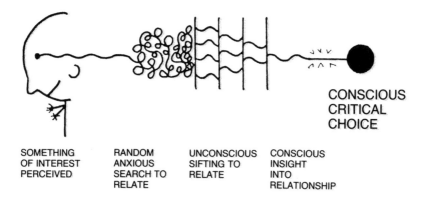

CONSCIOUS
CRITICAL
CHOICE

SOMETHING   RANDOM   UNCONSCIOUS   CONSCIOUS
OF INTEREST   ANXIOUS   SIFTING TO   INSIGHT
PERCEIVED   SEARCH TO   RELATE   INTO
               RELATE   RELATIONSHIP

If you decide to search further, the process repeats itself—again there's your random and anxious searching, your unconscious sifting, and your conscious insight. This phase can be repeated as many times as you choose to do so.

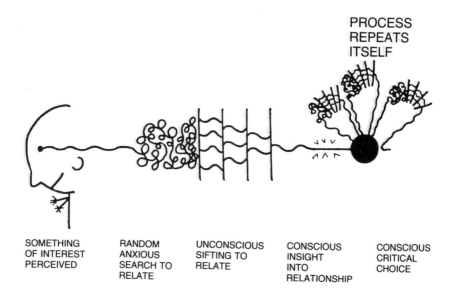

| SOMETHING OF INTEREST PERCEIVED | RANDOM ANXIOUS SEARCH TO RELATE | UNCONSCIOUS SIFTING TO RELATE | CONSCIOUS INSIGHT INTO RELATIONSHIP | CONSCIOUS CRITICAL CHOICE |

When you decide to accept an insight and shape it into an *externalized art form*, the process is complete. The insight is communicated through the elements of your chosen art form and something new comes into existence. A picture is painted, an opera composed, or a screenplay written.

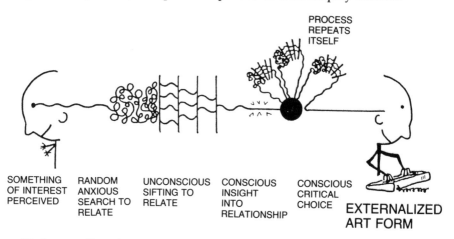

| SOMETHING OF INTEREST PERCEIVED | RANDOM ANXIOUS SEARCH TO RELATE | UNCONSCIOUS SIFTING TO RELATE | CONSCIOUS INSIGHT INTO RELATIONSHIP | CONSCIOUS CRITICAL CHOICE | EXTERNALIZED ART FORM |

Understanding the creative process is of importance to you. By knowing what happens and how it happens, you can control it. You'll be in charge. You can intentionally build a large inventory of life experiences. You can *will* your encounter with things of interest by opening yourself to new experiences. You can accept and embrace the feelings of anxiety that begin the process. You can continue "mulling things over" in your conscious mind to stimulate your unconscious mind to continue or hasten its sifting. You can insist on looking for alternative insights and deliberately delay the gratification of immediate solutions. If you do these things, you promote creativity. If you do not—if you avoid the anxieties of ambiguity and rush to quick answers—you will stifle creativity.

As you've probably already noted, the description of your creating process parallels the description of your information retrieval process. The conscious random and anxious search to relate the "something of interest" to "something else" is analogous to the selection of an information probe. The unconscious sifting to find relationships is similar to sending information probes into the permanent memory to find and retrieve an appropriate search set. The conscious insight into percieved relationships is the same as the appearance of an appropriate search set in the temporary working memory. The conscious choice to recycle the process and seek other insights is like free associating to discover additional information. *The creating process is a process of retrieval.*

Also, *the creating process is a process of discovery*—a process of discovery common to all artists. What H. W. Janson describes as "a long series of leaps of the imagination and the artist's attempts to give them form," (2) is as true for the screenwriter as it is for the fine artist.

> The hand tries to carry out the commands of the imagination and hopefully puts down a brush stroke, but the result may not be quite what had been expected, partly because all matter resists the human will, partly because the image in the artist's mind is constantly shifting and changing, so that the commands of the imagination cannot be very precise. In fact, the mental image begins to come into focus only as the artist "draws the line somewhere." That line then becomes part—the only fixed part—of the image; the rest of the image, as yet unborn, remains fluid. And each time the artist adds another line, a new leap of the imagination is needed to incorporate that line into his ever-growing mental image. If the line cannot be incorporated, he discards it and puts down a new one. In this way, a constant flow of impulses back and forth between his mind and the partly shaped material before him, he gradually defines more and more of the image, until at last all of it has been given visible form. (3)

The creative act is an act of integration—of unity and wholeness. It's the discovery and expression of what you have experienced and how these experiences have shaped the person you've become. Your conscious mind is the threshold of your expression. Your unconscious mind—memory— is your reservoir of experiences to be expressed.

Gaining access to this reservoir of experiences is a challenge that all creating people have to deal with, and each must find his and her way. There are, however, certain things that can work for everyone.

CONTROLLING THE CREATING PROCESS

You are in control of your creating process. You make the choices to do the things that stimulate, nurture, allow, sustain, and fulfill it. The creating process doesn't just happen. It happens because of the choices you make—because of the way you manage your time, control your space and focus, and direct your feelings and thoughts.

Time and Schedule Control

Screenwriters write. This is what they do. This is how they spend a certain number of hours *each day*. Just as a painter paints *each day*, and a violinist plays *each day*—screenwriters write *each day*. If you don't, you aren't a screenwriter.

You must set aside a certain amount of time each day to write. At the beginning—while you're studying to become a screenwriter—it may only be an hour a day, but it must be *that* hour. As you continue and your projects become longer and more complex, the one hour will become four, five, or six. When you write is your choice. You determine the hours that work the best for you—the hours when you're wide awake and most open to hear your inner world of wisdom and memory.

Your writing time must be scheduled. It is best if it can be the same time each day. It must be constant and inviolate. It can't be just whenever you "feel like it" or "get around to it." It's your job. You clock in. You clock out. But, unlike a job, you're the one who sets the hours and checks the time cards. You're the boss. You decide.

For many of us, the most difficult thing is to get ourselves to the writing place. There are always so many other pressing things to do—like vacuuming the "very dirty" floors, going to the store because "there's nothing in the house for dinner," making some "absolutely necessary" phone calls—and, of course, sharpening all of your pencils. Generally speaking, once you get to your computer—or typewriter—and get into your writing, these needs become much less compelling. So the challenge is to find ways to get yourself THERE. There are no universal methods for meeting this challenge—everyone has to develop their own ways.

Some screenwriters like to start early in the morning before anyone is there to distract them. Some prepare for the next day's work by leaving a sentence or thought that can be easily completed. Some create a system of rewards—work in the morning and play in the afternoon; work an hour and then fifteen minutes off; a certain number of pages before breakfast; a "cookie break" every hour. Whatever the trick, it doesn't matter, just so you get yourself THERE.

Writing Space Management

THERE needs to be a special place—a place that's always there for you and conducive to writing. It needs to be a place that's quiet, comfortable, and free of interruptions. A place where telephones and doorbells can't be heard or can be ignored. A place that's warm enough, but not hot. A place where only you and your characters talk, enter, and exit. It needs to be a place you can enter, sit down, and start writing. It needs to be your own "secret garden"—a special place that's free of any interference for your thoughts and feelings.

"Self" Management

Your choice of writing space eliminates physical interferences and you must also choose to eliminate psychological interferences. These are the things inside of you that make you endlessly "sharpen pencils"; that send you off on unnecessary errands; that make the empty page an enemy; that keep you from getting feedback until "it's ready"; that never allow you to finish even a first draft. Eliminating these interferences—these obstacles—is not ever easy, but certainly possible and necessary.

Criticism

The beginning screenwriter must embrace constructive criticism—never avoid it. This is the way learning occurs. It is a necessary ingredient in the learning process. Constructive criticism is to be sought after and welcomed.

Every screenwriter needs to develop a circle of "critics"—people who are knowledgeable and caring about the craft and art of screenwriting, and people who are kind and knowledgeable about the fragile nature of the creating process. You don't want people who will simply pat you on the back and you don't want people who have nothing but negative things to say—neither will be of value to you. You want people who can and will honestly tell you what's working really well and what needs to work better. Cherish the people who can give you both negative and positive feedback and banish the ones who focus only on the negative.

The tendency for most of us—and especially beginning screenwriters— is to want to ask for immediate and total validation rather than criticism. We want to show our work to someone and have them unqualifiedly say, "It's Wonderful!!!" That's a very natural tendency—but one you need to guard against. Guard against it because it just isn't going to happen. Be kind to yourself and not expect this—then you won't be depressed when it doesn't happen. Be honest with yourself—recognize when you're asking for constructive criticism and when you're asking for immediate and total validation. If it's validation you're after, go for it with full recognition of the risk involved.

Excessive self-criticism is one of the most destructive obstacles you may have to overcome. If allowed, it can stunt your growth and dwarf whatever materials you produce. A certain amount of self-criticism is both necessary and productive, but excessive amounts manifest a fear of criticism from others and expectations of validation.

It's the recognition of the necessity for criticism—constructive criticism— and the implausibility of immediate and total validation that can help you overcome excessive self-criticism. But, like so many things, this is easier said than done. However, if this is one of your obstacles, there are things you can do to help yourself.

You can force yourself not to excessively re-read and rewrite your first draft material. You can decide—choose—to limit this first draft work. As you finish each page, put it in a drawer or some place you can't get to until you've finished the entire piece. Then, and only then, gather up your pages to re-read and rewrite *once* before showing them to someone for feedback. Let this become a habit. Feedback will give you some objectivity and stimulate alternative ideas. You'll use the feedback as the basis for your rewrites and move forward instead of endlessly and unproductively going over the same material. This does not in any way diminish the importance of rewriting—writing is rewriting—but it links the rewriting process to feedback and releases you from acting out your excessive fear of criticism.

Unrealistic Expectations

Related to the fear of criticism and the desire for immediate and total validation are the expectations of inspiration and immediate greatness. These expectations can immobilize any writer, and especially the beginning screenwriter. As commented on before, these expectations are based on the antiquated—and contradictory—cultural myths that the Goddesses control creativity, that writers are "born," and that you either "have it" or "don't have it." If you've internalized these myths, it's difficult to deny them, but, if you have, you can help yourself by also internalizing the notion that "the Lord helps those who help themselves." In other words, by expanding your "storyhouse," by gaining access to your thoughts and feelings, and by regular and scheduled writing, you will create the conditions within which you can become a screenwriter—with or without the help of the Muses and your ancestral genes.

Writer's Block

Writer's block is that dreaded state when "nothing happens," when every idea you have is "all wrong," when you don't like anything you've done, and when you question whether or not you'll make it as a screenwriter.

Very frequently what appears to be writer's block can occur when you simply haven't yet found the best solution to whatever problem you're working on. Remember, the creating process includes a great deal of random and anxious searching. This can sometimes be confused with writer's block.

Although writer's block may feel insurmountable, there are ways to circumvent it. There is always some way to get around it—or over it. Writer's block is a state of mind—a state of your mind—and therefore you are in control. Most frequently it's the result of excessive self-criticism, fear of rejection, the expectations of immediate greatness and spiritual inspiration, and focusing on the product rather than the process. If any of these are giving you trouble—and at least some of them give all of us trouble from time to time—the remedies as discussed above can help you deal with them. One of the most fruitful ways to deal with writer's block is to dig more deeply into your characters. Put them in very different situations—situations that have nothing to do with the particular story you're working on. Watch what they do. Listen to them talk. Ask them questions. Introduce them to new characters. Present them with almost impossible obstacles. Get to know them in totally new ways. They can lead you out of writer's block better than anyone or anything else. Also, asking, "What would happen if . . . ?" and doing further research will help. Either or both of these will create new ideas and new alternatives that can start you writing again.

"What would happen if . . . ?"   Creating different situations and asking yourself, "What would happen if . . . ?" is certainly not an activity limited to dispelling writer's block. This is a question you'll be asking over and over as you develop your plot and character progression. However, if consciously employed during periods of writer's block, it can hasten your re-entry into your screenplay and the creating process.

What would happen if the police never arrive and someone gets badly hurt? What would happen if other people start fighting? What would happen if I get hit? What would happen if an automobile accident occurs nearby? What would happen if . . . ? This is the way you discover new and fresh obstacles for your characters to overcome, new and fresh situations through which to reveal character, and new and fresh plot events to carry the story in different directions. This is your system of trying out different alternatives to see how they play.

Research
Research is also something you'll be doing as a regular part of your creating process, and is a very effective way of dealing with writer's block. Research can open up unexplored areas to provide new ideas, new alternatives, and generate renewed interest and excitement.

The more you know about the subject you're dealing with, the more alternative characters and events you'll have to choose from; the more believable each character and event will be; the more clearly you will grasp the essence of what you want to say. We've dealt extensively with your inner research—the discovery of your connections with the characters, events, and themes of your work—and you also need to involve yourself in other forms of research—exploring print resources, conducting interviews, and engaging in personal observations.

Libraries are your gold mines. Here you'll find the thoughts and works of other people—ideological kinsmen. They share their thoughts with you through books, periodicals, newspapers, reports, manuscripts, and audio and video tapes. The library card catalogues will take you in any direction you want to go.

Interviewing is listening to other people talk. It's asking the questions that will head the interviewee in a given direction. It's listening for the things that are especially pertinent to your topic and then asking the questions that will lead the interviewee more deeply into that topic. Every research interview has definite objectives. You need to be very clear about what these objectives are and why they're important. It's this clarity that helps you direct the interview and achieve the objectives. Also, you need to honestly share your objectives with the interviewee so he or she will know what you want and why you want it. The interviewee is giving you his or her thoughts and you need to handle their gifts with the appropriate care and concern.

Personal observations are, of course, the most effective research method. Whenever it's possible to go to the place or the person you're writing about, that's the very best thing to do. When Earl Wallace and William Kelley were writing about the Amish, they went to Amish country and talked with Amish people. Dan Petrie, Jr. visited the Beverly Hills squadroom. Your personal observations give you concrete images, the kinds of details that create authentic situations, verifiable information, and, perhaps most importantly, the emotional tones of the location.

TRUTH IN THE ARTS

The key to the creating process lies in your ability to focus on the process—not on the product. The more you become involved in *doing* rather than looking at what you've done, the more your work will be guided by the "truths" of your characters, themes, and events—the truths to be found in the arts.

When we talk about truth in the arts, we're talking about something very different from truth in the natural sciences. The natural sciences primarily concern themselves with the discovery and analysis of the physical characteristics and behaviors of a phenomenon. The focus is primarily intellectual. The arts are dedicated to the discovery and understanding of the essence of a phenomenon. Here the focus is primarily emotional. The natural sciences present reality. The arts provide an insight into reality. These differences are clearly seen in the two words in the German language that stand for the English word *knowledge—erkenntnis* and *erlebnis*. *Erkenntnis* is defined as a knowledge about things—a scientific analysis. *Erlebnis* is defined as an immediate acquaintance with things—a deep and meaningful understanding of their essence. We could say that *erkenntnis* gives us a knowledge *about*—cognitive information—and *erlebnis* gives us a knowledge *of*—affective information.

Obviously, screenwriters deal with both kinds of knowledge, but *erlebnis* is your primary concern. The knowledge *about* something comes easily but the knowledge *of* something requires more effort. The creating process is primarily the discovery of the truths—the human values—that lie within you and your experiences. It's a process that discovers the links between you and other human beings—the links that make universal statements.

The creating process is a system of inquiry and retrieval wherein you search for your own involvement—your own value system. An inquiry and retrieval system that can be consciously stimulated and directed by asking questions and seeking answers.

Why do I want to write this story?
Why is this theme important to me?
When have I experienced something like this?
What are the values involved in this theme?
What are the feelings this theme arouses in me?
Why have I chosen this theme to write about?
What kinds of people would become involved in acting out this theme?
Who have I known that are like the characters I am developing?
What are my experiences with those people?
What are my feelings about these people?
What would I like to say to my characters?
Would I enjoy socializing with my characters?
How am I different from my characters?
How am I like my characters?
What are my characters' goals?
Are my characters' goals one's I could believe in?
Have I ever felt like my characters do?
What kinds of situations can I put my characters in?
Do any of these situations violate my value system?
Have I ever been in a situation like I've put my characters in?
What would I do in the situation I've put my characters in?
How would I respond differently than my characters do?

The discovery of your involvement with your characters and plot events doesn't mean that they will become you or do the things you would do. It does mean that you establish some kind of a connection with them. It's this connection that taps into a "true" situation and "true" behavior. It's this connection that allows you to understand your characters and provide them with the passion and purpose that makes their actions understandable and meaningful—universal—as a vehicle for your theme.

The discovery of the truths of your characters, themes, and events reveals much more than abstract concepts—it finds very concrete and detailed imagery. Truth—insight into reality—is to be found in images and is expressed through images. As has been said many times, there is a direct relationship between the idea to be communicated and the form through which it is communicated. There is a necessary linkage between the two. Each truth has it location, color, texture, rhythm, tempo, and pace.

A FINAL NOTE

Rollo May, in his book, *The Courage to Create,* presents the notion that the reason creativity takes so much courage is because it precipitates "an active battle with the gods." He reminds us of "the timeless fear that every society harbors of its artists, poets, and saints. For they are the ones who threaten the status quo . . . ." (4)

> In ancient Greek civilization, there is the myth of Prometheus, a Titan living on Mount Olympus, who saw that human beings were without fire. His stealing the fire from the gods and giving it to humankind is taken henceforth by the Greeks as the beginning of civilization, not only in cooking and in the weaving of textiles, but in philosophy, science, drama, and in culture itself.
>
> But the important point is that *Zeus was outraged.* He decreed that Prometheus be punished by being bound to Mount Caucasus, where a vulture was to come each morning and eat away his liver which would grow again at night. This element in the myth, incidentally, is a vivid symbol of the creative process. All artists have at some time had the experience at the end of the day of feeling tired, spent, and so certain they can never express their vision that they vow to forget it and start all over again on something else the next morning. But during the night their "liver grows back again." They arise full of energy and go back with renewed hope to their task, again to strive in the smithy of their soul. (5)

The creating process is not for sissies or for people who are easily pushed around and knocked over. It's for those who have the courage to *know* life and to *know* themselves, those who believe in what they are doing, and those who are resilient—renewable.

REFERENCES

1. Richard C. Atkinson and Richard M. Shiffrin, "The Control of Short-Term Memory," *Scientific American* (August, 1971), pp. 82–90.
2. H.W. Janson, *History of Art: A Survey of the Major Visual Arts from the Dawn of History to the Present Day*, 2d ed., Harry N. Abrams, Inc. and Prentice-Hall, New York, 1977, pp. 10–11.
3. Ibid.
4. Rollo May, *The Courage to Create*, Bantam Books, New York, 1976, p. 22.
5. Ibid. pp. 23, 24.

---12---

THE LAYERS OF
WRITING

We've covered many concepts dealing with dramaturgy, the elements of the motion picture art form, and the practices and processes of screenwriting. We've ventured into seemingly unrelated disciplines and applied their knowledge and experiences to screenwriting. We've looked at screenplays in a new way—as the blending of form and content—and we've focused on the utilization of filmic elements as vehicles for communication.

Hopefully, in a number of ways, you're in a different place than you were when you started this book. Along the way, you've undoubtedly acquired some new insights, developed some new patterns of behavior, expanded your views of your world, and more fully recognized the importance of yourself and your chosen profession.

Perhaps you've already written a number of screenplays or maybe you'll be starting on your first one. You may have learned—or will soon learn— that talking about, reading about, and thinking about screenwriting is much different than writing a screenplay.

Certainly by now you've learned that a screenplay has many, many things happening all at the same time—that there are many layers of information to be transmitted simultaneously. At first, as you're learning to write, this knowledge can be quite overwhelming—*if* you think you have to simultaneously and *perfectly create* all of these layers in the first draft. You don't have to do that!

DRAFTS

You create one draft at a time and each draft will add to and polish each layer. Of course, you always work with all layers simultaneously. You integrate theme, structure, character, mise-en-scène, filmic time, filmic space, motion, imagery, and sound in every scene, but with each draft you will strengthen and perfect each of these elements and their relationships to each other. Each draft builds on itself. Each draft brings you closer to completion.

Your first draft needs to be like one long deep breath—getting it all written all at once—from beginning to end. Nothing should interfere with this first vision. No one should tamper with it—including you—until it's all in one piece. This is your starting place—your broad strokes.

Then, in subsequent drafts, you'll add some things and delete others. You'll probably do some restructuring. Your images will be more clear, more complex. Your characters will speak to you with greater depth and clarity. They may be the ones who add and subtract. They may want to pursue things you don't want them to pursue and you'll have to find the reasons to accept or deny their wishes. You're images will be more compelling. You'll think more about the expressive qualities of sound, lighting, color, and the juxapositioning of shots. You'll develop more effective interactions between the characters and the mise-en-scène. You'll be getting a stronger sense of tempo and pacing. You'll work more with the momentum of the accumulated information. Your screenplay will acquire its own life and you will begin to separate yourself from it.

FEEDBACK

Along the way you'll want to get some feedback. You'll want to know what's working and what needs further development. Certainly with some anxiety and yet with eagerness you'll give it to your "critics" to read. Hopefully they'll always return it to you with many ideas and suggestions about what you can do to strengthen and improve it further.

BUT BE CAREFUL WITH WHAT YOU DO WITH THIS FEEDBACK AND WITH WHAT YOU LET THE FEEDBACK DO TO YOU. It is best to sit on your feedback for a while. Read it or hear it. Take it all in but don't respond to it immediately. Let your creating process go to work again. Let your inner wisdom and original vision take over—they will tell you which suggestions to integrate and which to reject.

Our initial tendency is to defend what we've written and explain all of the reasons why we did what we did. This is *not* a good use of feedback. Remember—you asked for feedback to help you—not to validate you. Receiving the feedback and suspending the inclination to defend will allow you to analyze more accurately the feedback. Immediate and defensive responses tend to rigidify your thought processes—and that's the last thing you want to have happen. You need to bring all of your flexibility into action to help you maximize the good things that are working for you and fix the things that aren't working as well.

Writing is rewriting. As your material develops it reveals itself to you. To use Janson's words again, there's that "constant flow of impulses back and forth between his mind and the partly shaped material." (1) You know what the visual, audio, and dramatic ingredients are and you know the tools you're working with. TRUST YOURSELF. Be sure you retain the essence of that "something of interest" that excited you in the very beginning. Know that if you keep asking the right questions your mind will discover the right answers. Know that when the right answers emerge, you will recognize them.

When you're ready, incorporate your changes into a new draft and work with designing your pages. Then decide if you want more feedback. Perhaps you'll want to confirm whether or not you've fixed the things that needed fixing and/or receive suggestions for polish and "fine tuning."

This will bring you to a draft you'll probably want to start showing around. There are no rules about the number of drafts you write. This is a decision you'll have to make. But you must realize that creating a screenplay takes time and effort and that there are multiple drafts each screenplay goes through.

GUARD YOUR "SILVER ARROWS"

A word of caution. Before you send your screenplay "out there," you want to be fully satisfied that it's as polished as it can be. "Fix" everything that's not working for you. Your opportunities to have material read by the people who can option and purchase will be somewhat limited. Be sure you don't use up your "silver arrows" on partially polished screenplays.

OBSESSIVE REWRITING

Although writing is rewriting, rewriting can also become obsessive. You can rewrite too much—hang onto your screenplay too long. Your screenplay can become too precious. If you aren't satisfied with your work after a fourth—or fifth—draft it's time to set it aside to work on a new and different screenplay. Sometimes you'll get too close to your work and not be able to find your answers until you've given yourself some time and distance. The key is to write a new screenplay and then, after that's done, revisit the old one.

We've traveled over a lot of territory together—and now we've come to the end—or the beginning. It's my hope that your visions will find their expression in filmic terms—that the truth and power of those visions will be truly realized by utilizing the truth and power of the motion picture medium. When film form is blended with film content, the motion picture medium itself—as an art form—rises to new and yet to be fully explored heights. It is my hope that you will be among those who will lead the way.

REFERENCE

1. H.W. Janson, *History of Art: A Survey of the Major Visual Arts from the Dawn of History to the Present Day*, 2d ed., Harry N. Abrams, Inc. and Prentice-Hall, New York, 1977, pp. 10–11.

AN EXAMPLE OF IDEA SKETCHING

The writing task in this example is essentially the same as your experience with discovering and selecting the expressive material to communicate Cathy's struggle to make her career decision. The shot descriptions and sketches are those of a student, Richard Ollis. Richard, along with other students in a class, was asked to create and then sketch a non-verbal scene, in no more than twenty shots, that would portray the emotion felt by a mother facing the death of her only child. The location is the son's room with normal set construction and props.

1. FULL SHOT SIDE PROFILE of Agnes standing several feet in front of clothes dresser. She walks slowly forward to within touching distance and pauses.

2. MEDIUM CLOSE SHOT OVER her LEFT SHOULDER, slight HIGH ANGLE showing her approximate view. Her hands slowly enter frame, moving toward drawer handles.

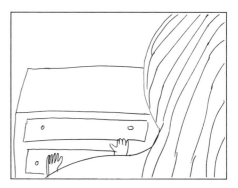

3. CLOSE UP of back of moving hand. Hand is shaking, pauses momentarily with slight hint of withdrawing, and then continues forward.

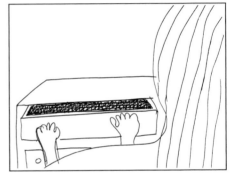

4. MEDIUM CLOSE SHOT OVER LEFT SHOULDER as before. Hands slowly pull drawer open.

5. CLOSE UP of her face. Slight LOW ANGLE. Tears running down cheeks, lips trembling.

6. CLOSE UP of hands slowly lifting folded boy's nightgown up out of drawer.

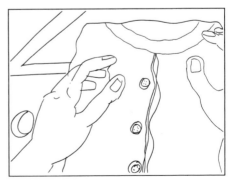

7. CLOSE SHOT hands holding top of nightgown. The rest falls to unfold itself and is slowly carried out of frame.

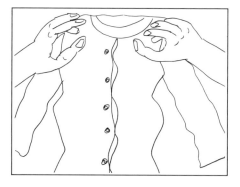

8. PROFILE CLOSE UP of Agnes' face as gown is brought up to her face. Her eyes close as more tears fall. Face turns slightly toward camera as gown is held against other side of face.

9. EXTREME CLOSE UP of smiling animal character printed on fabric of nightgown. A tear falls on it, glistens briefly and is absorbed.

10. MEDIUM SHOT Agnes carrying gown. She walks over to bed, sits down on the side, and faces pillows. She holds gown to her bosom and wraps the sleeves of the gown over her own arms. She slowly rocks back and forth for several moments and stops. She pauses, puts gown down on bed, and reaches toward pillows.

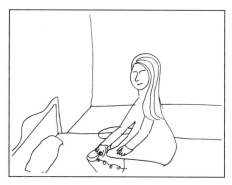

11. MEDIUM CLOSE SHOT of hand gliding up over pillows, grabs covers and pulls them down. Hand releases covers and very slowly moves up to middle of pillow and begins a soft caress. Hand is lifted slightly above surface of pillow and holds there—cup like.

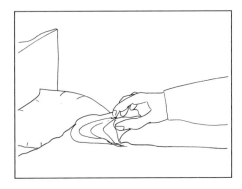

12. CLOSE UP SIDE VIEW of hand making gentle stroking motions in air above pillow in same location where son's head would be.

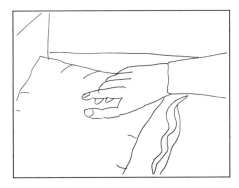

13. MEDIUM CLOSE SHOT of same action as seen over her left shoulder. She moves both hands to edges of pillow and begins to lean forward over pillow.

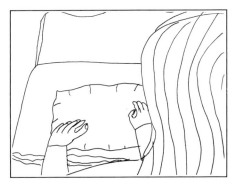

14. CLOSE UP PROFILE her face approximately six inches above pillow, eyes closed, tears falling, and gives a silent kiss.

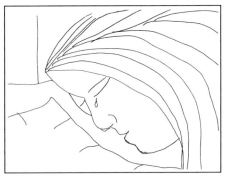

15. CLOSE UP of hand clenching edge of pillow.

16. MEDIUM CLOSE SHOT PRO-FILE as Agnes falls heavily onto pillow, burying face and sobbing uncontrollably. CAMERA DOL-LIES BACK slowly as screen FADES to black.*

What are the most expressive objects in this example? How are the mother's actions motivated by the objects? Do we clearly know what she is thinking? Is there a beginning, middle, and end? Does she finally accept the death of her son? If so, what is the action that shows this? Is there any extraneous material? Could anything be ellipsed? Does this example utilize filmic elements? If so, what and how?

*This is *not* an example of format for you to follow when writing your theatrical screenplays. This is the format often used for a shooting script. Unless you are writing a shooting script, be sure to follow the format examples in the manual referred to on page 233.

FILMIC ELEMENTS

Static Space

The Frame
  Size
  Shape
  Magnetism
  Planes
Lines
Shapes
Colors
Light
Texture
Space
  Negative
  Positive
Lenses
Camera Position
Montage
Image Selection
  Tensions/Resolutions
  Balance/Unbalance
  Rhythms
  Contrasts
  Complexity/
    Simplicity
Implied Movement

Filmic Time

Ellipsis of Events
Progression
  Beginning
  Middle
  End
Condensing Time
  Continuity
  Reaction Shots
  Cutaways
  Intercutting
Expanding Time
  Additional Actions
  Overlapping Actions
Camera Speeds
  Normal Motion
  Slow Motion
  Fast Motion
  Stop Motion
  Reverse Motion
Montage
  Elliptical
  Optical
  Symbolic
Transitions
  Optical
  Visual Similarities
  Visual Continuities
  Music
  Sound Effects
Reorganizing Time
  Flashback
  Flashforward
  Fantasy
  Dream

Filmic Space

Camera Placement
  Position
  Movement
  Angle
  Lense
Subject/Object
  Placement
Foreground
Middle Ground
Background
Subject/Object
  Movement
Horizontal
Vertical
Induced
Juxtaposition of
  Images
Contrasting
Similar
Foreshadowing
Juxtaposition of Sound
  Contrasting
  Similar
  Foreshadowing

Motion	**Imagery**	**Sound**
Natural Motion	Visual Symbols	Dialogue
Character/Object	Conventional	Narration
Primary	Natural	Situational Sound
Secondary	Semi-Conventional	Expressive Sound
Natural Motion	Visual Simile	Symbolic Sound
Camera	Visual Metaphor	Music
Induced Motion	Correlative	
Expressive Motions	Associative	
Editorial Motion	Mise-en-Scene	
Tempo	Location	
Rhythm	Set	
Pacing	Props	
Expressive Actions	Costumes	
	Hairstyles	
	Makeup	
	Composition	
	Linear	
	Layered	
	Tensions/Resolutions	
	Balance/Unbalance	
	Complexity/	
	Simplicity	
	Lines	
	Shapes	
	Colors	
	Lighting	
	Textures	
	Rhythms	
	Contrasts	

GLOSSARY

This glossary includes the terminology particularly applicable to understanding the integration of film form and film content and terminology that may deviate from conventional useage. It does not include definitions of "standard" motion picture design and production terms. The purpose of this glossary is to organize the main theoretical terminology employed in this work.

Affective communication   Arousing and influencing emotional understanding.

Beginnings   The introduction of the story problem to be solved. Act I.

Bridge   The transition from one sequence to another that sets the direction of the new sequence.

Catalyst   The character who introduces a new situation or new information that demands a response from the protagonist.

Change/growth   The essense of storytelling. A gradual and recognizable alteration of a character's response to a given situation.

Climax   The action (decision) that reveals the change/growth within the protagonist.

Cognitive communication   Arousing and influencing intellectual understanding.

Conclusion   What happens as a result of the protagonist's change/growth. The tag line.

Content elements   Characteristics derived from dramaturgy: theme, structure, character(s), and mise-en-scène.

Crisis   Events that complicate the story situation and demand action.

Dramatic objective   An objective that encounters conflict or contradiction.

End   The solution to the story problem. Act III.

External physical movement   Plot activities that allow characters to communicate their thoughts through actions.

Filmic   Any visual or aural device that utilized the potentialities basic and unique to the motion picture art form.

Filmic elements   The devices derived from the nature of the motion picture art form: filmic time, filmic space, motion, imagery, and sound.

Filmic writing   A process of discovery and creation that deliberately blends film form and film content.

Film content   What the screenwriter wants to say and the structure within which it is said.

Film form   The integration of filmic time, filmic space, motion, imagery, and sound into a unified and interrelated whole.

Final crisis   A final story complication that demands action and precipitates the story climax.

Internal movement   Actions that communicate thoughts and change/growth.

Middle   The struggle to solve the story problem. Act II.

Mise-en-scène   The total arrangements of time and space—to include character and camera placements and movements, locations, sets, and set dressings, props, and costumes.

Modifier   The character who forces and promotes the change/growth in the protagonist.

Opponents   Characters who initiate plot events that create conflicts which result in success or failure situations.

Personal goal   The character's psychological need that yearns for fulfillment.

Plot goal   The character's specific physical story goal.

Plot points   Major reversals that force the story to move in new and different directions. Generally occur at the ends of Act I and Act II.

Protagonist   The main character. The person who undergoes the most change and who most actively strives to achieve his or her goal. The one the reader identifies with and knows the most about.

Realization   The moment when the protagonist realizes and accepts the fact that a particular strategy must be abandoned.

Resolution   The climax. The growth/change in the protagonist.

Reversal   Unexpected and/or unwanted events that change the existing circumstances.

Screenplay structure   The aggregate of the elements of film form and film content in their relationship to each other.

Screenwriter   The person who has the original vision of a screenplay and who creates and blends the aural and visual filmic elements to dramatically communicate issues of human concern.

Sequence   A series of scenes tied together by a single unifying idea dealing with a major dramatic event.

Sequence plot goal   The goal which the protagonist believes will achieve his or her overall plot goal and personal goal.

Sequence strategy   The course of action the protagonist believes will achieve the sequence plot goal.

Scene   A series of shots taking place within the same location and same time frame.

Shot   A strip of film that represents the interval between the camera start and the camera stop.

Struggle   Strong and repeated efforts to overcome obstacles and difficulties preventing the achievement of the story goals.

Theme   The idea in the screenwriter's head and heart that he or she wants to get into the head and heart of the reader/viewer.

BIBLIOGRAPHY

PUBLICATIONS THAT CAN GIVE YOU A GREATER UNDERSTANDING OF DRAMATIC STRUCTURING

Aristotle, *Aristotle's Poetics*. Translated by S. H. Butcher with introduction by Francis Fergusson. New York: Hill and Wang, A Dramabook, 1961.

Armer, Alan A. *Writing the Screenplay*. Belmont, California: Wadsworth Publishing Company, 1988.

Egri, Lajos. *The Art of Dramatic Writing*. New York: Simon & Schuster, 1972.

Field, Syd. *Screenplay*. New York: Dell Publishing, 1982.

Froug, William. *The Screenwriter Looks at the Screenwriter*. New York: Delta, 1972.

Goldman, William. *Adventures in the Screen Trade*. New York: Warner Books, Inc., 1983.

Lawson, John Howard. *Film: The Creative Process*. Second Edition. New York: Hill and Wang, 1967.

Lawson, John Howard. *Theory and Technique of Playwriting*. New York: Hill and Wang, A Dramabook, 1960.

Mabley, Edward H. *Dramatic Construction*. Philadelphia: Chilton Book Company, 1972.

Macauley, Robie, and Lanning, George. *Technique in Fiction*. New York: Harper & Row, Publishers, 1964.

Miller, William. *Writing for Narrative Film and Television*. New York: Hastings House, 1980.

Raphaelson, Samson. *The Human Nature of Playwriting*. New York: The Macmillan Company, 1949.

Rilla, Wolf. *The Writer and the Screen*. New York: William Morrow, 1974.

Seger, Linda. *Making a Good Script Great*. New York: Dodd, Mead & Company, 1987.

Swain, Dwight V. with Joye R. Swain. *Film Scriptwriting*, 2 ed. Boston: Focal Press, 1988.

Vale, Eugene. *The Technique of Screen and Television Writing*. Englewood Cliffs, NJ: Prentice-Hall, Inc., 1982.

PUBLICATIONS THAT CAN GIVE YOU A GREATER UNDERSTANDING OF PERSONALITY DEVELOPMENT AND CHARACTERIZATION

Allport, G. *The Nature of Personality*. Addison-Wesley, 1950.

Erikson, E. H. *Childhood and Society*. Norton, 1950.

Erikson, E. H. Identity and The Life Cycle. (Selected papers.) *Psychological Issues*, 1, Monograph 1, 1959. Int. Univs. Press.

Horney, K. *Neurosis and Human Growth*. Norton, 1950.

Maslow, Abraham H. *Motivation and Personality*. Harper, 1954.

Maslow, Abraham H. *Toward a Psychology of Being*. Princeton, NJ: D. Van Nostrand Company, An Insight Book, 1962.

Rodgers, Carl A. *On Becoming a Person*. Boston: Houghton Mifflin Company, 1961.

Stanislavski, Constantin. *An Actor Prepares*. New York: Theatre Arts Books: Robert M. Macgregor, 1952.

Tillich, P. *The Courage To Be*. New Haven, CT: Yale University Press, 1952.

PUBLICATIONS THAT CAN GIVE YOU A GREATER UNDERSTANDING OF THE CREATING PROCESS, HOW YOU THINK, AND HOW YOU COMMUNICATE

Berlo, David K. *The Process of Communication*. New York: Holt, Rinehart and Winston, 1960.

Bois, J. Samuel. *The Art of Awareness*. Dubuque, IA: W. C. Brown, 1970.

Bois, J. Samuel. *Epistemics: The Science-Art of Innovating.* San Francisco, CA: International Society for General Semantics, 1972.

Brande, Dorothea. *Becoming a Writer.* New York: Harcourt, Brace, 1934.

Brian, Russell. *The Nature of Experience.* Riddell Memorial Lectures, Oxford: Oxford University Press, 1959.

Ghiselin, B. *The Creative Process.* University of California, 1952.

Hall, Edward T. *The Silent Language.* New York: Fawcett World Library, 1959.

Hall, Edward T. *The Hidden Dimension.* Garden City, New York: Doubleday & Company, Inc., Anchor Book, 1969.

Hayakawa, S.I. *Language in Thought and Action,* 2nd ed. New York: Harcourt, Brace & World, Inc., 1964.

Jung, C.G. *The Undiscovered Self.* New York: A Mentor Book, The New American Library of World Literature, Inc., 1957.

Jung, C.G. *Man and His Symbols.* Garden City, New York: Doubleday & Company, Inc., 1964.

Korzybski, A. *Science and Sanity: An Introduction to Non-Aristotelian Systems and General Semantics. (1933).* Lakeville, Conn.: International Non-Aristotelian Library Publishing Company, 3rd edition, 1948.

May, Rollo. *The Courage to Create.* New York: Bantam Books, 1976.

May, Rollo. *Man's Search For Himself.* New York: W. W. Norton & Company, Inc., 1953.

McLuhan, Marshall, and Fiore, Quentin. *The Medium is the Massage.* New York: Bantam Books, 1967.

McLuhan, Marshall. *Understanding Media: The Extension of Man.* New York: McGraw-Hill, 1964.

Maslow, Abraham H. Emotional blocks to creativity, *J. Individual Psychology,* 1958; 14, 51–56.

Perkins, D. N. *The Mind's Best Work.* Cambridge, MA: Harvard University Press, 1981.

Progoff, Ira. *At a Journal Workshop.* New York: Dialogue House Library, 1975.

Rothenberg, Albert, and Hausman, Carl, eds. *The Creativity Question.* Durham, NC: Duke University Press, 1976.

Ruben, Brent D., and Budd, Richard W. *Human Communication Handbook: Simulations and Games, Volume 1.* Rochelle Park, NJ: Hayden Book Company, Inc., 1975.

Samuels, M.D., Mike, and Samuels, Nancy. *Seeing With the Mind's Eye*. New York: Random House, The Bookworks, 1975.

Whorf, B.L. *Language, Thought, and Reality*. Cambridge, MA: M.I.T. Press, 1956.

PUBLICATIONS THAT CAN GIVE YOU A GREATER UNDERSTANDING OF FILM FORM AND MOTION PICTURE PRODUCTION

Baddeley, W. Hugh. *Documentary Film Production*, 4th ed. Boston: Focal Press, 1975.

Eisler, Hanns. *Composing for the Films*. New York: Oxford University Press, 1947.

Eisenstein, Sergei. *Film Form*. New York: Harcourt, Brace and Company, 1949.

Eisenstein, Sergei. *Film Sense*. New York: Harcourt, Brace and Company, 1942.

Dick, Bernard F. *Anatomy of Film*. New York: St. Martin's Press, 1978.

Bobker, Lee R. *Elements of Film*. New York: Harcourt, Brace & World, Inc., 1969.

Gessner, Robert. *The Moving Image*. New York: E. P. Dutton & Co., Inc., 1970.

Goldstein, Laurence, and Kaufman, Jay. *Into Film*. New York: E. P. Dutton & Co., Inc., 1976.

Huss, Roy, and Silverstein, Norman. *The Film Experience: Elements of Motion Picture Art*. New York: Harper & Row, Publishers, Inc., 1968.

Kindem, Gorham. *The Moving Image*. Glenview, IL: Scott, Foresman and Company, 1987.

Lindgren, Ernest, *The Art of the Film*, 2nd ed. New York: The Macmillan Company, 1963.

Maddux, Rachel, Silliphant, Stirling and Isaacs, Neil D. *Fiction Into Film*. New York: Dell Publishing Co., Inc., 1970.

Millerson, Gerald. *The Technique of Television Production*, 11 ed. Boston: Focal Press, 1985.

Nilsen, Vladimir. *The Cinema as a Graphic Art*. New York: Hill & Wang, 1959.

Pudovkin, V. I. *Film Technique and Film Acting*. New York: Grove Press, Inc., 1960.

Reisz, Karel, and Millar, Gavin. *The Technique of Film Editing. Second Enlarged Edition*. Boston, Focal Press, 1968.

Squire, Jason E., ed. *The Movie Business Book*. Englewood Cliffs, New Jersey: Prentice-Hall, Inc. 1983.

Wurtzel, Alan. *Television Production,* 2nd ed. New York: McGraw-Hill Book Company, 1983.

PUBLICATIONS THAT CAN GIVE YOU A GREATER UNDERSTANDING OF THEME

Benedict, Ruth. *Patterns of Culture*. New York: A Mentor Book, The New American Library, 1934.

Campbell, Joseph. *The Hero with a Thousand Faces*. 2nd ed. Bollingen Series XVII. Princeton, NJ: Princeton University Press, 1968.

Dewey, John. *Art as Experience*. New York: G.P. Putnam's Sons, 1934.

Hospers, John. *Meaning and Truth in the Arts*. Chapel Hill, NC: The University of North Carolina Press, 1940.

Langer, Susanne K. *Feeling and Form*. New York: Charles Scribner's Sons, 1953.

Langer, Susanne K. *Philosophy in a New Key*. New York: A Mentor Book, The New American Library, 1942.

Langer, Susanne K. *Problems of Art*. New York: Charles Scribner's Sons, 1957.

Larue, Gerald A. *Ancient Myth and Modern Man*. Englewood Cliffs, NJ: Prentice-Hall, Inc., 1975.

PUBLICATIONS THAT CAN GIVE YOU A GREATER UNDERSTANDING OF VISUAL DESIGN

Adonis, Donis. *A Primer of Visual Literacy*. Cambridge, MA: Massachusetts Institute of Technology Press, 1973.

Arnheim, Rudolf. *Art and Visual Perception,* Revised. Berkeley: University of California Press, 1974.

Arnheim, Rudolf. *Visual Thinking*. Berkeley: University of California Press, 1969.

Arnheim, Rudolf. *Film as Art*. Berkeley: University of California Press, 1953.

De Sausmarez, Maurice. *Basic Design: The Dynamics of Visual Form.* New York: Van Nostrand Reinhold Company, 1964.

Feldman, Edmound Burke, *Art as Image and Idea.* Englewood Cliffs, NJ: Prentice-Hall, Inc., 1967.

Fry, Roger. *Vision and Design.* London: Chatto & Windus, 1925.

Kepes, Gyorgy. *Language of Vision.* Chicago: Paul Theobald & Company, 1944.

Kepes, Gyorgy. *Module, Proportion, Symmetry, Rhythm.* New York: George Braziller, Inc., 1966.

Kepes, Gyorgy. *Sign, Image, Symbol.* New York: George Braziller, Inc., 1966.

Kepes, Gyorgy. *The Nature and Art of Motion.* New York: George Braziller, Inc., 1965.

Klee, Paul. *The Thinking Eye: Notebooks of Paul Klee,* ed. Jurgen Spiller and trans. Ralph Manheim. New York: George Wittenborn, Inc., 1961.

Moholy-Nagy, Laszlo. *The New Vision.* Translated by D.M. Hoffmann. New York: W. W. Norton & Co., 1938.

Moholy-Nagy, Laszlo. *Vision in Motion.* Chicago: Paul Theobald, 1947.

Zetti, Herbert. *Sight Sound Motion.* Belmont, California: Wadsworth Publishing Company, Inc., 1973.

Index